Austin Airways
Canada's Oldest Airline

Austin Airways
Canada's Oldest Airline

Larry Milberry

CANAV Books

**Canadian Cataloguing in
Publication Data**
Milberry, Larry, 1943 —
    Austin Airways : Canada's oldest airline

Includes index.
ISBN 0-9690703-3-0

1. Austin Airways — History. 2. Air Lines,
Local service — Ontario — History. I. Title.

HE9815.A97M54 1984 387.7065'7131
C84-098436-7

EDITOR AND DESIGNER
Robin Brass

TYPESETTING
Arlene Weber, Second Story Graphics

PHOTO RETOUCHING
Stephen Ng, SNG Retouching Studio

REPRO ASSEMBLY
Rob Devine and Betty Mason, Printart

ADDITIONAL PROOFREADING
Ralph Clint

Printed and bound in Canada by the Bryant
Press Limited, Toronto

Published by
CANAV Books
51 Balsam Avenue
Toronto M4E 3B6
Canada

Front endpaper
*Austin personnel change an engine
on one of the company's famous
Fairchilds. The locale is Ramsey Lake,
1939. (Sid Bennett)*

Title page
*One of Austin's famous black and
red Norsemans in a typical Northern
setting. (Jeff Wyborn)*

Back endpaper
*Austin Airways Cansos at their
Moosonee buoys, circa 1960. (Bill
Eccles)*

Fairchild 71 CF-BVI in a typical James Bay winter scene in the 1940s. (NFB via Paddy Gardiner)

Contents

Foreword   7

Preface   8

Austin Airways: The Beginnings   11

Wartime Adjustments   36

Post-War Growth   55

Hunting for Nickel   79

More of the Bush   97

Of Cansos and DC-3s   117

Austin Airways Today   141

Appendices   150

Index   159

A drizzly scene at Whale River in October 1963 as an Austin Airways Norseman is off-loaded. (Bill Eccles)

MOOSE FACTORY, ONTARIO

AUSTIN AIRWAYS LIMITED
Seventeen Years Continuous Service

	1951		**JANUARY**		**1951**	
SUN	**MON**	**TUE**	**WED**	**THU**	**FRI**	**SAT**
	1	2	3	4	5	6
7	8	9	10	11	12	13
14	15	16	17	18	19	20
21	22	23	24	25	26	27
28	29	30	31			

TORONTO
EM. 3-3522

SOUTH PORCUPINE
911

SUDBURY
8-8033

NAKINA

MOOSONEE

An example of Austin Airways' famous calendars.

Foreword

The first commercial air service in Northern Ontario was sparked by the mining industry and the need to link Haileybury with the goldfields of Quebec. Laurentide Air Service Ltd. used war-surplus HS-2L flying boats to open the first Canadian scheduled air service and flew its first paying passenger in the spring of 1924. The same year the Ontario provincial government took delivery of similar flying boats and began patrolling the forests north of Sault Ste. Marie. These two organizations share the honour of opening Ontario's northland to aviation, but the company that later became synonymous with the region was Austin Airways Ltd.

To those of us who watched Austin's Waco biplanes at the Toronto Air Harbour in the summer of 1934, and later at the flying club field in Downsview, it was one more company trying to introduce commercial aviation in the Canadian north. We wondered if it would survive. But Austin weathered the hard economic times of the thirties. Its growth to airline status shows it had the "magic formula of success" that let it survive when others so often failed.

Jack and Chuck Austin began with a desire to provide aerial transportation across Northern Ontario. They combined sound business sense with adequate funding and had the perseverance to stick it out when the going got tough. Jack Austin played an undisputed leadership role for 40 of the company's years but left the daily operation to the people he put in charge. The result was a nucleus of skilled, loyal employees who stayed with the company and made it grow. Austin treated its employees well, and established sound relationships with customers and suppliers.

Ingenuity and integrity were part of the survival game in early bush operations. The Austin brothers had both. They knew when to sit tight and when to expand, when to purchase new aircraft and when to lease. They had their share of bad luck but accepted it along with the good as they rode the highs and lows of the industry. They spread their wings occasionally beyond the borders of Ontario but continued their main objective of linking the isolated communities from Sudbury to James Bay and beyond.

The Austin story is about business, airplanes and geography, but more than anything it is about people. Larry Milberry's book is a tribute to these people, many of whom have contributed to the book. Though Austin Airways now has a new image, its success today is based on the accomplishments of the dedicated "survivors" who laid a firm foundation many years ago.

Fred W. Hotson

Fred W. Hotson
Chairman,
The Canadian Aviation Historical Society

Preface

The feeling runs deep among veteran bush fliers: "We've seen the best of aviation in Canada — the bush flying years." Few with any sense of history would quarrel with pilot Jeff Wyborn's claim. He, his contemporaries and those who came earlier were our modern-day "voyageurs," and their Bellancas, Fairchilds and Norsemans airborne "canôts du nord." These men and machines opened up the north and its riches as never before. They made the impossible possible.

For a long time the exploits of the early bush fliers were unrecorded. Finally, in 1954, Frank Ellis' *Canada's Flying Heritage* came along. Twenty years later it was joined by Ken Molson's classic documentation of Canadian Airways, *Pioneering in Canadian Air Transport*. Since then several valuable bush flying titles, mostly biographical, have appeared, books like *And I Shall Fly* by Lewie Leigh.

Some years ago I was reminded that Austin Airways' 50th anniversary was on the horizon. Though it doesn't hold Canada's oldest commercial licence, Austin is certainly the oldest of the major northern air carriers. As a microcosm of everything epitomized by the phrase "bush flying," the Austin story was too inviting. I set to work researching it, but the realities of being a small publisher, ever preoccupied with his financial juggling act, forced the Austin book onto the back burner. Finally, though, here it is.

As with the other CANAV books, *Austin Airways* is the result of much cooperation on the part of many people over years of scrounging for material. To start, Jack Austin was a great help in checking details, providing leads and reading galleys. Jack passed away in Toronto on December 1, 1984. Others who helped have also since gone, including the famous Jim Bell (Norontair's first Dash 8 is dedicated in his honour), George Charity and Moe Sears.

Always helpful too were Austin veterans Frank Russell of Grimsby, Rusty Blakey of Sudbury, Jimmy Cairns of Weston, John der Weduwen of South Porcupine, Frank Fisher of Port Credit, Hal McCracken of Timmins and Jeff Wyborn of South Porcupine. Without the support of these key people a book worth reading could not have been produced.

Many others have chipped in, including Les Ashcroft, Bob Baglow, Al Beaupré, Bill Bell, Eric Bendall, Sid Bennett, Dick Blakey, Ray Bradley (National Waco Club), Dave Brand, John Brown, Oscar Cecutti, Mr. and Mrs. Chaput, Sid Cleverley, Ralph Clint, Chuck Fowler, Hugh Fraser (Inco), Paddy Gardiner, Bruce Gowans, Bill Gwynn, Bob Halford (*Canadian Aircraft Operator*), Jim Hall, Len Harper, Eric Hazeldine, Walter Henry, Fred Hotson, Gil Hudson, Jack Humphries, Don Hurd, W.H. Kearns, Bob Kerr, Fred Knox, Cliff Larry, Victoria Lautens, James R. Lee, Graham Matthews, Nick MacDonald-Wolochatiuk, Archie MacDougall, Lloyd McTaggart, Peter Marshall, Morley McArthur, Don McIntyre, M.L. McIntyre, Ray McLean, Jack McNulty, Bob Mitchell, Ron Mitchell, K.M. Molson, Terry Monk, Mark Nieminen, Neil O'Brien, Holly Parsons, Jim Pengelly, R.N. Pettus, Bert Phillips, the late Stephen Piercey, J Pipe, Ron Preston, Bill Pullen, Gord Rayner, John Reid, Elmer Ruddick, Dave Russell, Phil Sauvé, R.L. Savage, Don Simmons, Brian Steed, Doug Taylor, David Thompson, Gerry Turner, Archie Vanhee, the late Spencer Woods and Glenn Wright (Public Archives of Canada). Thanks also to Austin Airways, Timmins, Ontario.

Many people kindly loaned photos for the book. As a result, here is what is to date the broadest and most finely reproduced collection of bush flying photos yet published.

As usual this CANAV effort includes some original artwork. Jack Austin commissioned the Peter Mossman profiles. By now all who follow my books will be familiar with Peter's fine renditions. Ron Lowry contributed three profiles, actually his first ever. Because of delays in getting this book out, subsequent Lowry paintings have already

8

Loaded with Christmas supplies, CF-BSC takes off at Nemiscau in this dramatic photo, Bill Pullen at the helm. (Paddy Gardiner)

been published in *The de Havilland Canada Story* and *Sixty Years: The RCAF and CF Air Command 1924-1984.* Ron is otherwise known as one of North America's finest modellers; two of his recent models, a Curtiss Shrike and a North American O-47, were commissions from the Smithsonian Institution in Washington. The detailed "Austin Country" map is primarily the work of Molly Brass, done while she was in grade 11.

Larry Milberry,
August 1985

Cape Dorset

SOUTHAMPTON I.

Hudson
Strait

RESOLUTION I.

Baker Lake

Chesterfield Inlet

Rankin Inlet

Whale Cove

N. W. T.

Dubawnt L.

Ennadai L.

Suglук

Ivugivik

CHUBB CRATER

AKPATOK I.

Cape Smith
(Akulivik)

Povungnituk

Ungava
Bay

Ft. Chimo

Hudson
Bay

Pt. Harrison
(Inukjuak)

L. Minto

Koksoak R.

Schefferville

Churchill

Brochet

Clearwater L.

Richmond Gulf

BELCHER IS.

Great Whale

L. Bienville

Labrado

Lynn Lake

Granville L.

York Factory

Ft. Severn

MANITOBA

Nelson House

Thompson

Winisk

Ft. George

Great Whale R.

Kaniapiscow R.

Sakami R.

in Flon

Snow Lake

Wabowden

Severn L.

Big Trout Lake

Severn R.

L. Sakami

Eastmain R.

The Pas

Norway House

Gods R.

Winisk R.

Attawapiskat

AKIMISKI I.

James

Old Factory River

Webequie

Eastmain

Nemiscau

L. Mistassini

Lake
Winnipeg

Sandy L.

Lansdowne House

Ft. Albany

Bay

Moosonee

Hannah
Bay

Rupert House

Rupert R.

Dauphin

Pickle Lake

Ogoki

ONTARIO

Moose Factory

Nottaway R.

Chapais

L. St. Jean

Gimli

Red Lake

Fraserdale

Matagami

QUEBEC

Harricanaw R.

randon

WINNIPEG

Kenora

Dryden

Armstrong

Sioux Lookout

Nakina

Longlac

Hearst

Kapuskasing

Cochrane

L. Abitibi

Senneterre

QUEI

L.
Nipigon

Geraldton

Jellicoe

Iroquois Falls

Noranda

Val d'Or

Trois Rivières

Hornepayne

Oba

Timmins

South Porcupine

Rouyn

Nipigon

Manitouwadge

White River

Foleyet

Kirkland Lake

Matachewan

Larder Lake

Belleterre

Red R.

Ft. Frances

Atikokan

Shebandowan L.

Franz

L. of the
Woods

Thunder Bay

Wawa

Chapleau

Gogama

New Liskeard

Haileybury

Cobalt

L. Timiskaming

Lake Superior

Biscotasing

Wanapitei L.

Temagami

North Bay

Ouaw R.

MONTRE

St. Je

Sault
Ste. Marie

Elliot Lake

Capreole

Falconbridge

Sudbury

Sturgeon
Falls

L. Nipissing

OTTAWA

St. Lawrence R.

Killarney

French R.

Huntsville

Austin Country

0   100   200   300   400 km

0   50   100 150 200 250 miles

MAP BY M. & R. BRASS

Georgian
Bay

Parry Sound

Peterborough

Barrie

Lake
Michigan

Lake
Huron

Lake
Ontario

TORONTO

MINNEAPOLIS

HAMILTON

Lake

Austin Airways: The Beginnings

Fifty years ago aviation in Canada was still in its infancy. Hardly a generation had passed since 1909 and the first powered flight in the country. Commercial flying, such as it was, went on mostly in the Northland, drawn there by mining, forestry, fishing, trapping and surveying. Though not lacking in enthusiasm, the newly-formed flying club movement was barely off the ground. The same went for military aviation: the RCAF was small and keen but woefully equipped. Any kind of expansion at this time was held back by the economic hard times of the Depression.

On the commercial aviation scene a big venture had been launched in 1930 with the formation of Canadian Airways. Founder James A. Richardson of Winnipeg hoped it would soon span the nation, but for now it could only operate regionally. Hard times kept it from growth and Richardson's wider dream was forestalled for a

University students turned businessmen, Chuck and Jack Austin stand beside one of their new Wacos. (via Larry Milberry)

decade. Meanwhile other operators were serving the North and constantly breaking new ground, though the going was rough. The Fokkers, Fairchilds and Bellancas of companies like Mackenzie Air Service, General Airways, Northern Aerial Mineral Exploration, and Dominion Skyways were crisscrossing the North, but in circumstances that were making nobody rich.

In this atmosphere of uncertainty, two young brothers decided to try their luck in the flying business. J.A.M. "Jack" Austin, 21, and Charles "Chuck" Austin, 23, were born in Renfrew in the Ottawa Valley. The family business was in lumber, run by two older brothers, Allen and Bill,

from head office in Chapleau along with senior partner G.B. Nicholson. Their saw mills were up the CPR from Chapleau at the small centres of Nicholson and Dalton. The Austins' father had died when Jack and Chuck were youngsters and, as they were minors, their inheritance had been withheld. When they reached 21, they received it and with some of these funds were able to buy out Mr. Nicholson, Jack becoming a company director.

In the summer of 1933 while studying at the University of Toronto, Jack and Chuck began taking flying lessons at de Havilland in North Toronto. Well-known local aviator and World War I flier Leigh "Cap" Capreol instructed them in Moths CF-APL and CF-ADG. Chuck went solo after about 12 hours of dual, but Jack was sent up on his own after about 3¹/₂ hours.

Chuck soon had his commercial ticket, but on account of wearing glasses Jack was temporarily limited to private flying. Things were slow around de Havilland for Cap and he began encouraging the Austins to get into the flying business. They talked it over and, using some of their inheritance, decided to give it a go. They hired Capreol and began operations as Capreol and Austin Air Services. The company came into being on March 1, 1934, noted in the official papers as: "conducting an aerial transport and passenger service, dealers in aeroplanes and aircraft supplies, aeroplane testing, instructing in flying, and generally in any business of an aeronautic nature." In a separate agreement, Capreol agreed to act as pilot for them,

(Above) A Sikorsky S-38 amphibian arrives at Toronto from Buffalo. The establishment of the Toronto-Buffalo service by Canadian Colonial Airways in 1929 encouraged air operations in Toronto Harbour. The Sikorsky service lasted only a year, but its facilities were later used by many visiting aircraft and became the base for Chuck and Jack Austin's flying venture. (Toronto Harbour Commissioners Archives)

On the waterfront, the Globe and Mail*'s de Havilland Rapide CF-BBG, before and after. The newspaper used the same seaplane facilities at the foot of Yonge Street as Austin Airways. It purchased the Rapide in June 1937. On August 21 the airplane was destroyed when it caught fire in a refuelling mishap. (via Fred Hotson and Larry Milberry)*

instruct flying, and generally promote the best interests of the company. He was to be paid $3000 a year plus a third of the commissions from the sale of aircraft and parts.

For two young and inexperienced businessmen, Chuck and Jack Austin showed real promise in the aviation business. They quickly organized good facilities, hired three first-rate employees and ordered two aircraft. The employees were Frank Fisher, Dick Preston and Frank Russell. As a base, they leased the unused facilities of the Toronto Air Harbour. These had been opened in 1929 and briefly hosted a variety of interesting visitors. For one season they were terminus for Canadian Colonial Airways' Toronto-Buffalo seaplane service; but thereafter they languished in the doldrums. The Toronto Harbour Commission was pleased that someone was showing an interest in the Air Harbour, and Col. Douglas Joy of the

Department of Transport helped clear the way for the Commission to turn over the facilities to Austin for a nominal amount.

Frank Russell was hired by the Austins after several years working for newly formed de Havilland Canada. Born in 1909, he had entered aviation in 1929 when he went to work for de Havilland in the company's original shops at de Lesseps field, a cow pasture on the northwest outskirts of Toronto. Soon after joining de Havilland, he had his first airplane ride when Phil Garratt took him up. Frank excelled at his new profession and was soon chief rigger. At the time there was plenty of work as de Havilland had an RCAF order for Moth trainers. Before long the company expanded to North Toronto where Frank was put in charge of Puss Moth assembly. It was feast or famine at de Havilland; he recalls working one continuous 54-hour shift.

When the Depression hit, things were rough all round and Frank recalls being forced to accept some public welfare. To qualify he had to turn over the licence plates from his car and from then on he pedalled the nine miles to work, where he was earning 40 cents an hour. On the side, he moonlighted as an auto mechanic to help make ends meet.

After five years at de Havilland, Frank joined the Austins on condition that he would take his air engineer's papers. Due to existing regulations he was still obligated by Col. Joy to spend two years as an apprentice, learning more about aero engines. Jack Austin too was studying for his engineer's licence, but Col. Joy, not one with a lot of time for book learning, wouldn't give Jack so much as a day's credit for having earned his B.A.Sc. at the University of Toronto! Jack's first air engineer's licence (No. A1144) was issued June 10, 1936.

Frank Russell was the first Austin employee actually to do any work. He cleaned out the Air Harbour buildings at the foot of Yonge Street and acted as night watchman. Years later he recalled how he had come to work for the Austins: "I was at de Havilland assembling a Bellanca Pacemaker belonging to General Airways at Rouyn. Leigh Capreol came up to me one day and asked if I'd be interested in a new job. He explained that two young men whom he had taught to fly were starting a charter flying service in Toronto Harbour. I said I'd be interested and asked if it would be steady employment. He assured me that it would be, at least for the summer. By coincidence I started with the Austins on April 28, exactly five years after starting at de Havilland. Little did I know that I was starting work for the airline that was to serve longer

Frank Russell paused for this snap while working on CF-AVN at Toronto in July 1938. (via Frank Russell)

than any other in Canada. The employment was not just to be steady: it was to be permanent!"

When Dick Preston joined the Austins as chief engineer in 1934, he brought a wealth of practical experience but at the time he had been temporarily grounded over a squabble with the DOT. He had begun flying in 1926 at J.V. Elliot's flying school near Hamilton. He received his licence the next year and worked for several firms, including Canadian Airways, International Airways, Canadian Vickers and Canadian Air Express. By 1934 he held coveted A, B, C and D air engineer's licences. Besides setting up the kind of engineering operation needed by the Austins, he became a valuable tutor to them and Frank Russell. Though he was to spend less than two years with Austin Airways, Dick was to make his mark on the company and would be fondly remembered by all for years to come. Half a century after he first met Dick, Jack Austin was to comment, "Dick Preston was one of the cleverest engineers I've ever met. I learned far more from him on the practical side than I ever did in university."

Frank H. Fisher was Austin Airways' first full-time pilot. Born in England in 1905, he left school at 12 and went to sea as a wireless watch. His earliest memories of flying were seeing Zeppelin and Gotha bombers on raids over England during World War I while lumbering Handley Pages flew the other way. Frank came to Canada in 1920 and spent three years sailing on the Great Lakes. In

(Above) Dick Preston, one of the most respected engineers in the country, came to work for the Austins in 1934. (Frank H. Fisher)

(Top right) Frank Fisher, Kelly Edmison and Sam Sainsbury beside a Buhl which Frank was flying for National Air Transport. (via Frank H. Fisher)

(Right) Two aircraft from Frank Fisher's early flying days: a Loening Air Yacht seen at Mile 187 on the rail line being surveyed to Churchill in 1928 or 1929, and a Fokker Universal at Hudson. (Frank H. Fisher)

1925-26 he was a Marconi operator with the Ontario Provincial Air Service (OPAS) at Gold Pines in northwestern Ontario. One day he bumped into legendary bush pilot Doc Oaks, who was flying director at the time for NAME. Frank, who had been taking flying lessons, asked Doc if he'd give him a chance to fly, to which Doc answered, "OK. You look eager enough!" So began Frank Fisher's flying career. After working with Northern Aerial Minerals Exploration (NAME), he flew for General Airways from such bases as Hudson, Chapleau and Rouyn. Usually he had a Bellanca, which he recalls as a real pleasure to fly, though there were times, he admits, when he was so overloaded that it was hard to get the plane into the air. Later Frank flew briefly for National Air Transport of Toronto. In the winter of 1931 he took a party of Harcourt Mines people headed by Sam Sainsbury

Austin Airways' D.H.60T which joined the company in July 1934 and was used briefly on a variety of general duties.

Illustrations by Peter Mossman

One of Austin's famous Waco UKC cabin biplanes. This one served from 1934 to 1942, and was finally written off after breaking through the ice at Biscotasing.

to the Belcher Islands in one of NAT's Buhl Air Sedans. The purpose of the trip was to stake, of all things, a coal mine. They had to take in their own stakes as no trees grew on the island!

While with General Airways, Frank had spent two years in Chapleau, where he and his wife lived in a house owned by Bill Austin, older brother of Chuck and Jack. Through this contact, Frank went to work with the Aus-

tins in the spring of 1934. He recalls what a hub of aviation Chapleau was in the early 1930s. General Airways, Eclipse Airways, Canadian Airways and the OPAS always seemed to have aircraft coming or going. One good source of revenue was the prospectors who arrived from the south; all the local bush pilots would meet the train to solicit business. There were some hard feelings among the competitors but everyone knew that,

The first Austin Airways aircraft, Waco CF-AVL, is seen on Toronto Bay upon its delivery in April 1934. This tough little biplane was to serve the company for over 12 years. It came equipped with the latest night flying equipment. Jack Austin called the DOT one night to ask permission to use the Waco to do some night-time joyriding. Only the janitor was available, but as he gave his permission, the flights were made! (K.M. Molson Collection)

Waco CF-AVL is shown in an early medevac demonstration at Toronto. The collapsible aluminum stretcher that can be seen behind the nurse has been preserved by Rusty Blakey in Sudbury. (via Rusty Blakey)

A view of newly delivered Waco CF-AVL, showing the greenhouse-type windows which were soon to be covered in. From the left, Frank Fisher, Jack Austin, Leigh Capreol and Chuck Austin. (K.M. Molson Collection)

A group shot taken when the Austins took delivery of their Wacos. Left to right: Sid Cleverley of the Toronto Flying Club, Leigh Capreol, Jack Austin and Dick Preston. (Frank H. Fisher)

(Left) A good detail of CF-APL, the Tiger Moth in which Leigh Capreol taught Chuck and Jack Austin to fly in the early thirties. The Gosport communications tubes can be seen in the front and back cockpits. (Right) CF-ATX, the Fox Moth owned briefly by the Austins in 1934-35. (Walter Henry, K.M. Molson Collection)

come what may, they all had to get along. Frank felt he often had the edge in this train station hustling as he knew a lot of the prospectors and mining engineers from his early days with NAME.

Sometimes, while working with General, Frank would have an Ontario government charter, usually to do with forest fires. He wasn't crazy about these jobs as the Department of Lands and Forests always seemed to want him to land on the smallest lake, full of rocks and closest to the fire. Besides, gas drums were usually the cargo and the pilot generally did his own loading. On top of this, the L and F always seemed in such a rush. Who needed it!

First Airplane Delivered

In February 1934 the Austins took delivery of their first aircraft. On Cap's recommendation they had chosen the cabin Waco (Weaver Aircraft Co.) and Chuck and Cap picked up the first one (on wheels) at Waco's Troy, Ohio, factory. Their second Waco was delivered (on floats) that May at Fleet Aircraft in Fort Erie. Jack Sanderson was running Fleet at the time and had established the company as Waco's Canadian distributor. The Austin machines were the UKC model powered by the Continental R-670-A radial of 210 hp. Choosing the Wacos proved a

fortunate move, for they served Austin Airways well for years to come, and helped put Austin "on the map" as a dependable operator. Interestingly, the sporty-looking cabin Waco had special appeal to a higher class of clientele, including the big-money names from Bay Street in Toronto. The Waco was like the Packard of the skies.

One of the aircraft, CF-AVN, was delivered with a unique modification for the day: a removable panel was installed on the port side behind the cabin to facilitate loading a stretcher. Thus the Waco became Canada's first commercial air ambulance and in the coming years was to serve frequently in this role, flying sick and injured northerners to hospital in places like Sudbury and Toronto.

In July, not long after the Wacos arrived in Toronto, the Austins purchased Tiger Moth CF-APL from de Havilland. The first Tiger Moth in Canada, it was acquired so that Chuck and Jack could build their flying time but also use it for business.

In August the Austins acquired the Fox Moth CF-ATX. This machine was taken on a trade from Bobby Cockeram of Prospector Airways when he bought a Waco through their dealership. CF-ATX, and another Fox Moth taken in on a trade when Norm Irwin also bought a Waco, were quickly resold.

The summer of 1934 proved a busy one in the charter

business. Many trips were made taking mining men from Toronto into the north where mineral exploration and mine development were booming. The Wacos were flying regularly into such places as Jellicoe, Geraldton, Long Lac, South Porcupine and Rouyn. Many of the passengers were becoming regular customers including George McCullagh of the *Globe and Mail*, a keen mining investor. His paper was always on top of the latest mining news and to improve communications McCullagh made regular use of the airways. George Drew, later premier of Ontario, was another Austin client. So was entrepreneur Harry McLean. Frank Fisher remembers that McLean was rather a nuisance to have along and was customarily late for the flight. One day Frank flew him down to North Beach on New York's Atlantic coast. McLean was making a pest of himself, so Frank took the plane down low over the trees, which sobered McLean and settled him down for the rest of the flight. McLean was a notable eccentric who was known around Toronto as "Mr. X." One of his pranks was to toss money from atop the Royal York Hotel. He once purchased an airplane from the Austins and paid for it in cash with a handful of thousand dollar bills.

J.P. Bickell, an important mining man (McIntyre Mines, etc.) and great booster of aviation, was another frequent client of Austin Airways. One day Frank Fisher flew Bickell to Yarmouth, Nova Scotia, for some tuna fishing. Frank had Duke Schiller, another of the legendary bush pilots, along for the ride. Off Yarmouth Bickell pointed down to a yacht and Frank landed. He and Duke were invited aboard to join in the activity, which included landing a 900-pound tuna. Meanwhile, all day long a fellow rowed back and forth from shore delivering up-to-the-minute stock market quotations!

The Pierce brothers of the *Northern Miner*, the famous mining journal, were also regulars with Austin Airways. Frank Fisher picked them up in the bush one day and found them quite distressed. They had been having a dreadful time with the blackflies and were very happy to see the Waco touching down on their lake. Fred Boylen was another famous prospector client who later on controlled some of Canada's biggest mines.

Another early charter took a government mining representative to investigate possible chrome deposits in Newfoundland in pre-Confederation days. When Frank Fisher and Jack Austin arrived in Corner Brook, after letting off their passenger in Port aux Basques, they were accosted by the local customs official. Their Waco was impounded for supposedly being in contravention of customs regulations. It was Saturday, so the matter had to be put off till Monday. At that point Frank, being "captain of the vessel," was charged with bringing in illicit goods. Luckily Jack was able to produce papers from Sydney showing that they were "in ballast" (carrying no goods). In the end, a $50 fine was levied, which was paid by the passenger who in the meantime had arrived by boat. The same day Frank and Jack took off and returned to Toronto, cruising at 110-115 mph and refuelling at Sydney, Saint John and Longueuil. The trio must have been pretty well worn out as they came in to land at Toronto a bit after sunset. After-dark landings were illegal in the harbour and, as fate would have it, Col. Joy of the DOT was watching a baseball game on the waterfront and heard the plane approaching. He made it his business to drive over to the Air Harbour to check things out. But by the time he arrived Frank Russell had the Waco away from the wharf and moored to a buoy, making it awkward for Joy to feel for a warm engine cowling. No, nobody around the dock had seen any airplane landing. No sir, Col. Joy.

Jack Austin remembers the Corner Brook flight for another reason: Frank Fisher's almost photographic memory for maps. The night before the trip Frank studied his maps closely and, as Jack recalls, during the whole trip never referred to them again. And another memory? After they got back to Toronto, Jack and Frank went up to Murray's restaurant for something to eat. People must have wondered why they ate standing up at the counter. It had to do with their sore backsides after a very long flight!

One day Frank flew George McCullagh to Montreal to watch a hockey game. They got home very late that night and while taxiing in Frank noticed a tic-tic noise. Problem? Airplane wingtip rubbing along a picket fence! Another of Frank's passengers was Denton Massey, famous Toronto evangelist, whom Frank Fisher often flew on his crusades. But besides flying interesting celebrities about, there was a lot of bread and butter work to be done. Whenever planes weren't on other jobs, they were pressed into service flying sightseers. Joyriding was the ancient name for this profession and on good days perhaps a hundred takers could be found willing to lay down $5 for a short flight around Toronto or wherever the plane was operating. Throughout all of this activity the "fleet" was kept in good trim by Dick Preston, Frank Russell and Jack Austin, while Frank Fisher, Chuck Austin and Leigh Capreol were taking care of the flying.

In the fall of 1934 Austin Airways ceased operations at

the Air Harbour due to the impending freeze-up and moved to the Toronto Flying Club field at Dufferin Street and Wilson Avenue in North York. This was just north of Barker Field, which was on the west side of Dufferin. At the TFC field Austin rented some hangar space and shop facilities and put a formidable sign over the hangar door. Over the winter the Austin fleet was thoroughly reconditioned, including the complete rebuild of CF-APL, which had been seriously damaged in a landing accident near Renfrew. The rebuild of the Tiger Moth provided valuable experience and the presence of Dick Preston was much appreciated as he taught the finer points of aircraft rebuilding to Frank Russell and Jack Austin. Other work done over that first winter included fitting skis to the Wacos, winterizing their engines, and overhauling floats for the coming spring. There was only one charter that winter, a trip to Timmins. But with spring breakup, the Wacos were towed back to the Air Harbour, minus wings of course, reassembled, and put on floats for another busy season's flying.

A minor anecdote relates to the rebuild of CF-APL. When it was finished, Leigh Capreol didn't want to test fly it, perhaps having doubts about the quality of the workmanship. So Dick Preston turned his cap around backwards and put on a pair of goggles. "There," he said, "do I look like a test pilot now?" And off he went in the Tiger Moth.

Austin's maintenance routine the following winter was to be different, as the aircraft were flown down to Whitby, about 30 miles east of Toronto on the Lake Ontario shore, and were changed over to wheels at Norm Irwin's farm. Irwin had his own airstrip there and called his spread the Red Wing Orchards (and his flying operation Red Wing Flying Service). It was adjacent to Whitby Harbour. Once changed over, the planes were flown back to Toronto where the mechanics got to work overhauling them after the busy summer season.

Austin and Eclipse

On May 22, 1935, the Austins incorporated under letters patent from the Dominion of Canada as Capreol and Austin Air Services Ltd. (This was amended later, by supplementary letters patent, to Austin Airways Ltd.) The three company directors were Chuck, Jack and Allan Austin. When Allan died in 1946, Bill Austin replaced him as director. Leigh Capreol left in 1935 to join Noorduyn in Montreal, which was just launching the Norseman. Later, when National Steel Car opened its plant in Malton in 1939, he would move there to test fly Lysanders.

That spring also marked the Austins' first northward expansion. This is where Phil Sauvé enters the picture. Sauvé, a native of Plantagenet, Ontario, had begun his aviation career in 1925 when he learned to fly on Jennies with a flying circus in Detroit. Thereafter he was involved

Over its first winter, 1934-35, Austin Airways established a maintenance base at the airport on Dufferin Street near Wilson Avenue in North Toronto, using it mainly for overhaul work. Shown here is their hangar, with the company's Tiger Moth, CF-APL. The picture was taken by a young lad, Walter Henry, who would cycle out to the airport to take pictures. Nearly half a century later he related how he'd risk being chased off the airport by grown-ups who didn't appreciate his enthusiasm.

Phil Sauvé and trapper Jack Stevens pose with an Austin Waco and a typical load of freight. By selling his operation and joining the Austins, Phil helped give them their foothold in the North. (Rusty Blakey)

Allan Austin, one of Chuck's and Jack's older brothers from Chapleau. (Frank H. Fisher)

in a variety of flying. He flew a Pitcairn gyroplane in 1927, had various adventures flying through the Prohibition era in the States, was a test pilot for Capital Aircraft and for Stinson, was an air mail pilot for American Airlines in 1929, and in 1931 returned to Canada to fly for National Air Transport in the North.

In 1934 he started Eclipse Airways at Chapleau and for a few months had a very busy time, mainly serving the mining industry. His business partner was an American, Mike Thorn, and Herb Beatty was his mechanic. When business slackened off, Thorn went back to the United States, taking his airplane with him. Phil Sauvé, who was already on terms with Bill and Allan Austin at Chapleau, took up an offer to sell out to Austin Airways and hired on as a pilot.

So Eclipse wound up its operation and its Waco YKC, one with the Jacobs L-4MA engine, went to work for Austin. The plane had been bought from Jack Sanderson in November 1934 and became Austin property the following June. Phil Sauvé flew it to Sudbury where he established a new base for Austin on Ramsey Lake, close to downtown Sudbury. Sudbury was soon to become Austin's primary base and remained so for over 20 years. Centring operations here as opposed to 250 miles south in Toronto was sensible, considering the amount of business in the hinterland where mining was booming. To establish this base, Jack Austin made a deal with Al "Skipper" Chalmers of Sudbury Boat and Canoe. Initially a dock and a small shack constituted the Austin operation there.

Also in 1935, the Tiger Moth, CF-APL, was sold and replaced by a Fleet 7, CF-AOC, which had been acquired in the Eclipse deal. The Fleet, with its five-cylinder Kinner engine and big metal prop, was to put in four years of service with Austin and, in spite of the cantankerous Kinner, was to do a great amount of work in the bush. Many a pilot got his wings on 'AOC, some of whom went on to long and successful careers in aviation. The Tiger Moth went to the Ottawa Flying Club, still wearing its black, red and silver paint job. So attractive was it that the club did not repaint it but instead used it as a model when repainting its Avians.

Fires and Emergencies
The flavour of bush flying in the mid-1930s comes across clearly in this description of Austin's 1936 season. The writer is Frank Russell:

"Come May in 1936 it was decided that Chuck Austin and I should take one of the Wacos and go down to St. Michel-de-Saint north of Montreal. We left on May 25 and were to supply transport to a fishing camp. But after three weeks we had found that the mosquitoes were biting much better than the fish. There were very few fishermen in sight!

"A phone call from Jack Austin saved us from this predicament and was to reshape my destiny for years to come. A diamond drill crew had started drilling at the Halcrow Swayze Mine east of Chapleau and required an aircraft three times a week. Chuck and I arrived at Chapleau on June 16 and it looked as if we'd be there till freeze-up or at least until October. I found a couple of furnished rooms and wrote my wife, Jess, that she should come up. On July 3 Jess and Mary, our five-year-old daughter, arrived, all happy to be together again.

"The morning of July 6, Jack Mathews, who was the chief ranger at that time, came over to our base and advised us that they had requisitioned our Waco to help fight the forest fires in Sault Ste. Marie district. After checking our aircraft and putting tools and equipment on board we were off to our first assignment, moving 24 men with their gear from Adelaide Lake to Batchawana Bay on Lake Superior, a short hop of about 10 miles over the hills. We carried two men and equipment on each trip. The lake was teeming with trout and as the men waited their turn they would go a short distance out from shore on a makeshift log raft and catch three or four fish to take home. The foreman and myself flew out on the last trip. I then went down to Sault Ste. Marie by truck, arriving late that night. Next morning we were out at daybreak doing two or three trips north of the Soo. We were then dispatched to Big Bend on the Spanish River where we worked until dark. As we had a cracked exhaust pipe, Bill Piggot, the ranger in charge, agreed that we go to Sudbury on condition that we be back at the crack of dawn next morning.

"We flew to Sudbury and upon landing looked back towards the west. There we saw an amazing sight. All along the horizon, for perhaps 70 miles, the forest was ablaze.

"The cracked exhaust was soon removed and with the help of Andy Carroll, the base assistant, we found a garage with a welding torch and repaired the damage. Realizing that time was short, I crawled into the back seat of the Waco and dozed until Chuck arrived and we flew back to Big Bend for another busy day on the fires.

"About 10 in the morning Bill Piggot asked me if I'd ever had one of the shore lunches put up by the forestry branch. I was a green city boy so that was new to me. Some of the men set up rocks and a fire was started on the shore. A big 2-foot by 4-foot by 8-inch pan was placed on the fire and meat and vegetables were poured in. A very large stew was produced and about two dozen men had a good feed. Tea was made in a 10-gallon pail.

"Day three at Big Bend was more of the same. It was 90°F and new fires were constantly breaking out. By now aircraft were arriving from wherever available. We were suddenly moved over to Wawa for 10 trips, then down to Biscotasing. By now our engine needed some attention and as our spares were in Sudbury another rush trip there had to be made. After some speedy servicing we made some trips out of Sudbury, then Chuck was dispatched to Gogama in CF-AVN. I stayed to service CF-AVL, which Frank Fisher had brought up from Toronto. He and I

(Left) Fleet CF-AOC seen at the Jerome Mine seaplane dock. The mine was about 25 miles north of Biscotasing on Opeepeesway Lake. Rusty Blakey recalls: "The Fleet with its big metal prop had lots of pep, especially on takeoff. When it was working, that is." It seems that the 5-cylinder Kinner engine was a bit of a nuisance. (Rusty Blakey)

CF-AOC while still owned by Fleet Aircraft. Company president Jack Sanderson flew it as his personal aircraft. The coupe top was unique for the time. (via Russ Martin)

then flew out to Bisco to work under forestry chief Jack Dillon. Meanwhile Chuck had been sent to Chapleau.

"Frank and I were together three days when one morning we awoke to a cloudy sky. As there was a shortage of fire hose at Chapleau, we took a load over and I was back where I had started 10 days before. That night it poured rain, giving everybody an easier feeling. At last we would catch up on some much needed rest. As I recall, over that 10-day period, three hours a night was a long sleep! During that time we had each flown 110 hours on endless 10-15 minute trips.

"Some of the other pilots working beside us during this emergency included: Paul Davoud (Canadian Airways, Fairchild 71), Ed Ayr and Harold Smith (Fokker Super Universal), Vern Gillard (OPAS, Hamilton Metalplane), George Phillips (OPAS, Moth), Carl Crosley (OPAS, Moth), Dick Overbury (OPAS, Moth), Archie Vanhee and Earl Hickson (Commercial Airways, Travelair and Fairchild 51/71), Jock Jarvis (Curtiss Robin) and Jack Austin (Fleet 7).

"As long as I stayed in the North there were forest fires, but rarely as bad as in 1936. Today, with big water bombers, bush roads, bulldozers and modern communication systems, fire fighting is much more sophisticated compared to the Wajax pumps, hoses, saws, axes and shovels used in our days. Fires can be controlled much more readily these days, but if they weren't in 1936, it wasn't for lack of trying. There was never a dull moment for us and knowledge we acquired could never be obtained in any university. And the friends and other personalities are unforgettable."

On July 14, 1936, the *Globe* reported on the northern Ontario forest fires in a story headlined "5 New Outbreaks in Sudbury and Algoma District:" "Weary firefighters anxiously scanned cloudless skies in the faint hope of rain last night as fires on several fronts once more assumed menacing proportions after earlier reports had indicated the danger was abating. Sault Ste. Marie, Nakina, Geraldton and Sudbury all reported increased danger to surrounding country. Flames broke out afresh, with winds fanning old blazes into renewed life. Five new fires were reported in the Sudbury District, bringing the total to thirty-five.

"All the resources of the Sault Ste. Marie Forestry Branch were pressed into service as flames, which have already destroyed 12,000 acres of pineland, raged out of control. The situation was regarded as the most serious in the area for several years. About 400 men were fighting outbreaks in Chaplin Township near Franz, eastward to Blind River . . .

"Nearly 4000 acres of the best white pine have been burned over in the Ranger Lake area of Algoma. Observation pilots have difficulty in spotting the fires which are believed to range in extent from 500 down to a few acres . . .

"At Nakina a strong wind was blowing that carried the fire Monday night away from the town where 700 inhabitants were ready to leave on a special train . . .

"Geraldton itself was safe after several terrifying hours Monday night. The whole town of more than 400 inhabitants hurriedly packed belongings and piled trunks, suitcases and boxes on the station platform while flames licked up the nearby bush . . ."

There had been some other excitement in 1936. On April 12 three Toronto men were trapped below ground in the Moose River gold mine in Nova Scotia. The incident made headlines and, as the operation to save the men got under way, aircraft began converging on the region with rescue equipment, newsmen and others. Frank Fisher flew down in a Waco carrying the *Toronto Star*'s top reporter, Frederick Griffin. They put up in a Halifax hotel where another Toronto newsman, rushed down by Phil Sauvé, was staying. Frank later flew the first pictures of the two survivors to Boston, from where the pictures were wired to Toronto to meet that day's press deadline.

Jack Austin was involved in another "dire emergency" about this time. There was a call from Franz that someone was in deep trouble and needed an airplane immediately. Jack and his brother Allan rushed up in the Fleet. Sure enough, there was a fellow in the greatest need. He had missed the train and was about to miss his own wedding! Jack hustled him into the Fleet and flew him up the railroad to Oba, where he was able to catch up to the train. As if that wasn't enough for one day, Jack then took off and became entangled in a vicious storm. He had no choice but to fight it out and when he finally got back into Franz, soaked to the bone, he found that his brother was very much "in the dumps" and about to begin composing Jack's obituary!

Jim Bell Meets the Austins

Over the winter of 1936-37 Jack Charleson and Red McCray operated a flying school at Ramsey Lake using an Avro Avian of the Ottawa Flying Club. It is said that the DOT encouraged the venture in hope of getting some of Sudbury's self-taught, unlicenced fliers legalized. Jack and Red were quite successful and became popular chaps around the Austin base. Rusty Blakey, working at the

(Left) Red McCray and Irene Bell (Jim's wife) along with Doug Reed who's draining oil from one of the Austin Fairchilds. Red McCray had come to Austin after experience in the RCAF, with General Airways, and with the Ottawa Flying Club. (Right) A young Jimmy Bell about to fly a Waco-load of Christmas parcels into the New Golden Rose Mine. (Jim Bell Collection, Rusty Blakey)

time for Skip Chalmers, described Jack as "the most comical character" and relates how one day Jack told him about one of his students who just didn't seem cut out for flying. Jack said, "The only way I could convince him that he couldn't fly was to let him go solo!"

Seeing how well Jack and Red had done, the Austins decided to start up their own flying school. This brought Red McCray and Jim Bell into the Austin fold, hired by Phil Sauvé. Red was a kind of remittance man who allegedly dabbled in aviation (and he was good at it) to fulfill the stipulation in an inheritance agreement that he hold down a paying job. Jim Bell was an aspiring young flier from Copper Cliff. Over the seasons preceding World War II, the new Austin venture was to train about 35 pilots.

Jim Bell had been determined to get into aviation since his boyhood. He obtained his private pilot's licence in 1932, having completed his training course under Tom Senior at Barker Field. In Sudbury he flew a variety of aircraft including the rare McVean Valkyr. Early on he was involved in the crack-up of a Church Midwing, a

homebuilt of his own making. To save him from further misadventure, Jim's father sent him and his brother Bill to Parks Air College in St. Louis, where the Bell brothers were given a more solid foundation in aviation. Then, under Gordy Steeves of the Ottawa Flying Club, Jim received his commercial ticket in 1936. Later that year he bought CF-ABX, a Curtiss-Reid Rambler, from Tom Senior and for the six months he had it was able to build more flying hours. When Phil Sauvé hired Jim, he put him right to work as Austin's flying instructor on the Fleet. Student rates at the time were $8/hr. solo and $12/hr. dual.

Within a few months Jim Bell had upgraded his qualifications by taking an instrument flying course at the Toronto Flying Club. The North was to see much of this fine pilot in the years that followed. Jim Bell was to become a legend.

Jimmy Cairns

Also at this time the Austins hired James T. "Jimmy" Cairns. Jimmy had begun flying May 28, 1928, when he

---

Austin Airways fliers listed among Canada's first 500 civilian pilots:

Pilot	Where Instructed	Lic. No.	Date Issued	Misc.
George Delong "Dick" Preston	J.V. Elliott	238	6-6-1927	Air Engineer Cert. No. 290 issued 8-6-1927
Erskine Leigh Capreol	de Havilland Canada	271	24-3-1928	
James Thomas Cairns	Toronto Flying Club, and Aircraft Ltd.	435	14-3-1929	Air Engineer Cert. No. 538 issued 2-5-1930
Frank Henry Fisher	NAME	496	17-7-1929	Air Engineer Cert.

took his first flight aboard the Toronto Flying Club's Moth G-CAJU with R.C. Guest as his instructor. On October 4 he passed his test for a private pilot's licence and on March 14, 1929, was issued commercial licence No. 435. Later in the year he was hired by the OPAS, making his first trip with them on October 29 in an HS-2L. He stayed with the OPAS until 1936 flying the Gipsy, Cirrus and Giant Moth, H-boat, Fairchild KR-34, and Fairchild FC-2 and 71. During that time he had received air engineer's licence No. 538. His two "tickets" and 11 years as an auto mechanic before going into flying made Jimmy a valuable asset to any aviation operation.

In August 1936 Jimmy left the OPAS and took a job with Starratt Airways at Hudson. On August 24 he checked out on CF-AJB, Starratt's Super Universal. Until October 31 he was busy flying it and the Moth, CF-AGX, and his log notes flights to such places as Sioux Lookout, Red Lake, Woman Lake, Jackson Manion Mine, Rat Rapids and Dog Hole Bay. He finished up with 202½ additional hours. At this point his pay was $375 monthly, a good wage for the day.

Early in 1937 Jimmy was hired by Austin Airways to replace Dick Preston. His pay was to be $200 a month plus a dollar a flying hour. Jack Austin chuckled that at the time the Austin planes were the slowest in the sky. Austin later changed their bonus system to a mileage basis, and all of a sudden the planes seemed to start moving a lot faster.

Jimmy's first flying for Austin was on January 5 in CF-AVL from Toronto. Until August he was based there, flying charters from the flying club in winter and the harbour after breakup. Aside from many flights with sightseers there were charters, often to summer cottage territory north of Toronto. Typical trips logged were: March

(Left) The Curtiss HS-2L was the mainstay of the Ontario Provincial Air Service from 1924 to about 1930. Many bush pilots served on these lumbering flying boats and it was in one of them that Jimmy Cairns made his first money paying flight in 1929. (Frank H. Fisher)

(Below) The D.H.61 Giant Moth on which Jimmy Cairns served as engineer before joining Austin Airways. It's seen at Pays Platt alongside a Moth. CF-OAK often served with Austin aircraft during forest fire fighting operations in Northern Ontario. (Jimmy Cairns)

1, CF-AVL, Toronto-Ottawa, 2 hours; April 15, CF-AVL, 2 trips Sudbury-Afton Mine, 5 passengers, 2 hours; May 12, CF-AVN, Toronto, photography, 1 hour; May 16, CF-AVN, Toronto-Whitby (wheels), 30 min.; May 19, CF-AVN, Whitby-Toronto (floats), 20 min.; May 24, CF-AVN, Toronto local, 12 flights, 29 passengers, 3 hours; May 28, CF-AVN, Toronto-Jackson's Point-Toronto, 1½ hours; July 17, CF-AWI, Lake Simcoe return, Fort Erie return, 3:10 hours. A long tour in August sent Jimmy and CF-AVL from Toronto to Winnipeg via such stops as Sudbury, Iron Bridge, Three Ducks, Oba, Port Arthur and Kenora. The trip lasted from August 25 to September 5 and took 42:25 hours. The day after his return Jimmy made 17 sightseeing hops with 48 passengers on what was likely the Labour Day weekend.

Over the winter of 1937-38 Jimmy took blind flying instruction on the Toronto Flying Club Fleet 7, CF-CET, plus some night instruction from Ernie Taylor at the Hamilton Flying Club on their Moth, CF-CBT. The summer of 1938 he continued flying from Toronto, usually with CF-AVL. Trips included June 26, Toronto-Lake Couchiching-Toronto, 2:35 hours; July 2, Toronto-Baptiste-Petawawa-Pembroke-Petawawa-Toronto, 6:05 hours; July 14, Burlington Beach return; July 28, Toronto-Buffalo-Rochester-Toronto, 2:55 hours; August 1, Toronto-Port Dover, 1:15 hours. Part of October and

November was spent flying CF-AVN from Sudbury.

One flight Jimmy Cairns always remembered was an ambulance call. A hunter had been accidentally shot at the north end of Algonquin Park and Jimmy flew him to North Bay. On arrival he asked around to see who might pay for the flight. Someone pointed to the hunter. Jimmy was not amused. The wounded man died a few hours later. When Jimmy left Austin Airways he had flown 430:45 hours with the company. This figure included more hours on the Waco than any other type.

Enter Rusty Blakey

In 1937 Austin Airways opened new bases at Gogama and Biscotasing, each about 80 miles from Sudbury. From either base aircraft could service the busy gold mine at Jerome. Gogama and the summer base at Temagami also served the New Golden Rose Mine 44 miles northeast of Sudbury operated by Consolidated Mining and Smelting, which was using Austin Airways but also its own aircraft at Ramsey Lake—A D.H. Dragon and a D.H. Hornet Moth. Mine personnel from the Temagami region could fly quickly into New Golden Rose on Emerald Lake. This saved hours as the land route was south to Warren, then north up a rugged bush road. The fare in from Temagami on the Waco was $5 ($10 from Sudbury). Other mining developments being served at the time were the Swayze Mine from the Chapleau base, and the McIntyre Mine at Belleterre, Quebec, from the Temagami base.

A key personality came to Austin Airways in the late thirties. A young fellow named Thurston A. "Rusty" Blakey had been working as a jack-of-all-trades around the dock for the Sudbury Boat and Canoe Co. Rusty got to know the Austin crowd and before long Phil Sauvé had hired him away from Skipper Chalmers as a helper. This was fine by Chalmers so long as Austin agreed to train Rusty as a pilot. The next thing Rusty knew, Jim Bell had him in the Fleet giving him flying lessons off the ice. Jim realized that his student was a "natural" and sent him solo after just 3½ hours. Phil Sauvé was keeping an eye on Rusty and insisted that he fly every day to learn the ropes as quickly as possible. In August 1937 Rusty received his licence, but not a private one: he went straight to a commercial ticket. One of his first trips after receiving his licence was out to the New Golden Rose Mine to pick up its first gold brick. Some of the men at the mine were a bit perturbed that Austin would send a "green" young pilot on such a responsible mission.

Rusty Blakey's first assignment was as base pilot at Biscotasing. He arrived there about Christmas 1938 with

(Left) Air engineer/pilot Jimmy Cairns is remembered by Rusty Blakey as "a thorough fellow—he'd check an airplane out very carefully before sending it out on a flight." (Right) Mechanics' wives, Marg McCarthy and Elsie Cairns, dressed for the weather, pose by an Austin Fairchild (Rusty Blakey, Jimmy Cairns)

Mining became big business in Northern Ontario in the early part of the century. Gold fever was sweeping the province with Toronto as the financial and supply capital. Great complexes like this one, Hollinger's Porcupine gold mine, were springing up, and the impetus provided to the economy was immeasurable. The transportation business was bound to be a winner in this setting. Roads were built, the railroad system expanded into the North and it was only a matter of time before aviation would reap some of the financial benefits. Several great pioneer aviation operations trace their roots to this high-spirited era. One is CP Air . . . another, Austin Airways. (Public Archives Canada PA15719)

(Right) The innocent-looking package being handed over to Jimmy Bell contains a $20,000 gold brick. Jim was about to fly it from the mine at Horwood Lake in CF-AWP. Austin pilots from the early years recall how sometimes gold bricks would sit unattended (and unmolested) on a dock waiting to be flown out. (Jim Bell Collection)

(Below) The waterfront at Jellicoe, Ontario. Austin Airways provided invaluable service to this mining centre in the 1930s and 1940s. The scene is typical of the small communities which depended so much on Austin. (W.N. Millar via K.M. Molson)

the Fleet to fly primarily on the 15-minute run to Jerome Mine. Fritz Kohls was to be his helper at Bisco. The Fleet wasn't an ideal aircraft for the work, having a load capacity of either one passenger or a small amount of freight, but it could get into all the local camps, including those on lakes too small for bigger planes. Thus Rusty was able to give the service required plus make a lot of good contacts for the future. The Fleet served well for several months until replaced by the Waco CF-AVL. Meanwhile Jim Bell was flying out of Gogama with the Fairchild CF-AWP and also serving the Jerome operation. While at Bisco in these days the Austin crews stayed at Bill Orange's place or at Jack Dillon's. Dillon was chief forest ranger in the region. Besides Austin Airways, few other bush operators were working in the region beyond Sudbury. Rusty recalls bumping into only one bit of competition at Bisco his first year. That was Stu Hill, flying a Bellanca for Dominion Skyways.

Ever since they had acquired their Wacos, the Austins had had considerable trouble with the engines and were hard pressed to get 400 hours between overhauls. As the engine wasn't self-lubricating, the rockers had to be manually greased. Every few days there would be trouble with a flat cylinder and the valves would have to be ground. Dick Preston eventually concluded that a lower octane gas (80 instead of 90) should be tried as it would have less lead. The results were positive. While at Bisco Rusty

was the first in the company to fly a Waco past 400 hours without having to change a cylinder. He notes that the improved performance, even with the more appropriate gas, had a lot to do with careful engine handling by the pilot.

And Then There Was the Time . . .

High adventure entered the Austin Airways annals on October 14, 1938, involving a crankshaft failure in flight and some very good flying by Phil Sauvé. The incident with Waco CF-BDN is described by Phil in his report to the Department of Transport on October 19, a few days after it had occurred:

"Left Gogama on Friday Oct. 14 at 15:00 hours with one passenger for Ronda Mine. Motor and aircraft checked before flight and found airworthy. Arrived at Ronda at 15:25. Picked up two more passengers and left Ronda at 16:15. After being in the air 45 minutes flying at an altitude of 5000 feet the propeller came off and swinging to the right cut off the lower wing just outside the wing struts and also doing considerable damage to front wing strut thus bringing leading edge of upper wing down. This decreased incidence on upper wing considerably and having lost most of the lifting surface of the lower wing, the plane was very hard to keep under control. Picking out a lake about five miles east of my track, I started to glide. By keeping machine at 80 mph I man-

(Left) Bert Jerome, on the left, along with his brother Jack, discovered one of the most productive gold mines in Ontario. He is shown here with a young helper. The Jeromes were flown north from Toronto to stake their claims by Austin pilot Jim Bell. (Right) The Jerome Mine around 1940. (Rusty Blakey, via Sid Bennett)

Austin Airways' "terminal" at Biscotasing, with a Waco awaiting its next trip; and a winter scene at Bisco, with a sled loaded with the inbound freight. (Rusty Blakey)

aged with full opposite control to keep machine fairly level and steered towards the lake. Pieces of fabric, ribs and spar were tearing off all the way down due to hard vibration. I do not think it would have held together for another 1000 feet.

"The passengers [Les Ashcroft, Don Groome and Joe Laflamme] were very good after I told them to fasten safety belts and they kept very silent. There wasn't a sound heard until we were on the water, which helped things a great deal. After landing, the machine was paddled to shore and we stayed there until Sunday, October 16, when we were picked up by C.C. Austin. There were no hardships and no one suffered from either lack of

food or cold. Our rations could have kept us going for another five or six days and we were very comfortable with one eiderdown and four pairs of blankets.

"We have now shipped motor to Continental factory for complete overhaul and there is a new lower right wing being shipped up. Also, upper right wing is going to have a new front spar put in. New wing struts and a new propeller are being shipped in. We expect to have the machine flying again in about three weeks."

Phil had landed the cripped Waco on Fraleck Lake north of Sudbury. When he failed to show up in Sudbury, a big search was begun. Progress was hampered by smoke and haze and after three days hope was fading. The search was concentrated mainly along the CNR tracks where people had reported hearing an aircraft. This line runs north from Capreol. Meanwhile the Waco was sitting on the shore of Fraleck Lake eight miles east of the tracks and about mid-way between them and the Wanapitei River. But the downed men had few worries. Bushman Joe Laflamme, the famous "wolf man" of Gogama, had brought along a shipment of moose meat. At last, on the third day of the search, Chuck Austin, detouring around some bad weather, spotted the stranded group.

Forty-four years after this incident, Les Ashcroft of Sudbury added some details of what happened when the Waco lost its prop: "Phil cut the engine and Joe Laflamme immediately asked, 'Did we hit a goose?' Don replied, 'No,' so Joe said, 'Well, it could be worse. We could have lost a wing.' Then Don added, 'Hell, the wing's tearing off right now!'

"Then Phil put his hand up for silence as he started to glide down. He had to glide to the right to keep the plane under control. With iron nerve, Phil got the plane down safely. It was the most remarkable flying I have ever seen or heard of.

"We didn't suffer at all waiting to be rescued. The plane carried a supply of rations, and a shipment of the wolf man's moose meat bound for Sudbury. Actually we had fun out there. We had nice warm blankets and kept a good fire going. The wolf man commented several times, 'No need for my wife to worry about me, but I sure hope she's feeding my wolves.' The wolf man sure kept things humming."

As soon as the men were picked up, plans were made to salvage the damaged Waco. Jack Austin, Frank Russell, Phil Sauvé, Jim Bell and Jimmy Cairns established a camp at Fraleck Lake. Jimmy Cairns recalled that after a hard day's work on the Waco, evenings were spent relaxing, aided by a case of rum which someone had thoughtfully flown in. After a suitable period of unwinding, Frank and Jimmy would keep Jack up late, explaining to him all he didn't know about running a flying business.

As to the Waco, its lower right wing was in tatters, but the upper one was removed and taken by canoe and portaged along the Wanapitei River to a road where it was trucked to Sudbury. Once repaired, it and a new lower wing were brought back in the same way. CF-AWP was used to bring in a new engine. Before too long CF-BDN was back together and Phil Sauvé flew it out to Sudbury.

Aerial Surveying

From its first year on the Toronto waterfront, Austin Airways was involved in photographic charter work, frequently taking up photographers from Toronto newspapers. Soon there were jobs doing photo work for the provincial government and, before long, major contracts developed, covering vast areas of the province, especially in the North. Complementing the photographic work, there were major contracts doing timber surveys for the province and the big forestry companies such as KVP. In this part of the Austin Airways story, two names stand out: Dusey Kearns and Holly Parsons.

Aerial photographer William Harvey "Dusey" Kearns got his start in flying when he was hired by the Ontario Department of Lands and Forests in 1924, the year the Department set up its aviation branch, the Ontario Provincial Air Service. In *Skyview Canada*, Don W. Thomson writes of Kearns: "In those early days Kearns cranked 75-foot long rolls of film that were 10 inches wide, with 110 exposures to the roll. Over the years since 1925, Kearns rose in the ranks to become chief aerial photographer for the OPAS. His nickname was derived from jocular references made by his postwar companions. Because of the well-known speculative plunges by Kearns in German marks he was called 'Von Dusenburg' and subsequently the title became abbreviated."

Kearns' first flight with Austin Airways took place from the Toronto Flying Club field in 1938. He recalls, "The flight was with Jimmy Cairns in a Waco on wheels. We carried the skis in the cabin and landed at Huntsville to change over. When we got to Sudbury, we cut a hole in the floor for a camera and left for Franz where photography was done for the Department of Mines."

The Waco (CF-AVL) was only a makeshift photo plane, so in May 1938 Austin purchased CF-AWP. This was a Fairchild 51/71 which had been used previously by Johnny Fauquier. It was properly modified for Dusey's needs and thereafter was to be seen far and wide across the

Waco CF-BDN after its prop-throwing episode. The photo clearly shows just how badly the lower starboard wing was torn up. Cowl damage is also evident. Jack Austin and two others work on removing the engine. (Jimmy Cairns)

Joe Laflamme, the famous "wolf man" of Gogama, raised a team of wolves as sled dogs and showed them in New York in 1938. He's on the left while some fearless lad helps him board his pets. Prudently, pilot Jim Bell is out of the picture on the other side of the aircraft. (Jim Bell Collection)

(Below) Happy survivors of the Fraleck Lake incident. From the left: Phil Sauvé, Les Ashcroft, Don Groom and Joe Laflamme. Rescue pilot Chuck Austin is on the right. (via Les Ashcroft)

W.H. "Dusey" Kearns (above) with one of his big aerial cameras. (Sudbury Star via W.H. Kearns)

(Right) An AWP gallery on floats, skis and even wheels. Air operations during the Fairchild years at Austin were still generally a "seat-of-the-pants" affair. Pilots flew without radio and their success depended on a combination of flying ability, a thorough knowledge of the countryside and weather, and top aircraft maintenance. (Gord Mitchell Collection)

Ontario bush country, in Manitoba and as far west as the Rockies.

Holly Parsons was for many years the best timber sketcher in Ontario and much of his work was done viewing the forests from a perch in one of Austin's aircraft. Like Dusey, Holly started his flying in the rickety HS-2L flying boats owned by the Ontario Provincial Air Service. Bruce West in his book *The Firebirds* describes Holly's profession: "On such missions the observers usually carried outline maps already drawn on heavy material which wouldn't flap to pieces in the aircraft's slipstream as it whipped around an open cockpit. To these outline maps such accomplished artist-observers as Parsons deftly add-

ed the required details concerning such things as the type and distribution of timber stands, while the airplane soared at altitudes up to about 5000 feet over the bush country." By the late thirties, Holly Parsons seemed as much part of the furniture around Austin Airways as any of the "regulars."

Keeping Them Running

Aircraft maintenance was a top priority with Austin Airways. Once Dick Preston left the company this vital aspect was mainly the responsibility of Jimmy Cairns and, later on, Frank Russell. Frank had moved to Sudbury in 1936 to take over this job. While running the main base at Sudbury, he was to spend plenty of time in the field as well, though the Austin pilots were either licenced engineers or knew enough about engineering to keep their machines running smoothly, usually with the help of a competent helper/mechanic.

Keeping the aircraft running during the busy summer season was a taxing business. Frank Russell recalls that as a rule flying was on a dawn-to-dusk basis. The mechanic would be down at the dock before sunrise to check out his aircraft. Weather permitting, the pilot would usually be off as soon as the sun appeared on the horizon. From then till sunset the airplane would be flying back and forth between base and wherever it was serving—a mine, a camp site, a forest fire, and so on. Each time the plane returned, the mechanic would usually pitch in with loading or unloading, fuelling, and keeping on top of any mechanical snags as well as paper work.

Often the engineer or helper would be away from base with his airplane. He would keep everything shipshape, drawing whatever he needed from his tool box. His main concern was the engine, and this he, and the pilot, babied as if everything depended on it. And it did! Among other engine maintenance routines, plugs were cleaned every 25 hours.

Frank seemed to be forever on the move, on routine visits to Austin bases, and on special trouble-shooting trips. He recalls that the Toronto-Sudbury run could be made via Waco in 2:10 hours. By Model T the trip took eight hours, while the train could do it in one, maybe two, hours less than that. As Frank remembers, out-of-pocket expenses while on the road in 1936 were modest. At the Queen's Hotel in Chapleau, pilot and engineer could get lodging for $25 a month, with the best in meals at 35¢ each or three for a dollar.

One trip in particular that Frank couldn't forget took place over the winter of 1937-38. An Austin machine was unserviceable in Belleterre where McIntyre Mines had an operation. Frank had to get in there on a propeller-driven snowmobile from Haileybury, a trip of about 50 miles. It was bitterly cold and they stopped half way at an RC rectory where they received a "wee drop" to bolster their morale. They then pushed on to Belleterre to service the plane. A good example of old-fashioned commitment!

A case of major aircraft maintenance from the Waco era with Austin Airways is shown in this report by Frank Russell to the DOT. The work was done to CF-AVL at Sudbury:

Fuselage: "All fabric and woodwork removed, tubing

A good overview of Austin Airways' Sudbury base in 1937. The long buildings to the left belong to Sudbury Boat and Canoe. The shack with the checkered roof is the original Austin building at Ramsey Lake. Two buildings to the right is the house which was later added to to become Austin's main office. Inco's Copper Cliff stacks loom in the distance. (Jim Bell Collection)

(Left) A nice snap of Chuck Austin with helper Britt Jessup. Chuck spent 15 years flying with the company and with the RCAF. (Rusty Blakey)

In the "men at work" photo Bill McCarthy and Frank Russell pose atop a Waco at changeover time. (Jimmy Cairns)

An Austin Waco is the subject of this Sudbury Star *photo. The* Star *caption read: "Winter's a long time coming, and so far as Lake Ramsey is concerned, it has got no further than CPR Bay. The faint white strip seen in the background at the right is ice, reported about three inches thick. The Austin Airways Waco has been changed over from floats to wheels, and these will be used on the lake when it freezes over, and until the snow is five or six inches deep. One other plane is fitted with skis while the third plane is still on floats in readiness for mercy flights or any other emergency. (Rusty Blakey)*

cleaned and painted with two coats of P27 primer and two coats of Lionoil and aluminum powder. All woodwork replaced and repaired where necessary.

"Stretcher compartment installed complete with necessary fittings and attachments.

"All cowlings repaired where necessary.

"Battery cables run direct to starter and starter switch to correct compass deviation.

"Woodwork given two coats of Lionoil, and fuselage covered with Flightex Grade A fabric, given 14 coats of dope as per Berry Brothers specifications, finished black and rubbed down with Berry Brothers Superfine Rubbing Compound."

Wings: "All woodwork repaired or replaced as necessary, new trailing edges installed and covered with Grade A fabric. Given 11 coats of Berry Brothers dope, finished in Fokker red with silver letters. Rubbed down with Berry Brothers Superfine Rubbing Compound."

In a June 1937 C of A renewal inspection, the following problems were noted for Waco CF-AWI: trailing edge of lower wings badly warped, soggy fabric on lower wing, #2 and #3 main ribs broken at trailing edge on lower port wing, top front cross member in fuselage found badly rusted and pitted beneath trim, excessive play at aileron guy strut. Repairs took from June 29 till July 19 when the new C of A was granted. This sort of work was routine for Frank Russell's maintenance organization.

Rusty Blakey remembers an amusing little anecdote about aircraft servicing from his days as a young pilot. He was flying a Waco at Bisco when his engine started missing. Chuck Austin and Frank Russell landed by chance and Frank looked over Rusty's engine. He interchanged some plugs and the engine ran smoothly. He then said to Rusty, "There, young man. Let that be a lesson to you. You had the front plugs in the back." Something like yelling at a cyclist, "Hey, your back wheel's going forward!" Rusty was taken in by this trick—Frank knew that his tinkering around probably hadn't done much except maybe dislodge some deposits on the plugs.

Waco Roundup

After thousands of hours of service, each of Austin Airways' Wacos was to meet an undeserved ending. The first to go was CF-BDN. Gordy Mitchell was flying it near Chapleau one day when the engine quit. The Waco crashed through trees and was a complete loss. Amazingly neither Gordy nor his passenger was severely injured.

A letter to the Department of Transport from Jack Austin sums up the demise of CF-AVN on December 8,

CF-AVN was Rusty Blakey's first aircraft with Austin Airways. Before he could get his hands on the Waco as "his" airplane, Jack Austin insisted that Rusty have 1000 hours under his belt. In this photo CF-AVN is seen at Eagle Nest Lake, about 50 miles northeast of Sudbury. (Rusty Blakey)

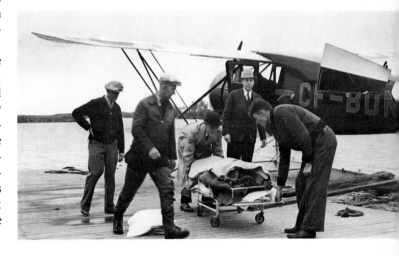

Austin Airways flights have saved many lives over the years. Here a patient is transferred from Waco CF-BDN at Sudbury. The stretcher hatch is clearly shown. Jim Bell is assisting, while Dr. Stanley Polack is seen behind him. Ambulance cases were frequently men injured in the mines or lumber camps. Those who recall the Austins tell that no medevac was ever refused for lack of funds. Jack Austin authorized many an emergency flight without concern for payment. The main thing was to get the sick or injured patient to hospital first, and settle up later. This was long before the days of provincial medical insurance. (Rusty Blakey)

(Top left) Waco CF-BDN as plunked into the woods on January 8, 1942, by Gord Mitchell after his engine quit. Four men and a horse salvage what they can (above) and Sid Bennett (left) retrieves the bent prop. (Gord Mitchell Collection, two via Sid Bennett)

Waco UKC* (CF-AVL, CF-AVN)

Length	25'2½''
Wing span	33'2⅝''
Height (wheels)	8'6''
Empty weight (land)	1923 lb**
Gross weight (land)	2850 lb
Useful load	927 lb
Engine	Continental R-670-A, 210 hp
Floats	Edo P-3300
Fuel	58.4 Imp.gal.
Oil	4.0 Imp.gal.
Passengers	Pilot plus three
Airframe hours	To July 1945, 3086 hrs.
Cost	$8203.67 on wheels, incl. taxes, duty

*Figures drawn from DOT file for CF-AVL.
**As noted in DOT file for CF-AVN, empty weights land, sea and ski respectively were 1909 lb, 2210 lb and 2017 lb. Gross weights were respectively 3000 lb, 3250 lb and 3000 lb.

Waco VKS-6 (CF-BDN)

Length	26'8''
Wing span	35'
Height (wheels)	8'8''
Gross weight	3250 lb
Engine	Continental W670M, 240 hp

Waco YKS (CF-AWI)*

Length	25'2½''
Wing span	33'2⅝''
Height (wheels)	8'6''
Empty weight (land)	1853 lb
Gross weight (land)	2963 lb
Gross weight (sea)	3250 lb
Engine	Jacobs L-4MA, 225 hp

*CF-AWI was transferred from Eclipse Airways to Austin Airways via Jack Sanderson on July 1, 1936. Austin paid $8512.00 for it. CF-AWI had been built in 1943.

1942: while taxiing, the aircraft "broke through the ice on Upper Green Lake, about 25 miles south and west of Biscotasing, and submerged." Pilot Elmer Ruddick and two passengers got out. The insurance company insisted that the Waco be salvaged. Pilot Frank Fowler organized some help and got the plane up onto the ice and dried out. Then he and Jack Austin flew it down to Sudbury, where it was put in the hangar overnight. Next morning, imagine their surprise when they came to work—there was the Waco with its wings pulled away from the fuselage and drooping sadly. It seems the warmth of the hangar had melted the ice which was all that had been holding the wings together. The glue had become unstuck while the plane had been submerged!

CF-AWI, originally Phil Sauvé's machine, saw only about a year's service with Austin before being traded off to Jack Sanderson for Waco CF-BDN. It met a not uncommon ending for bush aircraft. On October 15, 1946, the pilot was preparing to preheat his engine with a blow pot. As it was windy, he placed the burning blow pot in the cabin. All of a sudden, poof! No airplane. This incident took place at Latham Island near Yellowknife.

CF-AVL was lost on October 24, 1946. It had been dispatched from Sudbury that morning for a trip to Killarney and Little Current on Georgian Bay. Taumo "Tommy" Mattinen was the pilot. While taxiing in rough water at Little Current the Waco flipped. The pilot reported later that, "Mr. Fabbro and myself were able to get out of the aircraft and sat on one of the floats until a boat came out and took us both to shore." The Waco was salvaged in a few days but considered beyond practical repair. Tommy Mattinen had had a couple of other brushes with the Wacos. One day he returned to base with damaged wingtips, having landed too close to a rocky cliff. Another day he took out hydro wires at Matachewan, blacking out the mine and townsite there. Tommy later left Austin Airways to fly in Newfoundland, where he was lost in a crash.

Waco CF-AVN went through the ice on Upper Green Lake on December 8, 1942. Frank Fowler salvaged the plane, and with Jack Austin flew it back to Sudbury. After it thawed overnight in the hangar, the wings fell apart—they had only been held together by the ice! (Gord Mitchell Collection)

One of Johnny Fauquier's aircraft, a Waco UKC, over northern Quebec. Occasionally the Austins would bump into aircraft flown by Fauquier, General Airways, Wheeler Airlines and other bush operators. As a rule, the rivalry was strictly friendly. (Bert Phillips)

(Below) Part of the General Airways fleet at changeover time. The scene is at Noranda, the company's main base. General Airways was the biggest bush operator in northwestern Quebec during the 1930s. As a rule, there was little competition between companies like Austin and General, even though they were neighbours. General usually stuck to the Quebec side of the border, except for cases such as major forest fires. Note CF-AWP, at the time operated by Johnny Fauquier. (via Bert Phillips)

Wartime Adjustments

The coming of war in September 1939 influenced every aspect of Canadian life, bush flying not excepted. Immediately there were restrictions. Flights connected with things like sport fishing or hunting were cut out, and only necessary commercial flying was permitted. Generally essentials like gasoline and oil were not hard to come by, but some parts and aero engines could be. Overall, companies like Austin Airways had to adapt to conditions. It wasn't quite business as usual.

On one occasion, Austin needed a new Pratt and Whitney engine for a Fairchild. Jack Austin had to go to Ottawa to make arrangements and meet with none other than C.D. Howe, Mackenzie King's minister-of-just-about-everything. Howe agreed on the spot to get Jack the

engine, telling him, "You're going to get your engine. That's the simplest request I've had all day!"

The war had another effect on Austin Airways—a number of employees left to join the war effort. These included Jimmy Cairns, who went to No. 1 Air Observers School at Malton then to No. 4 at London as superintendent of maintenance; Red McCray, who left for No. 2 Elementary Flying Training School at Oshawa; Bill Sumner, who quit for work at another EFTS; and Les Compton, who became an AOS pilot flying Ansons. He was killed one night in 1942 while on a training flight from No. 5 AOS, Winnipeg. At the time, Rusty and Dusey happened to be on a stopover at Winnipeg in CF-AWP. Chuck Austin and Phil Sauvé also left the company.

Hundreds of World War II trainers being taken west via the Northern Ontario ferry route refuelled and had minor servicing at Nakina. Here Cornells are being readied for their next leg. An Austin Airways tent and blowpot have been pressed into service to help the cause. (Right) A quartet of sergeants from No. 124 Ferry Squadron outside their Nakina hotel. For decades this was a familiar spot for fliers passing through (few regretted having to leave) and for all involved with Austin's Nakina operation. (Both, H.A. Maguire)

Chuck was posted to Borden, then Jericho Beach, where he became chief instructor on flying boats. His wartime years were spent first on Stranraers then on Cansos. Jim Bell also left Austin at this time. At first he was among a group of pilots heading for England to fly with Imperial Airways, but instead he joined the RCAF and served for a time at Borden, Trenton and Dartmouth as a flying instructor with the rank of flight lieutenant.

Jack Austin relates one amusing little incident early in the war when one of his employees came to him to report that he was going into the AOS system. He said he wasn't giving any notice but was quitting on the spot. He explained it simply and with a certain logic: "You pay me by the hour, so I'm quitting by the hour."

One interesting wartime job undertaken by Austin Airways came about when surveying for the Alaska Highway had fallen behind schedule. Aerial surveyor R.N. "Reg" Johnson recommended the team of Kearns and Blakey to help get the project caught up. "If only they were here," he lamented, "the lack of aerial photos would soon be remedied." A US commander replied, "Well, if they're so damned good, get them out here!"

Dusey and Rusty were soon on their way west with the Fairchild, CF-AWP, but no sooner had they arrived at Fort St. John than they realized they were in trouble. The photographs were required to be taken from 11,000 feet above sea level with the surrounding mountains up to 16,500 feet! To lighten the plane, Rusty flew back to Winnipeg where he changed the Fairchild's floats for wheels, but that was an exercise in futility. There was no way the old Fairchild could ever operate in such rarefied air, so after two months in the west back it went to Ontario where it was more at home.

Those Tiny Aeroncas

Beginning in 1939, Austin Airways acquired three Aeroncas, the first two with 50-hp engines. These were for flying instruction and general duties, and were CF-BLM, 'BLN and 'BLO. For three such innocent-looking airplanes, they were to have exciting careers. Forest sketcher Holly Parsons recalls using the little Aeroncas for his work: "On one flight at around 4000 feet, upward air currents took us up to 8000 feet with full motor on. We thought we were chosen. Only with the nose down and full throttle were we able to regain our former required elevation. This aircraft worked well for our purpose but was so sensitive that one could put his arm out the window and the nose would start coming around in a turn."

Aeronca CF-BLN was bought by Austin Airways in

Aeronca CF-BLM photographed at Hamilton in 1939 while still owned by aircraft broker J.B. Dunkelman. (Jack McNulty)

February 1939 and was wrecked on February 9, 1941, in a freak mishap. While taxiing on skis on Ramsey Lake, the engine quit. Student pilot Peter Laurin got out and swung the prop, and the engine fired. Away went the Aeronca, sans pilot! Jack Austin's letter to the DOT of February 11 elaborates: "The student grasped a hold on the starboard wing strut and attempted to stop the airplane. In doing so he slipped on the snow and, losing his hold on the strut, caught hold of the rear check cable on the starboard ski. From a prone position he managed to guide the aircraft in circles until his hands became too numb to hold on longer. This was just before assistance arrived. The airplane then started down the lake taxiing

All that remained of CF-BLN after it ran away on Ramsey Lake in February 1941. (Gord Mitchell Collection)

with no one at the controls. It gradually gathered speed and after travelling about half a mile crashed into the trees on the shoreline."

Austin Airways bought CF-BLO from the Aeronca plant in Cincinnati and it was delivered in July 1939 for a grand total of $3270. Its life was to be short but included one of the minor tragicomedies of bush flying. On October 16, 1939, it was stolen from Ramsey Lake. Within hours the RCMP had sent out dispatches alerting a wide region to the theft. Its initial report noted, "thief tied up night watchman and cut all wires on other planes lying at anchor . . . thief is well armed."

This sounded like real intrigue. The report even alluded to the possibility of the plane being in the hands of an enemy agent. All was made clear, however, when CF-BLO was found damaged along the Pickerel River south of Sudbury. The thief was a New Liskeard man going by the name of Farrendon. He had a record of minor offences, including car theft. He had also had an introduction to flying so knew how to start a light airplane. Sometime earlier he had attempted to steal an airplane. When he appeared at the Austin base that October night, Farrendon was an unemployed, homeless, friendless and seriously ill man. His plan was to steal an airplane and commit suicide in it.

At the dock Farrendon got talking with Austin's night watchman. The pair began drinking and eventually Farrendon climbed into the Aeronca and took off. He tried to crash the plane a short time later but botched his effort. Later it was determined that the watchman had cooked up his story of being accosted by an armed man and tied up, in order to cover up his own slackness. At their trial, both men were found guilty. Farrendon received a year's imprisonment and the watchman a suspended sentence.

A busy day's work with CF-BLO was recorded February 16, 1940. Two fishermen from Killarney on Georgian Bay, Fred Prouls and Frank Webberfield, had been ice fishing with their dogs when the ice broke up and they went adrift in Georgian Bay. After they had been out of touch with the mainland for several hours, the villagers put in a call to Austin Airways in Sudbury for help. Jimmy Cairns took off immediately and soon had the lost men spotted. A stiff wind was blowing across the narrow dimension of the floe, forcing Jimmy to make a tricky approach. He then made six trips to remove the men, their dogs and their fishing gear. In all, Jimmy was in the air 2:20 hours.

On October 11, 1940, one of Austin's instructors, Bad-

en Brownlee, was up in CF-BLO with student pilot Theodore Perron. They were practising spins over Ramsey Lake and an attempt was made to land out of the last spin. The air was calm and the water glassy as the aircraft descended. Something went wrong at the last moment and the Aeronca crashed into the lake killing both men.

Of the three Aeroncas, CF-BLM had the most varied existence. It was brought into Canada in March 1939 by General Aircraft Dealers of Toronto at a cost, taxes and duties included, of $2350. It was demonstrated around southern Ontario that summer then sold in July to Wally Siple of Larder Lake. Using it and a Taylorcraft, Siple ran a small flying school called Kirkland Air Services. In March 1940 he sold the airplane to Leavens Brothers, who in turn sold it to the Austins.

On March 26, 1943, Frank Fowler of Austin Airways was coming in to land on Indian Lake near Bisco in CF-BLM when he was caught in gusts and crashed into the trees. Frank escaped all right, but the plane was a mess. The insurance company paid Austin the claim, but Frank, by now on his own, went to the insurers and bought the wreck from them for $200. He hauled the parts to Sudbury and by the end of the year had the Aeronca rebuilt. He applied for a Certificate of Registration and in his inimitable use of the English language wrote on the line showing intended use of the plane, "commercial, passenger and fright."

Frank soon had CF-BLM hard at work. He hauled fish

CF-BLM pranged at Indian Lake in March 1943. This was hardly the end of the tough little Aeronca, as it was later salvaged and rebuilt by Frank Fowler. (Gord Mitchell Collection)

with it, cruised timber, and flew the game warden around. Then, more trouble. On May 14, 1945, Frank was preparing to land near Foleyet when he inexplicably blacked out and crashed. This time he wasn't so lucky and was badly banged up with two broken legs and other injuries. Yet neither he nor the Aeronca was down and out. Frank continued flying and a succession of other operators kept the again-restored Aeronca on the go. But enough is enough, and CF-BLM cashed it in for good on June 17, 1954. While taxiing at Wasaga Beach on Georgian Bay, it flipped and sank. It suffered irreparable damage and never flew again.

Walter Frank Fowler qualifies as one of the real "characters" in the Austin annals. He was born in Muskoka in 1901 and got into aviation towards the end of World War I when he took a job with Canadian Aeroplanes. This got him the occasional flip in a JN-4. Through the twenties

Frank Fowler stands beside his little Heath Parasol sometime in the late thirties. (via Charles Fowler)

he worked as a truck mechanic, but in the early thirties did some part-time work with Leavens Brothers in their barnstorming operation. During this period he acquired a basket case of a Heath Parasol, CF-BJB. It had been built from a kit by the Chandler brothers of North Bay, who eventually lost interest in it and shipped it to Frank as a heap of loose bits in the back of a truck. He went to work and made it look like an airplane again, but was soon up against Col. Joy, the DOT inspector. Joy adamantly refused to licence Frank's Heath and upon each inspection was able to come up with plenty of excuses to justify his decision.

Frank flew the Heath regardless. He devised a platform atop his '32 Plymouth which accommodated the little homebuilt without having to disassemble it. With this contraption, he travelled to any convenient field (out of Col. Joy's sight!) and flew to his heart's content.

Early in the war Frank realized that if he was going to get anywhere professionally in the flying business he'd have to be licenced. He won his commercial ticket and in 1942 was hired by Austin. The following year he obtained an air engineer's ticket. Though he was only to spend a brief time with Austin, it was long enough to make him a local legend.

Frank was a most ingenious fellow and never seemed to be stuck for long, no matter how awkward the situation. This had nothing to do with his education, for he had dropped out in grade four when he was barely literate. Writing Col. Joy's examinations was one of his toughest challenges. His spelling was atrocious, and Jack Austin used to coach him: "Frank, make sure that if nothing else, when you misspell a word on the exam, misspell it consistently right through the whole paper." Frank, it seemed, could misspell a word in an infinite variety of ways.

One day Frank was flying an Austin Waco south of Sudbury when it threw a propeller tip. He had to glide down to a landing in Johnny Creek, a very tight, oversized beaver pond. How to get out? To an ordinary pilot this would have been a hopeless predicament, but not to Frank Fowler. He surveyed the pond and its hydrology. He would have had no idea what "hydrology" was, but he knew enough to do a bit of stream diverting. Before long he had raised the water level enough that he could squeak out of there and get home.

Frank's tough luck with the Austin Aeroncas has already been mentioned, but he still liked the docile little planes. In 1941 he purchased a K-model and rebuilt it as a KC, but there was one problem: on floats it couldn't get airborne with himself (at 240 lb.) and his brother aboard. Undeterred, Frank devised a solution. He installed Bellanca-like winglets on the struts. This bit of added lift was just enough for CF-BIL to get off the water with its two hefty passengers.

After about a year with the Austins, Frank left to seek other work. He did some flying for Pineland Timber in their Cessna Airmaster and later flew a bit for Nickel Belt on the Husky. He was also involved in a number of ingenious aircraft salvage operations, including a sunken Goose, a battered Husky and a Rearwin (CF-BEX). The Rearwin was down in a lake in the Hornepayne region of

(Above) A Sudbury Star *portrait of Bellanca CF-AND at Austin's Sudbury wharf. This tough bushplane served with Austin for nearly five years before being lost in a fire at Nakina. Rusty Blakey remembers it as "a very good aircraft. It performed well, though its Wright engine was not as good as a Wasp. You hand-cranked it from inside the cockpit then pressed a starter button on the floor to get her going." In this picture CF-AND is seen on skis at Nakina. (via Peter Marshall)*

The Old Red Hen, *so called for its orange paint job, at Bisco loading hay and oats, feed for the work horses at Jerome Mine. (Left) Elmer Ruddick on the float of the Bellanca. (Below) CF-AND roars into the air at Nakina. (Rusty Blakey, via Elmer Ruddick, Elmer Ruddick via M.L. McIntyre)*

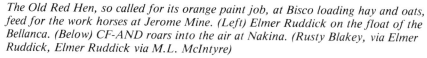

northern Ontario. Frank raised it from the lake bottom and readied it for ferrying out, but on takeoff from a logging road broke its prop on a stump. This left him stranded, but not for long. He picked out a suitable piece of wood and chopped and whittled a new prop complete with copper leading edges. Like most of Frank's ventures, this worked quite nicely and he flew safely back to Sudbury. The propeller has hung for many years over the fireplace at his son Chuck's place in Oak Ridges, Ontario.

In 1951 Frank Fowler had to quit flying for medical reasons. He returned to his Muskoka home and led an active life until he died in 1979. Nobody who knew him would be surprised to hear that at the time he was busy with a project to install a water wheel on his property.

Bellanca Workhorses

One of the greats of the Canadian bush flying scene was the Bellanca CH-300 Pacemaker. Two such aircraft served with Austin Airways. The first was CF-AND, acquired in June 1939. CF-AMO followed in 1944.

CF-AND was built at Bellanca's Newcastle, Delaware, plant in 1930 and was imported into Canada at Montreal as a demonstrator. It operated briefly during 1931 with Coastal Airways of Vancouver, then was sold to General Airways, based, among other places, at Hudson in northwestern Ontario and Elk Lake in north central Ontario.

When General went bankrupt, CF-AND was purchased by Austin. At the time it was being overhauled at Fort William by Canadian Car. Phil Sauvé accepted the aircraft there and flew it to Sudbury. It became one of Austin's workhorses, primarily in the Biscotasing and Nakina regions, much of its work being in support of mining and prospecting activity. Les Compton, Rusty Blakey and Elmer Ruddick did most of the flying.

A sample of Rusty's flying from Bisco in CF-AND follows. The legs between the mining towns noted were short, but the airplane was vital to the life of these isolated centres:

Jan. 29, 1943	Jerome	1:00
	Gogama	:15
	Jerome	:15
Jan. 30	local	:10
Feb. 1	Bisco	:15
	Cinquisle	:25
	Jerome	:15
	Gogama	:15
	Jerome	:15
	Sudbury	1:00

Elmer Ruddick logged these trips from Nakina on March 2, 1943:

O'Sullivan Lake	:20
Ara Lake	:15
Robinson Lake	:20
Ara Lake	:15
Robinson Lake	:20
Ara Lake	:15
Robinson Lake	:20
Nakina	:30

On February 7, 1944, Elmer made several trips from Nakina to Robinson Lake, Marshall Lake, Melchett Lake and Goode Lake. This was a commercial fish haul operation. The return flight from Goode Lake was to be the Bellanca's last. The following morning as mechanic Charlie Kohls was preheating it with a blowpot, it caught fire and was burned to destruction.

Bellanca CH-300 (CF-AND)

Length (landplane)	27'4"
Length (seaplane)	30'
Wing span	46'4"
Height (landplane)	8'
Height (seaplane)	13'9"
Empty weights: land	2596 lb
sea	2993 lb
ski	2676 lb
Gross weights (payload in brackets):	
land	4300 lb (817 lb)
sea	4835 lb (955 lb)
ski	4300 lb (737 lb)
Engine	Wright R-975 Whirlwind, 300 hp
Propeller	Hamilton Standard, 9'3"
Skis	Elliott Brothers
Floats	Edo 2015 or 2009
Fuel	94 Imp. gal.
Oil	5 Imp. gal.
Passengers	Pilot plus six
Hours noted to July 12, 1943	1454:30
Purchase price (Austin Airways)	$5465.00

Hauling Fish at Nakina

In the early 1940s Austin Airways began operations at Nakina. Just before this the territory north of there was being worked by Baillie-Maxwell Ltd. with their Bellanca, CF-AMO, and their Fox Moth, CF-API. This operation, run by Frank Baillie and Roy Maxwell, held a fish hauling monopoly granted by Ontario's Liberal government under Premier Mitch Hepburn. Their

Baillie-Maxwell's Fox Moth runs up at Nakina during winter operations along the Albany River. Before the airplane began service, Nakina's vast hinterland was served mainly by canoe in summer and tractor train in winter. It was not uncommon for mail to be delivered by Indians snowshoeing between places like Ogoki Post and Fort Albany! (Bert Phillips)

Weighing sturgeon near Ogoki Post on the Albany River in 1938. On the right is Baillie-Maxwell pilot Eric Bendall. To his right are some Ogoki people, starting with Gilbert Baxter and his father, John, behind the scale. The others are unidentified. (via Eric Bendall)

domain stretched all along the Ogoki River and down the Albany River to Fort Albany. In 1942 Austin bought out Baillie-Maxwell and Gord Mitchell (later Elmer Ruddick) set to work hauling sturgeon out of the hinterland aboard CF-AND. The fish was flown back to Nakina, where it was processed, Emile Coté being in charge of

that for Austin. The fish was put aboard the train daily, destined for such places as Chicago and New York. Caviar went to North Bay to be pasteurized before going to market.

Eric W. Bendall was pilot for Baillie-Maxwell beginning in July 1938. He provides the following details about the fish hauling business. Though he describes the pre-Austin years at Nakina, the technique didn't change much after Austin took over:

"Baillie-Maxwell established a base at Cordingly Lake about three miles north of Nakina. My first trip to Fort Hope and Osnaburgh House on the Albany River was July 20, 1938, where Roy Maxwell had set up a deal with the Hudson's Bay managers. The scheme was simply to haul HBC freight northward and pick up sturgeon and caviar at selected spots along the Albany, then head home to Nakina. There were two main triangular routes: Nakina-Ogoki Post-Fort Hope, and Nakina-Fort Hope-Osnaburgh House. Each fishing area was visited every other day.

"Using nets or hooks, the Indians would start fishing and keep the fish they caught alive in log cribs built in the river, or by staking them in the river on four or five foot cords tied to their tails. When they had fish, they displayed a white flag which could be clearly seen from the air. No flag, no stop. When the Indians heard or saw the aircraft, they went to work gutting and dressing the sturgeon. By the time I got down and tied up, and set my scales on a tree, there would be several hundred pounds ready to weigh and pay for.

"I weighed each fish in full view of the owner, recorded each weight in a receipt book with the owner's name, totalled it up and gave him his copy. He in turn would take the receipt to the Hudson's Bay post and trade it for whatever he wanted. This continued until I had about 1200 lb aboard the Bellanca, and I would then return to Nakina.

"Since I was just a dumb pilot, I did not get involved in the dollars and cents of the operation. But you didn't have to be a financial wizard to know that someone was making money. Full loads both ways!

"The caviar was processed at Nakina and packed in tins. The sturgeon was iced and packed in large boxes for shipment by rail each evening. The fishermen were receiving 5¢ a pound, and even though the railhead price was much higher, some families were clearing $200 a month, double what the captain of CF-AMO was making. At one time I considered moving in with the Indians and fishing for sturgeon!''

One big difference between the way Baillie-Maxwell and Austin Airways did business on the Nakina fish haul was that Austin didn't use scrip. Instead it used cash. Two cash boxes were carried. From one, fish was paid for directly to the individual fishermen. From the other, business was done selling groceries and other supplies to the Indians. Prices were at the going rate in Nakina, so the usual freight tariffs didn't apply. Besides this, Austin Airways also provided the Indians with nets, fishing line and hooks at no cost.

The arrival of Austin Airways in a new town invariably had important effects on life. In the case of Nakina, it meant that those in the hinterland, in places like Ogoki Post and Fort Hope, had a reliable new connection with "the outside." Food and other supplies were

Another Albany River sturgeon fishing scene, this one dating to 1944. (George Charity)

now easily obtained without the usual long waits. And an ambulance service was available. Nakina became what in former days would have been called a rail-head — the jumping off point for trade and other day-to-day activities for a vast region. The impact included a boom in the wholesaling of food and dry goods, and all the details connected with fish hauling, such as a flourishing ice cutting business in winter.

The Fabric Fairchilds

One of Canada's classic bushplanes in the early years in the North was the Fairchild. Beginning in the twenties, the brainchild of Sherman Fairchild, the Fairchild line became one of the most suitable for the Canadian bush and tundra. In his book *Pioneering in Canadian Air Transport,* K.M. Molson notes of the Fairchilds (and their rivals, the Fokker Super Universal), "These aircraft . . . may be considered as the aircraft that put the air transport business in northern Canada on a practical basis. Western Canada Airways seemed to prefer the Super Universal, which became the standard aircraft of their fleet. Most of the other operators seemed to prefer the Fairchilds. . . ."

Austin Airways was to operate five Fairchilds over the years, the three earliest being a 51, a 51/71 and a 71B. The first, CF-AWP, was the 51/71, purchased in May 1938. Next to join the fleet was CF-BVY, a 51 purchased in March 1942 when it was declared surplus by the RCAF. CF-BVI, the 71B, was a former CPA machine bought by Austin in February 1944. These aircraft were to give the company excellent service. Years later, two Fairchild Huskies were added.

Engineer Frank Russell has provided a short history of Austin's early Fairchilds. In a letter to K.M. Molson of February 4, 1979, he writes: "We purchased our first Fairchild in 1938 from John Fauquier. This was the only 51/71 at the time. It came with a Wasp Jr. T1B but the blower speed had been reduced to cut the horsepower to 320 hp. The propeller was also adjusted to control the rpm for this power at takeoff. CF-AWP was for some time on photography. At full throttle it could just maintain 10,000 feet, due to lack of supercharger or impeller speed. All-up weight was 4370 lb on floats and 4600 lb on wheels or skis.

"We purchased CF-BVY in 1942. It had an early 300 hp Wasp Jr. A. It was originally a razor back with a Wright engine but was converted to a four-longeron type with the Wasp. We operated CF-BVY until we ran out of engines and couldn't get parts. In 1947 we retired this Fairchild as the DOT would not allow us to install a de-rated P&W 985 engine. We removed the wings and tail and stored them.

"Meanwhile we had purchased CF-BVI from C. Babb at Winnipeg in February 1944. This aircraft had been in the RCAF and was a 71B with a Wasp C engine. It had a gross weight of 5500 lb. We operated CF-BVI until breakup of 1944 and then, as we had not been able to obtain floats, as the engine was time expired, and as the

Austin Airways' Fairchild 51 (above) in a typical winter setting. (Left) CF-BVI at a remote Northern Ontario dock. (Rusty Blakey, Gord Mitchell Collection)

"We had obtained a set of floats good only for 5500 lb so we didn't get the 6000 lb that we had hoped for. We test flew the aircraft after conversion. Takeoff was normal but we found that cooling left something to be desired on continuous climb. Otherwise we considered the aircraft acceptable.

"In 1948 we decided to convert CF-BVI to a 51/71, using the wings, tail and floats from CF-BVY. The engine was de-rated to 320 hp by installing a ground-adjustable propeller and a placard not to exceed rpm. This aircraft performed as well as CF-AWP. All-up weight was 4600 lb on Edo 670 floats. All conversion work was done at Sudbury."

When Austin bought CF-BVI, the old CPA machine, there was an undue delay by CPA in delivering its floats. As these were urgently required at Sudbury, Allan Austin called the railroad (CPA's parent) to discuss the matter. He presented his enquiry in terms of whether or not the CPR wanted its flow of railway ties from Austin's sawmills to continue. The floats were shipped immediately!

Typical of the Fairchild line, CF-BVI served Austin Airways well for over five years, then met its fate. On July 17, 1949, with pilot Chuck Austin and two passengers aboard, it crashed on takeoff from English Lake, 33

aircraft was due to be recovered, we decided to modify it to a 71C and also install a 450 hp Wasp Jr. R985 AN 14B. The mods from 71B to 71C consisted of installing heavier longerons and adding a gussett here and there on the clusters. The wing had heavier plywood gussetts added to the spars at the fittings. The engine change was discussed with Pratt and Whitney, and Ken Dawson of P&W was sent to Sudbury to oversee and assist in the installation. We decided to use a constant-speed propeller in place of the variable pitch one, and this greatly improved the plane's ability to hold altitude.

Fairchild CF-AWP sets out from Sudbury with two canoes strapped to the floats. (Right) CF-AWP at Gogama at spring changeover in 1938. (Rusty Blakey, Jim Bell Collection)

miles south of South Porcupine. The aircraft was wrecked but nobody was hurt.

Additional CF-BVI history has been documented by M.L. "Mac" McIntyre in the Fall 1965 CAHS *Journal.* His story, "Three Rare Birds," describes some of the aircraft recovery and restoration work done by Gordon H. Hughes of Port Stanley, Ontario:

"More evidence of the fascinating activities of Northland Aircraft Services is to be seen at the back of Mr. Hughes' shop. There is a Wasp engine, a rusted and broken fuselage, wrecked floats, and bits of rotted wood and patches of dope — the remains of Fairchild 71B, CF-BVI, another real old timer. . . .

"On 17 July, 1949 she stalled on takeoff at English Lake in Temagami Provincial Forest and dropped into eight feet of water at the end of the lake. No one was seriously hurt and the cargo of drilling equipment was removed, but the rest was left in the lake to be almost forgotten for 13 years . . . Mr. Hughes bought salvage rights from the insurance company.

"In late September 1962 the salvage job was started, the engines, floats, wings and tail surfaces being brought out at that time. It was very cold and snowed and rained almost steadily during the six days of this operation. The water was frigid, black, and full of blood suckers. No

diving equipment of any kind was used except a diving mask and a bottle of whiskey. The motor mounts had to be cut under water before anything could be moved and most of the wooden parts fell away as the larger parts were lifted. Big patches of red, black and silver dope remained in almost original condition, with the underlying fabric rotted off except where it was being protected by being doped directly onto metal parts. Oil drums and a raft were used to float the parts to the other end of the lake, then they were trucked over 43 miles of bush road to the highway at Matachewan. The remainder was brought out the following spring under somewhat more pleasant conditions. . . ."

Fairchild 51 (CF-BVY)

Wing span	44'
Length (seaplane)	32' 7¼''
Length (landplane)	30' 11¼''
Height (landplane)	9'
Height (seaplane)	11'3''
Empty weight (landplane)	1890 lb
Empty weight (seaplane)	2290 lb
Gross weight (landplane)	3600 lb
Gross weight (seaplane)	4000 lb
Year built	1927
c/n	23
Former RCAF registrations	G-CYYT
	627
Acquired by Austin	March 3, 1942
Airframe hours to June 28, 1945:	2726:20 hrs

Originally built as an FC-2, the aircraft was converted to Fairchild 51 specs in July 1931. With its 300 Wasp Jr. CF-BVY had a marginal payload. Austin Airways wanted to update its power plant, but the DOT refused to allow this. This led to the aircraft being scrapped in 1947.

Fairchild 71B (CF-BVI)

In 1944 Austin Airways purchased the Fairchild 71, CF-BVI. This aircraft had been built in 1930 at Fairchild's Hagerstown plant and sold to the RCAF as G-CYWE (later renumbered as 674). In 1941 it was acquired by Winnipeg-based Wings Ltd. and re-engined from a Wasp C engine to a Wasp SC-1 of 420 hp. Wings was then absorbed into Canadian Pacific. In late 1943 CP sold the aircraft to the Babb Co. of Glendale, Cal., for $5000. Finally, in February 1944 it was purchased by Austin Airways for $7660. It was immediately re-engined with a Wasp Jr. of 450 hp. This brought CF-BVI up to 71C standards.

Length	32'10½''
Wing span	50'
Weight (landplane)	8'8''
Height (seaplane)	9'4''
Empty weight (skis)	3505 lb
Gross weight (skis)	5500 lb
Engine	Pratt and Whitney Wasp Jr. 450 hp
Propeller	Hamilton Standard 9'6''
Floats	Edo 5300
Fuel	132 Imp. gal.
Oil	10 Imp. gal.
Passengers	Pilot plus seven

The Bay Region Opens Up

During the war Austin Airways began developing interests centred on James Bay. Few aircraft had ventured into the area since the first, a Vickers Viking, had visited in 1924. On that trip, Roy Grandy and B. McClatchey had flown a government agent on his annual tour as far north as Attawapiskat. The main object of the trip was to deliver treaty money. What was a trip of a few days in the Viking had previously taken many weeks by canoe. Even so, another 20 years would pass before any sort of regular air service would come to the James Bay region. It would take Austin Airways to realize the potential for aviation there.

The key personalities in the Austin Airways James Bay venture were Jack Austin and Gord Mitchell. Gord was one of Austin's stalwarts through the war years. He had begun flying lessons in 1939 at Larder Lake where Wally Siple was running a small flying school. He won his private pilot's licence March 15, 1940, his commercial a few months later on October 23, then joined the large number of civilian instructors in the British Commonwealth Air Training Plan, being posted to the Leavens Brothers flying school at Barker Field in Toronto.

In the winter of 1941 Gord moved his family to Sudbury and went to work for the Austins. He and Jack made the original trip to Nakina to set up Austin's base there. Flights to James Bay were to begin from South Porcupine, another base opened up by Gord. Austin had moved there when old-time bush pilot Ed Ayr ceased his South Porcupine operation.

In 1944 Gord Mitchell flew a Fairchild to Moose Factory on a proving flight. Once word got around that he was there, many enquiries came in. His plane was soon busy serving the small and widely separated population in the frozen, desolate country. But what made operating on the Bay feasible was a mail contract won by Austin in 1944. This came about in an unusual way. That March Austin received a contract to fly Dr. Orford on his spring medical mission to the James Bay Indians. Jack Austin flew up to Nicholson to meet Gord coming down from Nakina in CF-BVI. The same day, March 4, they arrived at Moosonee. Next day they set off with Dr. Orford and Hugh Conn of Indian Affairs and visited Eastmain and Fort George. The same week, Jim Bell, flying a Norseman for CPA, was in the area with Matt Cowan, district manager for the Hudson's Bay Company.

While taxiing out in the morning from Eastmain, Jim had the misfortune to break his tail ski. He was obliged to fly Cowan back to Moosonee, then return to his base

These photos, provided by Paddy Gardiner, were taken by the National Film Board during one of Doc Orford's medical tours along the east coast of James and Hudson Bay in 1946. The contrasting shoreline scenes are Moose Factory and (with igloo) Port Harrison. In the centre photos Fairchild CF-BVI is readied for flight and Gord Mitchell is shown in the cockpit. During the early years on the Bay most flying (about 700 hours) was done in summer. Only 50 hours of work could be expected in winter. (NFB 21207, 21195, 21203, 21208)

at Roberval for repairs. Meanwhile Jim Soper, the HBC manager at Fort George was in a bit of a fix. He had been counting on Jim to fly some freight deep inland to Kaniapiscau and asked the Austin twosome if they could help. Gord flew one proving flight and determined that the distance was some 40 miles less than the competition had been billing the HBC for! Soper then asked Jack if Austin might be willing to fly some regular trips and to check with his boss when he got back to Moose Factory (not realizing that he was talking to the boss).

Gord's proving flight to Kaniapiscau had taken place March 9, the previous three days having been weathered out. A 1200-pound load was delivered there to Glen Spears of the HBC. Next day Gord flew 1400 pounds of flour into Great Whale and returned with a sick Eskimo who required Dr. Orford's attention. On March 10 Gord *et al.* flew to Factory River and Rupert's House. At Factory River Jack managed to break some ribs trying to hold down the tail of the Fairchild to help Gord turn. Next day the Fairchild was back in Moosonee and, after another day lost to weather, it headed off up the west coast with Dr. Orford. They visited Attawapiskat and Fort Albany and were back in Moosonee on the fifteenth.

As soon as the Fairchild was released by Dr. Orford, Matt Cowan chartered it to complete the work he had originally planned with Jim Bell. So on March 16 Gord and Jack flew off to Fort George. They then moved 1400 pounds of flour to Great Whale and returned with a load of fur. Next day a load of fur was taken to Moosonee via Factory River; and on the 18th Cowan and a Mrs. Anderson were flown into Fort Albany. Next day more fur was flown from Factory River to Moosonee. CF-BVI then headed south, arriving at Sudbury March 21.

While at Moosonee, Matt Cowan and Jack Austin had discussed the role the airplane could play in moving the mail. Till then it had been delivered up and down the coast by the time-honoured methods: coastal boats in summer, dog teams in winter. The dogs posed a real headache for Cowan. As local postmaster, he had to keep a large number of dogs over the summer doldrums. They were literally eating him out of house and home. Cowan agreed to use his influence to try to get a mail contract for Austin Airways. The Post Office was agreeable and soon Austin was moving the mail in days where it used to take months. The airplane had cracked another northern frontier. Later on Jim Bell was to ask Jack Austin, "How much are you going to pay me for breaking that ski?"

When Gord Mitchell first visited the James Bay region, the native inhabitants were still living according to their traditional lifestyles. Gord was often to find himself overnighting with Eskimos in an igloo and as an avid film maker was to shoot many rolls of 8mm movie film showing igloo-making, the beluga whale hunt and other features of coastal life. On most of his trips Gord's companion was his trusted mechanic Fritz Kohls.

Besides his flying on the Bay, Gord Mitchell was busy with other tasks. One Lands and Forests contract was to restock areas where wildlife had been trapped out; for several days his passengers were beavers. There was also plenty of flying with Dusey Kearns and Holly Parsons. An emergency flight involved rushing diphtheria serum from South Porcupine to Moose Factory in marginal weather after an epidemic had broken out. The *Toronto Star's* headline describing Gord's flight read "Flier Risks Death to Get Supplies into Stricken Area."

Holly Parsons wrote of Gord: ". . . while based at Moose Factory after a drawn out winter mapping stint, we were returning to Kapuskasing airport. Gord Mitchell was my pilot. We were thankful to be returning, as uncertain weather had hampered and prolonged our program. We were within sight of the Kapuskasing runways, possibly a bit over 20 miles away, when ice began to form on our wings. We returned the 150 miles to Moose Factory, the last place in the world we wished to see again at that time." Disappointed or not, Parsons knew that Gord had made the right decision. Another pilot might have pushed on, might have made it, but to a professional it wasn't worth the gamble.

In its September 1945 edition, *Canadian Aviation,* in an article by Jim Hornick, gave a profile of Gord Mitchell and his work with Austin:

One of the few remaining outposts on the North American continent where flying by the seat of one's britches is a necessity rather than a novelty is Canada's poorly charted, sparsely populated Hudson Bay country whose white residents you can easily count on a few pairs of hands.

This is a land where airplane and dog team reign supreme as vehicles of transportation and a place where weather-wise Gordon Mitchell, a pilot for Austin Airways in Sudbury, is friend and flying mailman to fur traders and missionaries scattered along the barren coasts of Hudson and James Bays.

Mitchell and his old reliable Fairchild 71 were a familiar sight to Indians and Eskimos up in the Moosonee district last year. This winter he will be back on his mail "beat" again but this time in a newer, faster machine—a Norseman.

The ten-year-old Fairchild whose 330-horsepower engine bounced her off a tiny lake like a frightened mosquito, went into involuntary retirement recently when engine failure at takeoff forced her to crash into a lake near the home base of Sudbury. But Mitchell is going back because the hardy pioneers of Rupert House, Eastmain and Factory River need him, need more contact with the outside world than a battery-powered, crackling radio.

Last year, rushing to finish all his air freight assignments before an early thaw suspended flying operations, the Sudbury airman was trapped by nature at Moose Factory and for several days both he and his mechanic, Fritz Kohls, spent several anxious hours directing the preparation of a water strip to facilitate operations on floats.

Without any dynamite to blast a channel in the ice, he and Kohls used axes and, with the aid of Indian labour, were able to cut through four feet of ice a path 20 feet wide.

Between these assignments he takes mail up the east side of the big bay to the Great Whale River, 350 air miles north of the base at Moose Factory. On the west side, he travels as far up the coast as Winisk, a distance of 300 miles.

And just for a change, he converts his plane into an ambulance to rush patients from isolated communities down to the hospitals at Fort George and Moose Factory.

Relying solely on contact flying, he receives fairly accurate weather reports through the Hudson's Bay Company's post-to-post communications system. Before taking off for a distant point he has the local factor radio ahead to check on flying conditions.

But there are always the unforeseen factors, the unexpected developments which tend to make bush flying a hazardous occupation. Like the time he ran into an unpredicted snowstorm over the bay and flew like a brick to the nearest point of land with a two-inch crust of hard-packed snow on his wings.

'Way up the bay, the problem of mooring is complicated due to strong, changing currents in the rivers. A pilot's only alternative is to beach his craft, and to do this successfully, he must be a fair judge of ocean tides.

One time, Mitchell landed up the bay at high tide and several hours later, after the water had receded and his Fairchild was nesting far from the river on dry land, word came in that an Indian from a nearby settlement had but a few hours to live if he wasn't immediately rushed to hospital.

This posed a real problem but when the local tribe came down to the plane with offers of aid, Mitchell was able to leave in a matter of minutes.

"There were so many of them," he related afterwards, "that they just picked up my plane and carried it down to the water."

The patient was rushed to Moose Factory but despite emergency treatment, died a few days later.

This airman's live cargo is not always human as was proved a year ago when he ferried several beaver up the Bay for the inauguration of several big, federally sponsored beaver preserves.

"They're all right," he told the writer, "as long as you've got them in something they can't eat. Wooden boxes never bothered the beaver because they just ate their way out but we got some tin and that fixed them."

When freeze-up comes in the north, ice formations extend 25 miles into the Bay, breaking up, freezing again and flowing out to sea with the tides. Some are washed back, piling up and forming steppes.

Last summer, there were only two weeks when Mitchell didn't sight big floes out in the Bay. Some of the icebergs were several miles in length and a mile and a half in depth, looking for all the world like islands.

The ice and snow are so bad that often you can't tell land from water. Not so long ago, Mitchell landed five miles from a trading post, taxiing two miles and travelling the remaining three by dog team.

For this reason and for many others, he is never without the services of a good mechanic. And despite the fact that he flies a comparatively small airplane, he carries with him complete emergency equipment—a sleeping bag, rifles, sufficient food for three weeks, axe, fish net, snowshoes, first-aid kit and oil stove.

A wood stove would be of no use in some sections because north of Richmond Gulf, there is no fuel. The natives keep warm by burning whale oil and seal blubber.

At Port Harrison, 400 miles north of Great Whale, the few white residents burn coal which has to be shipped in by boat during the summer.

The record load of mail ever carried by the Austin Fairchild into the land of ice and snow took up 30 cubic feet of cabin space in 1944. Since service is only twice a year, it is allowed to pile up.

Three or four days are required for a complete "run" and a trip is made up each side of the bay. Often, there is so much to be carried, double trips have to be made.

Missionaries and traders are so glad to have "company" they always insist that Mitchell and his mechanic stay the night before proceeding.

The best illustration of this unorthodox northern flying Gordon Mitchell can call to mind is to recite the true story of a "green" mechanic's experiences on the mail run.

This particular engineer's pilot landed on a far northern river at high tide one night and after securing his machine to a nearby tree, took his weary companion to the trading

*One of Austin's rugged Bellanca
CH-300s — "The Old Red Hen."*

Illustration by Peter Mossman

factory to rest. During the early morning hours, when everyone was asleep, the tide sneaked out again, leaving the plane high and dry.

Bright and early in the morning, the pair walked down to the water and a wide-awake mechanic exclaimed, "Wow, did we land in there?"

Jim Hornick

Gord Mitchell left Austin Airways in 1948 to fly for McIntyre Mines and to pursue his interest in prospecting. On December 3, 1966, he was flying CF-HKK, his Piper PA-11, over Nighthawk Lake near Timmins. It was a calm clear day and Gord was spotting for moose. In a seemingly impossible happening in the wide expanses of Northern Ontario, Gord collided with another aircraft (which came into his blindspot) also out moose spotting. Both aircraft crashed to the ice killing those aboard.

The Bay region had many a well-known character. Some of these rose to the calling of "institution," men like free traders Bill Anderson of Fort Albany, and George Papp at Richmond Gulf. These were the most hospitable of people and few would be more welcomed at their posts than the men of Austin Airways. It is said of George Papp that when he went north originally he was headed for Port Harrison, but he was shipwrecked at Richmond Gulf and simply stayed there instead. One day Hal McCracken was to fly a trip for George to a point 100 miles inland. Hal asked George for a map. George quickly scratched a few details on a paper bag and away went Hal in his Norseman.

The following winter, George had another trip for Hal and once again Hal asked for a map. "Another map?" he replied. "I gave you one last year!"

Austin pilot George Charity recalls George Papp: "George and his wife were Hungarians and George used to trap far inland from the Hudson Bay coast. After a couple of seasons of this he built a trading post at Richmond Gulf and when I went on my first trip to Port Harrison I stopped there with the mail. The Papps were wonderful friendly people and always happy to have us drop in for a meal or stay overnight. George built at least two good-sized boats at Richmond Gulf. One was the *Swan,* about 35 feet long. He made a number of voyages to Moosonee for supplies, some of the trips being hair-raising as both Hudson and James Bays can get very rough. George used to find it rather difficult raising a crew to go with him on those trips."

Hard Luck Freighter

One of Austin Airways' most unusual and distinctly Canadian aircraft was its Fleet 50K Freighter. The brainchild of Jack Sanderson, the Freighter was designed in the late 1930s to provide for bush operators a rugged twin-engined utility aircraft. The prototype aircraft flew initially on March 1, 1938, and was followed by a further five aircraft. A combination of untimely factors eventually conspired to relegate this sturdy and versatile design to the footnotes of Canadian aviation history. Nonetheless CF-BJW, the fourth Freighter built, did find its way to Austin Airways in 1945. It was bought as a replacement

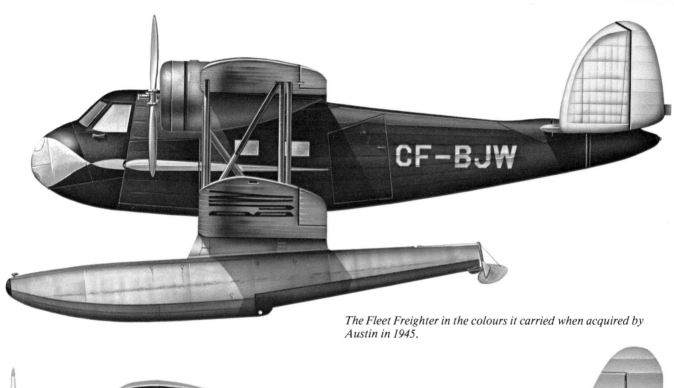

The Fleet Freighter in the colours it carried when acquired by Austin in 1945.

Austin's hard-working old Fairchild 51/71.

Illustrations by Peter Mossman

for Bellanca CF-AMO, which had cracked up early that year.

The detailed history of the Fleet Freighter has been researched by M.L. "Mac" McIntyre and published in the *Journal* of the Canadian Aviation Historical Society. Excerpts from the story of CF-BJW during its Austin Airways era are reprinted here:

Frank Russell, chief engineer of Austin Airways, provides further details on the last remaining Freighter. BJW had been stored out behind the Fleet plant more than two and a half years when she was bought by Austin Airways in

May 1945. She was dismantled and trucked to the Island Airport, Toronto. The engines were overhauled and the aircraft reconditioned, but no major work was undertaken in order that she be ready for the busy summer season. She had 383 hours at this time.

The original BJW colours of blue fuselage and orange wings with aluminum tail suggest a hope that she would be sold to Canadian Airways, but she never carried the familiar goose insignia. Quite possibly BJW was going through the paint shop at the factory about the time BJU was being made ready for trials with Canadian Airways and these colours were chosen so that BJW would be

Fleet Freighter CF-BJW alongside the dock at Sudbury (top) and burned out on O'Sullivan Lake north of Nakina in 1946. The Fleet's rigid gas lines were known to leak and may have contributed to the fire. At the time Frank Russell had replacement flexible line on order, but it arrived too late. (via L.B. Best and M.L. McIntyre)

ready for a sale that never materialized. A fresh coat of dope was applied and Chuck Austin took her north to Austin's main base at Sudbury where she proved an immediate success in spite of much engine trouble during the summer.

During the winter overhaul at Sudbury, Frank made a number of modifications to the aircraft. The original engines with grease lubricated rockers were replaced with a later model of L-6MB with pressure lubricated rockers, and constant speed props were installed. The oil rads and engine control system from a Cessna Crane were installed. The original Fleet system of wire sliding in a fibre-lined tube had a tendency to pick up moisture which could freeze, so these were all replaced. The old slow acting tailplane trim system was redesigned to eliminate the need for excessive trim wheel spinning. The floats had been damaged and replaced during the previous summer. She

was recovered and finished to the Austin colours of black fuselage with silver trim and red wings, and the Austin Airways crest was applied on both sides of the forward fuselage.

After a few flights from Sudbury and South Porcupine bases, BJW worked almost exclusively from the base at Nakina, northeast of Lake Nipigon. Freight and passengers were carried throughout the northern midwestern part of Ontario during the summer. A colony of beavers was relocated to an area near the Albany River where the Department of Lands and Forests found need for more beaver dams. A steady backlog of jobs which required the large doors and floor hatch of the Fleet was soon developed and she was often seen swallowing or disgorging refrigerators or machinery while sitting astride a dock.

Austin put over 500 hours on BJW before she was burned at O'Sullivan Lake, 25 miles north of Nakina on 6 October 1946 as a result of a backfire while starting the starboard engine.

Chuck Austin, who flew BJW, Frank Russell, Rusty Blakey and Elmer Ruddick, of Austin, are all high in their praise of the Freighter, with that one exception of the engines. At the time she was burned, plans were being made to replace these with Wasp Juniors during the following winter.

Much has been said of its inability to hold altitude on one engine when fully loaded. Chuck Austin found that, while this was true, the rate of loss was so slow that it was possible to stretch the glide for many miles on one engine, so this was no great problem with the many lakes in Northern Ontario. Austin had obtained BJW for $10,000, along with spares, and this had proven to be a real bargain for an aircraft of its capabilities. They would have liked another to match it, but by now even the unknown Freighter in Mexico had been dismantled. So this was the end of the Freighters.

A few extra fuselage frames had been built during the production run, partly perhaps to keep the welders busy while waiting for RCAF orders. These were seen in various places in later years; in the roof trusses at the plant, in a field back of a local factory, and one is said to have been dumped in the Niagara River. Other parts were stored in a warehouse under the Peace Bridge, and in an old winery on Garrison Road. The two wrecks remaining in the bush seem to be well stripped. Very few useful parts appear to have survived with the exception of one Curtiss Reid prop, a tail ski, and possibly a pair of oleo legs. The floats from BJW, which were used to make a barge, have been located still in good condition. Frank

Two Fleets. The prototype Freighter tied up beside Austin's Fleet 7 at Sudbury. Austin was generally pleased with its Freighter, though Jack Austin, like many others, felt that Fleet's choice of Jacobs engines was a fatal mistake. (Rusty Blakey)

says the control column was identical to that in a Custom Waco, and the cowlings were from a Fleet Fort with a few other Waco parts. So we can at least hope that enough parts may be located to make the eventual restoration of the Freighter in the Museum at Ottawa a distinct possibility.

No doubt some people would question the value of salvaging the remains of BXP from Labrador and considering a restoration. But there are a number of men with personal knowledge of the subject who would insist that the Freighter is well worthy of a place in our National Aeronautical Collection as a fine example of Canadian enterprise and ingenuity, but one which just failed to make a mark in our aviation history only because of a few unfortunate circumstances.

Tommy Williams, the dean of Canadian pilots, sums it up quite nicely, I think, when he says, "I liked the aircraft and feel that its potential was sadly limited by factors not connected with its design. The burnings, crashes, and engine failures, all add up to an assessment in my mind that the aircraft was never given a fair break. It was nice to handle and I found no fault in it. It deserved more than it got in power plants and ancillary equipment. . . .

In August 1968 this writer camped for five days beside the remains of Fleet Freighter CF-BJW, 25 miles north of Nakina, Ontario, to salvage any material which might be useful in the eventual restoration of the Freighter in the Museum. She has lain here on the north shore of O'Sullivan Lake for 22 years since she was burned in a start-up fire after unloading freight at a now abandoned gold mine, a mile across the lake.

Gord Hughes holds an oleo leg from the Austin Freighter after he and Mac McIntyre had salvaged parts of the wreck in 1970. (M.L. McIntyre)

On 6 October 1946 when the fire started, Chuck Austin emptied the fire extinguisher, then jumped in the lake where he was picked up in a boat by Webb Thompson. They dragged the burning machine out in the lake away from the mine and an adjacent gasoline cache. The starboard engine blew off but a control cable held and anchored the machine to the engine on the lake bottom. Next morning they beached her in the small sand-beached bay where she still rests. Elmer Ruddick of Austin's removed the port engine, which, along with the fabric on the port wings, was undamaged. The following spring BJW drifted away in the high water and Thompson dragged her back to the beach where he removed the floats to make a barge for his drilling equipment. The tail and rear fuselage were cut off, apparently in two stages, and now rest in about 12 feet of water in the bay.

As I began the job of dismantling and removing struts and fittings from BJW, I felt somewhat as though I was desecrating an old grave. She rested on the lower stub wings at the water's edge, and the port upper wing drooped with its interplane struts anchored to pieces of lower spar half buried in the sand. Everything aft of the rear doors was missing and the starboard side showed the effects of tremendous heat. As late as five or six years ago, vandals had not bothered it too much, but now it has been badly mauled and stripped by souvenir-hunting fishermen and campers. The aluminum was not deteriorated, and except for where the paint had been burned off, the tubing was not badly rusted. Although some spar laminations had separated, much of the glue was still holding remarkably well for 22 years of weather. Casein was the standard aircraft glue at the time of construction, and the Sitka spruce in the spars was the only wood in the aircraft.

About 450 pounds of partly damaged, but potentially useful, material was recovered for the Museum, including one wing, three tips, two part ailerons, root ribs, most of the outer wing struts, most spar fittings, one or possibly two gas tanks, and other parts. In addition, both floats were located, still in useable condition. Only a rudder trim tab, attached to two rudder ribs and some rotten tubing, was recovered from under water, but the tailplane, fin and rear fuselage tubing is easily visible in the clear water. The fuselage and centre section assembly was left as it was—a landmark for years to come.

Quite understandably, restoration of the Freighter is well down the priority list for the understaffed Rockcliffe crew. They have several projects which they can complete with a smaller expenditure of time and money. However, since they had few wing parts and struts, and no useable tanks, the material from BJW will fill some of the blank spots on the parts list for the Museum Freighter and perhaps make its eventual restoration more practicable.

Fleet 50K - Freighter Version

Span	45 ft
Length	36 ft
Height	13 ft 6 in
Cabin	15 ft x 4 ft 6 in x 6 ft 1 in
Wing Area	528 sq ft
Wing Loading	14.2 lb (landplane) 14.77 lb (seaplane)
Power Loading	9.38 lb (landplane) 9.75 lb (seaplane)

Weights:

	Landplane	Seaplane
Empty	4,600 lb	4,975 lb
Disposable	3,726 lb	3,351 lb
Gross	8,326 lb	8,326 lb

Included in Disposable Load—1,331 lb for gas, oil and pilot

Performance:

Top Speed	150 mph	148 mph
Cruise	132 mph	130 mph
Land	61 mph	61 mph
Takeoff	14 sec	28 sec
Climb	1,000 fpm	950 fpm
Ceiling	15,000 ft	14,000 ft
S.E. Ceiling	4,200 ft	4,000 ft
Range	650 miles	640 miles
Extra Tanks	950 miles	936 miles

Chronology for CF-BJW, Fleet 50K #203

21.8.39	Fleet Aircraft
17.7.39	Dominion Skyways (lease)
8.42	CPAL (lease)
12.5.45	Austin Airways Ltd.
6.10.46	burned at O'Sullivan Lake, Ontario

M.L. McIntyre

A line-up of Austin Airways bushplanes on Ramsey Lake: two Fairchilds and a Bellanca. (via Sid Bennett)

Post-War Growth

A fine view of Norseman CF-GMM at Moose Factory with an Austin Bombardier alongside. The Hudson's Bay Co. post is in the background. (Jeff Wyborn)

The Norseman Appears

Radio was an important factor in Austin's plan to open up the James Bay area. In about 1940 the company had taken over the McIntyre Mines radio licence in South Porcupine. Radio was installed at Sudbury, then at Moose Factory. The Hudson's Bay posts along the coast already had Morse or key type communications, and were soon converting these to voice. This system was in place as far up the coast as Severn by 1945 and was used on a relay basis, with messages being passed up or down the coast from station to station. Farther south, Austin also began equipping tourist camps in the Sudbury area with two-way radios.

Another major innovation for Austin Airways, especially along the Bay, was the introduction of the Norseman. The company's first was CF-DCK. It was a former US Army UC-64 which was lying dormant at Dorval soon after the war. Frank Russell went down to inspect it and found it had a badly cracked wing spar. He studied the manuals and discovered that an approved repair existed, so the Norseman was bought in January 1946 for $13,000. To that point, the aircraft had a total time of 616 hours. It would be a fine replacement for the Fleet Freighter.

Once airworthy, CF-DCK was put to work from Moosonee, where its performance edge over the Fairchilds was a real boon: even on floats it could carry 7-8 passengers

Northern metropolis. This early fifties view down Durham Street in downtown Sudbury shows a booming urban scene of the day. In this milieu all forms of transportation were in demand and Austin Airways shared in the prosperity. (Right) One of three Harvards bought by Austin Airways from War Assets for $900 is seen on the ice at Sudbury on January 21, 1947. Felix Cryderman, seen here, had ferried these up from RCAF Station Jarvis. The Harvards were cannibalized under Frank Russell's supervision and the leftovers sold as scrap. (via Ed Kenyon, via Peter Marshall)

or over a ton of freight. It had improved performance with its 600 hp R-1340 engine, and better fuel reserves than Fairchild or Bellanca pilots had known. CF-DCK became the first of many Norsemen to fly in Austin colours in the next three decades.

With the war ended, commercial aviation was able to get back on a regular footing and renewed activities, such as prospecting, encouraged bush operators to expand. As well, surplus aircraft were available through War Assets at bargain basement prices and wartime pilots were back on the job market. In this setting, Austin Airways began a period of growth, expanding its fleet and hiring several new pilots. Among these were George Charity, hired in 1946, Hal McCracken (1947), J Pipe (1948), and two hired in 1950: Archie McDougall and Jeff Wyborn. When Gord Mitchell left Austin in 1948 to fly for McIntyre Mines, the only pilots from the pre-war Austin group still flying were the Austins and Rusty Blakey. Besides his flying duties, Jack had become manager of head office,

which in 1948 was moved from downtown Toronto to the Toronto Island Airport.

First of the new group of pilots was George Charity, who had started flying in 1935 when he was 24. He remembers how, as a lad of seven, he had met a pilot walking across a field in North York near Toronto. The pilot had just cracked up his airplane. Young George thought that that was just swell and decided on the spot that he'd be a pilot himself one day.

George took his flying lessons at Barker Field from Len Tripp and Fred Gillies. To help finance his lessons he did some trapping on the outskirts of the city. Frank Russell remembers doing the same in order to add a bit to the larder during the Depression. George received his private licence in 1937 then took a welding course at Central Technical School. With his welding papers he got a job at de Havilland, where he remained for four years. When war started, he tried to join the RCAF but was turned down on account of a previous leg injury.

Finally George got a job flying Ansons with the Air Observers School at Prince Albert, but the war ended before long. He then joined Lands and Forests in Lake Superior country, flying an old Buhl which he recalls as a good rugged aircraft but short on power. On one trip he had had to return twice to offload part of his cargo as the Buhl just couldn't make it. He was pleased when the Lands and Forests gave him a Stinson Reliant replacement.

George's first flight with Austin Airways was in CF-BVI in March 1946. He recalls, "There was a Fairchild 71 sitting on the ice at Ramsey Lake. As it had just one seat in the cockpit I was told to hop in and check myself out. I had never flown the 71 before. I started the engine, warmed it up and took off. I soon discovered what a delight the Fairchild was. From then on I enjoyed every trip, perhaps

because of the 71's stick control. It handled like a Cub."

Soon George was posted to South Porcupine, working with Gord Mitchell, then found himself on James Bay with Norseman CF-DCK, alternating with Rusty Blakey, flying a month along the Bay and then a month down south.

Next to join Austin as a pilot was Hal McCracken on February 1, 1947. As a teenager Hal got to know the Austin operation while he worked at Sudbury Boat and Canoe, and in 1939 he took flying lessons there from instructor Bill Sumner, training in the Aeroncas at $10 an hour. For a while in 1940 he worked in Austin's shop on Notre Dame Street, where Frank Russell was in charge; then he became involved with the air training plan, flying Ansons with the Air Observers School at St. Jean, Quebec, from 1942 to 1945. After the war, Hal returned to Sudbury, bought a Cub and did some instructing. Austin Airways had bought its first Stinson 108, and when Hal had a close look at one of the handsome four-seaters one day, he decided on the spot that he'd be better off if he could

(Left) George Charity, right, visits a trapper north of Cochrane. (George Charity Collection)

(Below) An early post-war view of Austin's Sudbury base showing dock and slipway. The small shack was Austin's first Sudbury facility. At the dock is a Fox Moth owned by prospector S.T. Lundberg of Toronto. (Maurice Labine)

Fairchild CF-AWP in its Austin Airways finery. (Hal McCracken)

get a job with Austin. He had no trouble getting a job and at first was based at Sudbury, where, among other jobs, he frequently flew Holly Parsons around in the 108 on forest survey charters. One March Hal and Holly did a complete survey of the vast Lac Seul watershed in northwestern Ontario.

Like the other Austin pilots, Hal spent a lot of time along the James and Hudson Bay coasts. There were routine trips deep inland where none but the Indian trappers ventured. The terrain was gently undulating Canadian Shield, carpeted, when not under snow and ice, with lichens and dwarf spruce. Lakes and rivers were everywhere and it was years afterwards that any detailed maps were available. Pilots in the 1940s flew with ancient marine or "aeronautical" charts, typical being the Port Harrison chart dated 1947. It shows the area inland for perhaps 100 miles from the Hudson Bay coast and is completely blank except for three rivers and two lakes. A caution on the map warns, "The topography shown on this sheet is from exploratory surveys and may be inaccurate; other features may exist of which no information is available."

To make up for the lack of official navigation aids,

Roughing it in the Chubb Crater during the federal government survey there in March 1965. George Charity built his own igloo (on the right) while the survey party slept in small tents in minus 30 degree conditions. (George Charity Collection)

Overall view at Moose Factory in the fifties. (Rusty Blakey)

pilots depended on the instinctive homing sense of their passengers. A trapper could guide a Norseman to his campsite by following his usual canoe route. Better still, the trapper could sometimes draw the pilot an inland map. These proved to be reliable, and by getting a number of trappers to fill their territory in on a sheet of paper, a pilot could end up with a useful map. Rusty Blakey and George Charity were the first to use such maps with Austin Airways.

Hal McCracken emphasizes one important factor in

the Austin Airways story. That was Frank Russell, head of maintenance. Frank was a superbly organized engineer and trouble shooter who kept equipment in the best of shape. He would accomplish what others would give up as hopeless. Over the years Hal had only three minor mechanical problems himself, but seems to have contributed to one of Rusty's. One day Rusty was about to take off from Sudbury with a load of passengers. As he fired up, Hal joked, "Look Rusty, if your engine quits, you be sure and come straight down." Off went the Norseman, but no sooner was it airborne than, sure enough, the engine quit. And Rusty did come straight down! That was one quip Hal probably didn't bother with again.

J Pipe's flying days dated back to the early thirties and by coincidence he and Chuck Austin had received their pilot's licences on the same day in February 1934. J made an early trip to James Bay in 1935 flying two fellows to Fort George, Cape Jones and Eastmain. They were looking into commercial fishing possibilities. In 1937 J began flying with Wicks Lumber of South Porcupine, first as

George Charity flying his Flut-R-Bug homebuilt at South Porcupine in 1972. Terry Monk recalls that this plane was built all over the north. Wherever George happened to be, he always seemed to have a former or stringer to whittle at. (George Charity Collection)

Get to work George! A mountain of sacks filled with oats waits for the weather to clear at South Porcupine, and for George Charity to move it over to Esker Lake in his Fairchild. (Right) Norseman CF-GMM delivers some bushwhackers and their gear to a northern lake. (George Charity Collection, Rusty Blakey)

engineer, then pilot, on a Waco. Two years later he was flying CF-BFA, a Bellanca, for Canadian Airways, hauling mostly flour and sugar on the Manouane dam project in Quebec. He left Canadian Airways in 1942 and took a job flying a Buhl, then a Norseman, for the OPAS at Armstrong, but in 1948 left there and began his association with Austin Airways.

One of J's first big jobs with Austin was flying Norseman CF-DCK on contract to Dominion Gulf Exploration. He supported Gulf's Goose and Canso survey operation over the summers of 1950-51. Over the first season, he flew the Norseman for 604 hours for Gulf and missed only one day's flying. He enjoyed this work for different reasons, one being that the Gulf boys would always make

Austin's first Norseman, CF-DCK, at Sugluk, with the usual crowd of curiosity seekers gathered around. (Rusty Blakey)

The Norseman in summer: CF-GMM at Moosonee with George Charity sauntering by and an RCAF Canso tied up offshore, and (right) CF-EIB at Port Harrison in 1948 with a crowd including RCMP and marine radio people. (Rusty Blakey, George Charity Collection)

sure that a good dock was built wherever they were camped. This was a real blessing for a bush pilot.

J recalls a trip up the Hudson Bay coast with George Charity. Due to weather, they had to spend three days at Little Whale River, staying in a tent in the "coaster" community (Indians dwelling on the coast as opposed to inland). He remembers that in no time at all the coasters had eaten up all his grub; and someone there owned an old phonograph and one record, which he played continually, using a bent nail in place of a proper needle.

Just before setting down at Little Whale, J had sent out a radio message telling of his weather problem. The message was not received, save by a ham operator on the West Coast. He relayed the message to Austin just in time

Norseman 'BSC taking off with a canoe at Rupert House. (Paddy Gardiner)

Arctic beauty. Norseman CF-GMM along the shores of the Richmond Gulf, well up the east coast of Hudson Bay, sometime in 1955. (Jeff Wyborn)

(Facing) Attawapiskat (top) and Povungnituk in the early fifties, typical Bay communities which relied heavily on the air service provided by Austin Airways. (Jeff Wyborn)

to save them the trouble of launching a search for the overdue plane.

Jeff Wyborn began flying at the Lakehead in 1937. He took his training from O.J. Weiben and when war broke out worked at Canadian Car and Foundry in Fort William on the Goblin and Hurricane production lines. Equipped with air engineer's papers, he worked as maintenance crew chief at No. 2 EFTS at Fort William. Next he was crew on Canadian Airways' Bellanca CF-AWR, which was freighting in northern Quebec. Later he flew Moths and a Buhl for the OPAS, and then worked for Severn Enterprises in northwestern Ontario.

In 1950 Jeff was hired by Austin Airways at its South Porcupine base. Many of his trips were along the James and Hudson Bay coastlines and, like other Austin veterans, he vividly remembers the long inland freighting trips by Norseman, navigating by hand-made maps. Most trips were routine but Jeff does recall a more memorable one: "One day I was flying a passenger home. After a while I realized the fellow was drinking. Before long he was passing the bottle to me. When I declined, he insisted all the

more. Enough is enough, so I had to backhand him one, and had a time keeping the plane out of the trees. My passenger was by then quite irate and no sooner were we down than he was yelling up to his wife, who'd come out of their cabin, to bring down his rifle. He was intent on doing me in! So away I went, oblivious to my tail ski which had broken during my hurried landing."

Rusty Blakey recalls that Norseman CF-EIB had been a mediocre performer. Then one day, Jeff, taking off from Attawapiskat in a crosswind, clipped the mast of a boat and holed a float. The Norseman had to be flown out for repairs, and when it returned, says Rusty, "it was a real bomb." He suggested to Jeff that he take the other Norsemen out and do the same thing with them.

Jeff relates another Norseman incident. While coming in to land at Moosonee, something went amiss and the aircraft crashed down onto the water, skipping several times in a nose-down attitude. After tying up, he got out to check the plane over. At first he couldn't understand what had gone wrong. Then Rusty spotted a tiny hole in the fabric of the tail. Closer inspection revealed the culprit.

Earlier in the day, someone, likely one of the local kids, had been winging pebbles at the Norseman. One had punctured the fabric and dropped down inside to eventually jam the elevator just when Jeff needed it most.

Like most of Austin's new pilots, Archie MacDougall came to the company as a wartime veteran. Archie had joined the RCAF in 1940, won his wings at No. 6 EFTS, Prince Albert, then instructed on Ansons and Cranes at Souris and Dauphin in Manitoba. As the war dragged on, he and a lot of other instructors became anxious about getting into the "real" war. In Archie's case, he volunteered to the Royal Navy and just as the war drew to an end went overseas to fly Seafires from carriers in the European theatre.

Archie came home to Sudbury in 1945, back to his old job in the purchasing department at Inco, but soon became involved with Hal McCracken, doing some instructing. A year followed at Chapleau, flying Cormack Lumber's Seabee before he joined Austin in 1950. Archie did the usual tour of the Austin bases but was to spend most of his career (until 1977) flying Beaver CF-GQQ from Geraldton.

Jim Hobbs had likewise come out of the RCAF, where he had been an instructor. After the war he did some flying from Buttonville near Toronto and in the Montreal area,

and owned a surplus Finch for a while. He then took a job flying for Nickel Belt Airways of Sudbury just before coming to Austin in 1952. Jim was another top Austin pilot who was to gain the respect of everyone in the business.

Sad Times

With the special attention the company paid to aircraft maintenance, and with top pilots, Austin Airways developed a reputation for safety. When one of its Aeroncas crashed in October 1940, the company suffered its first fatalities. Sadness hit the people at Austin again in 1949.

Pilot Felix Cryderman worked part time for Austin after his wartime career. One of his postings was as a fighter pilot aboard merchant ships equipped with catapult launchers to fire Hurricanes off their decks. The fighters would fly their missions, then the pilots would either ditch or parachute into the sea near the fleet. Felix was actually a prospector by trade and had gone to Nakina to fly for the Sullivan mine operation, but he also did some flying for Austin on CF-AWP and for Don Hurd in a Bellanca. On June 17, 1949, he was taking off from Cordingly Lake when the Fairchild stalled and dived straight in. Felix and his passenger died, and the cause of the mishap was never determined.

(Left) Rusty Blakey at the controls of CF-BSC the day it was delivered to Austin Airways. (Centre) Jeff Wyborn on the float of an old Gipsy Moth at Port Arthur in 1939. (Right) Fritz Kohls, Don Gosby of the Hudson's Bay Co., and Jeff at Old Factory in 1951. Jeff's Norseman is in the background. (via W.H. Kearns, two via Jeff Wyborn)

(Left) Felix Cryderman, wartime fighter pilot who lost his life in the crash of Fairchild CF-AWP. (Right) A classic northern scene: Norseman CF-EIB is serviced at Great Whale in August 1953. Jeff Wyborn was with a film crew from Paramount which was movie making all the way up the east coast. Here he poses with old-time DOT met man Fred Woodrow. Engineer Bill Montgomery takes care of refuelling while the ubiquitous kids get in on the action. (via Rusty Blakey, via Jeff Wyborn)

(Below left) Soon after the war Austin Airways bought the first of three Stinson 108 Station Wagons. The Stinson was ideal for a variety of jobs, especially in the summer tourist season. In this photo Rusty taxies CF-ESP, purchased in May 1947. With its 150-hp Franklin engine the four-seat Stinson could cruise at an easy 130 mph. (Right) Stinson 'ESM at Sudbury. A Norseman has just landed and is step taxiing to the dock. (Both via Hal McCracken)

Two-man kayak at the Belcher Islands in 1954. (Jeff Wyborn)

Eskimos at Great Whale during a routine visit by the Austin Norseman. (Jeff Wyborn)

Native encampments in the Austin Airways domain during the early fifties. An Eskimo group poses by their large hide tent at Ferguson Lake, and a family of Indian trappers is seen at their camp inland from Eastmain. (E.A. Kenyon, Jeff Wyborn)

The Mystery of CF-FXT

One of the most fascinating mysteries in the lore of northern Ontario had its beginning on April 26, 1951. That day Dr. Albert H. Hudson of Timmins and Toronto Maple Leaf hockey star Bill Barilko were flying south from Rupert House in Hudson's Fairchild 24W, CF-FXT. The two men were heading home from a fishing trip on the Seal River north of Fort George. Very stiff headwinds hampered their progress and the trip into Rupert House took an hour longer than usual. Once they had arrived, the young post manager tried to persuade them to stay overnight and wait for the weather to improve, but the travellers wanted to push on. The people at Rupert House were the last to see them alive.

It was soon realized that the Fairchild was down somewhere on the route to South Porcupine, and a huge search was begun which went on for weeks. In the end not one clue turned up. Many theories were discussed as to where the plane disappeared. One that persisted for years even revolved around a theft of gold! The excitement at the time of the search was heightened by a $10,000 reward offered by the Maple Leafs to whoever could locate the missing plane.

The search that had been organized by the RCAF had been carefully run, and the whole area within the Fairchild's range had been combed over and over. When

The Fairchild 24 in which Dr. Hudson and Bill Barilko disappeared in April 1951. (Jack McNulty)

the search was abandoned, it was with a sense that everything possible had been done. The experts felt that the two men had been killed in a crash. Had they gone down and survived, they believed that Hudson, an expert woodsman, would have pulled through with his friend. As the years passed, the memory of the lost Fairchild faded, but at the Austin staff house at Moose Factory and wherever fliers gathered in the North, the mystery was always a topic for interesting surmise. One thing everyone agreed

Austin's base at South Porcupine in 1955. (via Jeff Wyborn)

(Left) Austin's one-of-a-kind Aeronca 15AC, bought in 1949, is seen at the South Porcupine dock. (Right) In 1949 Austin Airways took delivery of its first Beaver, serial number 60. CF-FHX served the airline for many years and was finally sold to Lakeland Airways when Austin disposed of its float bases in the late 1970s and early 1980s. Sadly, 'FHX was lost on June 6, 1981; it was flying from Temagami when it crashed on Maple Mountain killing all four on board. Deteriorating weather was suspected as the cause of the tragedy. (Jeff Wyborn, Jack McNulty)

Austin Airways Beaver ('FHX) and Aeronca ('FNT) flying from Jeff Wyborn's log, March 1951. The flying was done from Austin's base at South Porcupine and included work for lumber operators at Esker Lake, Pine Lake and Horwood Lake, and for mining interests at Gowagamak (Hollinger Mines), Burrows Lake and Loonwing Lake (Dominion Gulf).

Date	Aircraft	Route	Time
March 2	FNT	Kapuskasing-Brunswick Lake-Porcupine	2:10
5	FHX	Esker Lake-Porcupine-Grassy River-Porcupine	3:10
7	FHX	Porcupine-Pine Lake-Porcupine	2:00
9	FHX	Porcupine-Esker Lake-Porcupine-Pine Lake-Porcupine	3:35
10	FNT	Porcupine-Papakomeka-Porcupine	:30
10	FHX	Porcupine-Muskasenda Lake-Pine Lake-Porcupine	1:45
11	FNT	Porcupine-Camp 16-Gogama-Porcupine	1:40
13	FHX	Porcupine-Camp 16-Opishing Lake-Porcupine	1:30
13	FHX	Porcupine-Peterlong-Kapiskong-Porcupine	:55
14	FHX	Porcupine-Pine Lake-Peterlong-Porcupine	1:30
15	FXH	Porcupine-Eskder Lake-Porcupine-Parting Lake-Porcupine	1:40
17	FHX	Porcupine-Gogama-Porcupine	5:00
20	FNT	Porcupine-Gowagamak Lake-Gravelridge Lake-Porcupine	1:20
21	FHX	Porcupine-Gogama-Burrows Lake-Porcupine	1:55
22	FNT	Porcupine-Loonwing Lake-Parting Lake-Porcupie	1:30
22	FHX	Porcupine-Loonwing Lake-Porcupine-Parting Lake-Porcupine	1:30
23	FNT	Porcupine-Washagami Lake-Porcupine	:45
23	FHX	Porcupine-Parting Lake-Washagami Lake-Porcupine	:35
25	FNT	Porcupine-Parting Lake-Loonwing Lake-Porcupine	3:55
25	FNT	Porcupine-Parting Lake-Loonwing Lake-Porcupine	3:55
25	FHX	Porcupine-Loonwing Lake-Porcupine	:35
27	FHX	Porcupine-Horwood Lake-Porcupine	3:15
31	FHX	Porcupine-Loonwing Lake-Porcupine-Washagami Lake-Porcupine	1:50

on though: Hudson had likely been beaten by the headwinds he had met earlier in the day. The same day, Jim Hobbs had flown the other way, from South Porcupine to Moosonee, a trip that normally takes two hours, but had made it 50 minutes faster.

On May 31, 1962, the ghost of CF-FXT finally appeared, and the mystery was solved. A helicopter pilot was flying in the area of Island Falls north of Cochrane when something in the bush caught his eye. He looked closer and identified a pair of floats. He reported this back at Cochrane and felt that he could probably relocate the floats. Soon a party was at the site where the wreck of Dr. Hudson's Fairchild was positively identified. The DOT carefully examined the remains and eventually concluded, "...the aircraft struck the trees in a 50° nose down attitude at an angle of bank of 25° to the left. It was apparent from the damage to the propeller that the engine had been either under power at the time of impact or windmilling at high rpm. The elevator trim tab was found in the almost full nose up position. The trim control in the cockpit corresponded to this position. There is no evidence available to explain this trim setting which is considered abnormal to cruising flight. There was insufficient evidence to determine the cause of the accident." Thus the story of CF-FXT was laid to rest. Well, not quite, for even these days pilots young and old still muse about what happened that fateful April day so many years ago.

The Church of the Airways

Stories abound of Austin Airways and its people from the post-war years, with much of the "action" centring on James Bay and points beyond. A lot of the flying in the area was done for the Anglican and Roman Catholic missions, with the former holding fort on the east coast and the RCs on the west coast. The Anglicans published the *Northland* from their South Porcupine diocese office and there were frequent mentions of Austin Airways and the fine relationship that existed between the two. The June 1952 edition of the *Northland* describes a typical swing by bush plane through part of the Church's domain within the James Bay watershed. The story gives an authentic slice-of-life picture of missionary activity among the Ojibway of the region. On this trip Elmer Ruddick was doing the flying;

On the Trail of the Ojibway

The year 1952 found me and my family in a different place in the work of the Church and among different people. For eleven years we had worked among our Cree Indians in the James Bay area, stationed on the shores of the inland sea of James Bay. Now we are far inland on a large lake (Attawapiskat) 150-odd miles from the nearest railway.

We are not as isolated as at Factory River. Planes

The Anglican bishop visits part of his flock at one of the James Bay settlements during the 1940s. (Sid Bennett)

bring us nearer to more settled areas, and travel of any sort is done by plane, and all freight and supplies for various people in this area is by air.

We are among the Ojibway people, I suppose an offshoot of the Ojibway around the islands of Georgian Bay.

Lansdowne House is the main centre in summer. In winter they are scattered around at different little villages in a radius of 50 miles. It was my privilege to visit them this winter when they were away from the Mission.

In company with John Yesno of Fort Hope and Austin Airways pilot Elmer Ruddick, we left Fort Hope, February 10, going to Meminquish, about 25 miles from Lansdowne. The Hudson's Bay Company operates a camp trade here and we found quite a number of our people awaiting us. Coster Wabasse is the catechist here. We shook hands with the people and asked if there were any babies to be baptized.

A fire was started in the log house set apart for the church. Benches had not then been made, as it was a new building erected last fall, so all sat on the floor. There was a Holy Table and chair up at the front, with a clean cloth on the Table. The babies (three) were laced in cradles with fancy bead work on the cloth. It was a heavy job to lift the babies in my arms, as one or two of them were over a year old. Immediately after the baptism service, we had Holy Communion, "Do this in remembrance

of Me." How many miles we were from the place those words were spoken, though we knew in a moment of time we travel in spirit and thought to the Throne of Grace. The people were very devout and reverent.

We arrived at Summer Beaver in about five minutes' flying time. Adam Big-John was away on his trap lines, but he had left the services in the care of Thaddeus Oshkineegeesh (Young). I never saw a man who so looked like an African, and expected at any moment for him to break out in some African dialect. When he spoke it was pure Ojibway. Thaddeus is a devout Christian and ably fulfilled Adam Big-John's trust in leaving the services in his care.

There is a very nice little church here. I saw inside, one of last year's posters which read, Read, Worship, Work. Thaddeus had translated this into, Pray, Work, Collection, in Ojibway; I thought that was just about what it was about.

We spent the night at Lansdowne House and next day went to Pememuta, about 40 miles west, where there is a church and village. Here we found James Nishinapao, the catechist. We were glad to see him and the people. As usual we had a Baptism and Communion Service. James told me there were a number of people at Birch Lake, and a number of babies to be baptized. So, we flew there, about 40 miles away.

The Chief of the Fort Hope Band, John Boyce, has his

Indian summer encampment at Richmond Gulf in the 1950s. (Rusty Blakey)

trapping grounds there, but we found him away. I baptized four babies, had one marriage service and Holy Communion. We stopped next at Mud Lake. Another baby to be baptized.

From here we flew to Memniska, a trading post and tourist lodge. We found the men away except for one woman. I baptized one baby. The plane left me at Fort Hope, returning to its base at Nakina.

Later on, I accompanied John Yesno to Kagangami Lake, 70 miles south of Fort Hope, by snowmobile. There are two camps here. I gave them Holy Communion and spent a night with them. John Rich has his trapping grounds here and also fished quite a lot of fish. He was an old Hudson's Bay Company man and his wife came from Rupert's House on James Bay.

Previously, in January, I had made a trip to Webequie, about 50 miles north of Lansdowne, taking in a load of roofing paper for their church. Simon Jacob is the catechist here with Edward Spence helping him. The H.B. Co. have a camp trade here (winter only). There were quite a number of people. I baptized four babies, had a marriage service and Holy Communion.

I distributed toys and clothing to the children which had been sent in from Christ Church Cathedral, Hamilton, Ontario.

I returned to Lansdowne. In all, we had covered some 200 or more air-miles and saw some 200 people. For me it was a happy experience. It was the first time I had seen many people after arriving last fall.

by The Rev. Redfern Louttit, one of our native clergy, Lansdowne, House, Ontario.

Dr. B.H. Harper served as National Health and Welfare medical chief in the James Bay area between 1947 and 1952. He worked both sides of James Bay and made frequent use of Austin Airways. As well he travelled by snowmobile and canoe with his companion, Jimmy Gunner, who was half Dane and half Cree. During emergencies, Dr. Harper sometimes did diagnosis and recommended treatment over the Austin Airways radio network. (via Leonard Harper)

Flying Doctor Service

The coming of Austin Airways to the James and Hudson Bay region was a blessing to the natives in many ways. One vital improvement was in medical care. With airplanes available on a regular basis, doctors and nurses could be flown up the coast from Moosonee to do regular rounds or make emergency trips and inhabitants needing emergency treatment could be flown from the hinterland to hospital at Moose Factory. The scourge of TB could now be tackled on more equitable terms.

One of the best known medical people in the region was Dr. B.H. Harper. In 1947 he moved to Moose Factory from South Porcupine as Dr. Tom Orford's replacement. His son Leonard recalls a few people and events from those days: "My father's practice extended from Winisk on the south shore of Hudson Bay, around James Bay, and up the east coast to Richmond Gulf and Port Harrison. While a lot of father's work involved travelling in the winter by snowmobile, and in the summer by boat and canoe in conjunction with the RCMP, he did a lot of flying. There were many emergency trips, and, as there were no nav aids, flights were sometimes far from routine.

"Gord Mitchell, Rusty Blakey and George Charity were father's pilots in those days, and the thing that impressed me most about father's association with these pilots was the utter confidence he had in them."

Leonard Harper's other memories of Austin Airways include how Austin would always bend over backwards to help. "I can remember my mother going down and giving a bag with some oranges and bananas to George Charity to deliver to Mrs. Sheppard at Fort George or some of the other wives up the coast. The goods were always delivered. Nothing was too small for the Austin pilots to help with.

"In 1952 my father was up the coast with the RCMP when my mother took ill and subsequently died. George Charity was up the coast at the time. He picked my father up and tried to head south, but bad weather caught up with them and forced George to turn back. As soon as it cleared he got father down to South Porcupine, where my mother was in hospital. This was Austin Airways."

One day word came that Eskimos were mysteriously dying at Port Harrison. George Charity flew in a doctor and nurse, and they found a young girl deathly ill—from what, nobody knew. The Norseman flew on to Cape Smith where other cases were found. Everyone in these centres had been eating muktuk—chunks of seal meat. Later it was found that people in Greenland had been falling ill with the same symptoms, and the problem there had been diagnosed as trichinosis. Having aircraft on hand and experienced pilots was a great blessing to tiny places like Port Harrison when such medical difficulties arose.

George recalls how from time to time, when medical people were hard pressed, he and other bystanders in a village would be pressed into service as paramedics, checking pulses and performing other minor tasks which saved vital time. On another medical emergency, George Charity and George Papp went into a settlement north of Richmond Gulf to aid an Eskimo who had been shot. When they landed, they asked around for the injured man. He was not there, they were told. He was out fishing! It seems that nature had taken over and the man had healed nicely before help arrived.

One of Hal McCracken's recollections from this period is of an ambulance case from Hartley Bay near the mouth of the French River. A call came in just as he was setting off in a Beaver with a load of freight for Blue Mountain Lodge. He delivered the freight then hopped over to Hartley Bay. Just as he landed, a crowd of Indians rushed down to the plane for a stretcher, but there wasn't one aboard. They hurried off, but just as quickly reappeared, bouncing an expectant mother along on an old bed spring.

The woman was hustled into the Beaver and a man climbed aboard to attend. Someone passed him up a knife and Hal took off. The trip back to Sudbury turned out to be more than Hal had ever bargained for. The patient put up a fair din and her companion kept shifting back and forth from the cockpit checking her out. Finally, knife in hand, he went back and delivered the baby. Not being used to such goings-on, Hal admits to having felt mild queasiness. Nonetheless, if his three passengers could survive the excitement, surely a rugged bush pilot could handle it!

More of Dusey

Aerial surveying continued throughout the fifties, though by this time electronic methods were being used as well as the tried and true photography. A 1952 story in the *Sudbury Star* by John Hunt described Dusey Kearns at work with Austin:

The big yellow Norseman plane tied up at the Haileybury dock attracts swarms of small boys, all anxious for a free ride and with a thousand questions to plague the pilot.

Sitting under the shadow of the wing, chewing a cigar and keeping one eye on the youngsters and the other on the weather, is W.H. ''Dusey'' Kearns, who has been flying over the forests of Northern Ontario for the past 28 years.

Using Haileybury as a base while making an aerial photographic survey of the forests, Dusey Kearns has photographed 250,000 square miles for the Department of Lands and Forests since he quit his job in a bank to take what he thought would be a short holiday as an aerial observer.

''I went up in a plane, and I seem to have been up in one ever since,'' he says.

When photography first began to be used for mapping of forests, Dusey lent a hand with cameras, then caught the shutter bug and has been a camera fan ever since.

An expert in his field, Dusey is not content with the big aerial camera that has a 10-inches-square negative, but also carries his own movie and still cameras.

The father of three children, and the grandfather of several more, Dusey does not regard his job as being very exciting.

''You just keep flying in a straight line, and making sure that the pilot is on course. You see a lot of trees and a lot of lakes, but you get used to them.''

Dusey has never had a crash, which he attributes to the high standard of bush fliers. He also rarely takes a bad picture, due largely to the mass of light meters, exposure tables, filters and other photographic equipment which he carries in his pockets, slung around his neck, and in various cases which fill up the Norseman's cabin.

''It's no good guessing, you've got to be sure, and sometimes a little luck helps,'' he says.

Although he has never been lost, Dusey was off course once and as a result, his name has gone down for posterity.

''It was in 1928. We thought we were north of the Albany River, but it turned out to be a river that wasn't on the map, so they named it the Dusey River and Dusey Lake just to remind me of my mistake.''

Sudbury Star

Rusty Blakey later described Dusey Kearns as ''the greatest guy . . . he had friends all over the country.''

(Top) Jim Bell, Bob Moore and two Cree guides show some of the take from a day on the James Bay goose hunt. Jim and Bob were two of the originators of the hunt which has become one of Northern Ontario's big autumn sporting activities.
(Below) Just in from the hunting grounds, a Moosonee guide shows the results of his efforts. An Austin Beaver bobs in the background. (Jim Bell Collection, Dave Russell)

Rusty remembers that one day he and Dusey were on a trip from Chapleau when they got into a fierce rainstorm. Rusty landed and they waited for the weather to clear. Around midnight the rain let up, and the next thing Rusty recalls, Dusey was out on the shore setting up camp and getting a fire going and doing his best to cheer the others up. Another time Rusty and Dusey went out to fish for

trout at a spot recommended by one of the rangers. They fished for hours and kept pulling in pickerel, which they just tossed back. No trout were to be had. Eventually the pickerel stopped biting, but Rusty pulled in a pike which he set aside. By then the boys were getting pretty hungry. But, not at all perturbed, Dusey got a good fire going and cooked the lone pike. "That old pike tasted just great," reported Rusty, "and Dusey was happy as could be, as usual."

The James Bay Goose Hunt

What was to become another Austin Airways tradition —the annual goose hunt on James Bay—had its beginning as a tourist activity back in 1946. Those involved at the start included Jim Bell of Nickel Belt Airways, Len Hughes, Bob Moore, and Bill Anderson, who operated a hunting camp on an island in the Albany River.

The November 1946 Inco *Triangle* reported on the first official goose season on the Bay: "Last month a group of nimrods embarked on a new and fully modern hunters' odyssey. In the brand new Fairchild Husky of Nickel Belt Airways, a party of marksmen took off on October 6 to bag geese in the James Bay area . . . The flight to Moosonee (from Sudbury), about 400 air miles, took four hours, including a stop at Cochrane to refuel . . . The party stayed overnight at the Hudson's Bay Company post at Fort Albany, enjoying to the full the excellent hospitality of the Scottish factor, Bill Anderson. Next day, under the watchful eyes of three Indian guides, they embarked with a full quota of supplies and their equipment in three 20-foot freighter canoes, each of which could carry at least two tons. Their outboards drove them down the Albany River about four miles, and then across an inland channel, on the shore of which they pitched camp. A two-mile walk distance, on the shore of James Bay, was their hunting grounds. There were the geese, feeding on the grassy flats or circling overhead.

"At the crack of dawn the hunters were up, breakfasted, and away. . . . The Indians quickly built blinds with grass and willow sticks, then set out decoys of goose wings and chunks of mud. Later, after some geese had been brought down, they were used as decoys, propped up in lifelike positions with willow sticks.

"Then the hunters sat in the blinds while the geese were called in. The Indians did the calling. First with a high-pitched bark and then with the feeding call, a low rumbling sound that really brought the big birds down within shooting range, the native guides did their stuff. And the nimrods banged away with zest and enthusiasm.

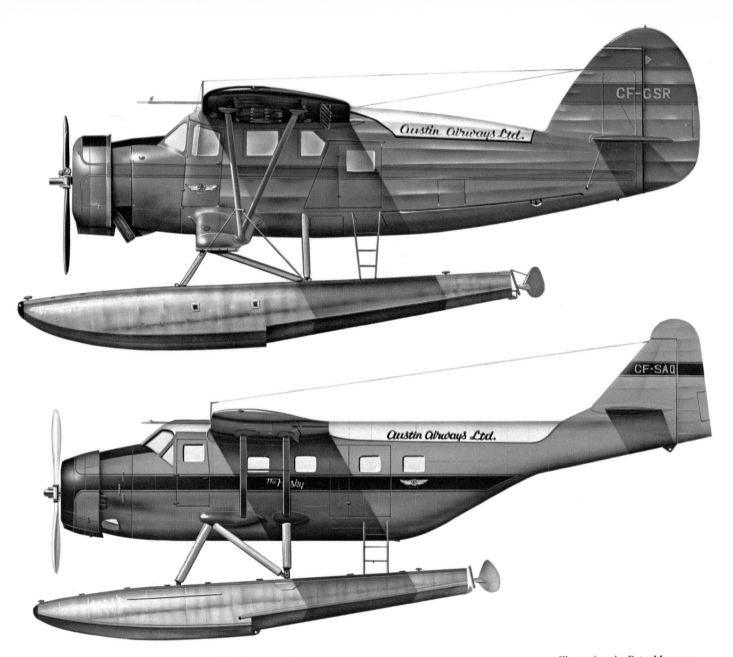

An Austin Norseman and Husky in 1960-vintage colours.

Illustrations by Peter Mossman

They were allowed a bag of 25 each, and their total bag for the trip was 115. . . ."

The main camp in the lower James Bay area was at Hannah Bay, 44 miles east of Moosonee. It was owned by the Ontario Northland Railway. Beginning every September and lasting until October, two groups of hunters per week would arrive by train in Moosonee. There were 20 hunters per group, and while one group was flown in to Hannah Bay, the other came out. Rusty Blakey notes

that Ozzie Saari of North Bay ran the camp and that it was a very fine set-up: hunters stayed in neat, clean cabins equipped with oil heaters. A railway cook prepared the finest of meals and hundreds of hunters were so satisfied that they returned year after year to the ONR operation.

In 1952 Austin Airways bought out Nickel Belt Airways and continued to promote the goose hunt. Through the 1950s the hunt grew steadily and aircraft like the Husky could not keep up with the demand. The Canso and DC-3 took over, flying hunters into the camps from Cochrane, Porquis Junction, Timmins and, later on, Mount Hope.

Tourism in general had long since become bread and butter for Austin Airways. Sport fishing and hunting were always reliable sources of revenue, as were charters for cottagers and tourist camp operators. Many an amusing story resulted from this work. One night Frank Russell (whose phone number happened to be listed in the Sudbury directory) received a call very late. It was from an American tourist wanting to arrange a fishing trip for his family the next morning. "Can you get a guide for us?" was the tourist's main concern. Frank informed him that this would be no problem, meanwhile harbouring a fear that he might have trouble rustling somebody up.

Frank spoke with Jack Austin in the morning. Since Frank had been the one who had given the assurances, Jack's words were simple: "If you can't find a guide, Frank, then you're it!" So off went Frank to see whom he could find, and after some scrounging he came up with a "guide" in one of the local beer parlours. The fellow was not in the best of shape, fresh from days of exhausting work on the fire lines, and quite a few beers into the afternoon. Frank persuaded him to abandon his brew

and took him over to the dock. Away went the fishing party and nothing else was heard of the incident, not, that is, until a year had gone by. The American tourist showed up in Sudbury for another fishing trip. "Where's that guide you sent me out with last year?" he asked. "He was the best darn guide I've ever had."

Fairchild Husky

One of Canada's most controversial bushplanes was the Fairchild F-11 Husky. Designed and built in Longueuil just after the war, the Husky made its first flight June 14, 1946. At this time the Ontario Department of Lands and Forests was in the market for a new bushplane and was looking seriously at the attractive Husky. It was a

Two photos of Husky CF-EIQ, one in its standard factory paint job taken at Toronto Island, and one in its Austin colours in northern Manitoba. (Jack McNulty, Bruce Gowans)

big, all-metal machine with a distinctive upswept rear fuselage and cargo doors that permitted loading from the rear of such awkward items as drill rods and canoes.

At first it appeared that the Husky would be a production success. Several were purchased by Sudbury-based Nickel Belt Airways, a thriving operation headed by businessman Ben Merwin that also controlled Boreal Airways in Quebec. But the Husky's promising start was soon stalled. De Havilland Canada had made it known that it too was developing a new bushplane in the same general category and on August 16, 1947, its entry in the market took flight: the DHC-2 Beaver. The Beaver soon showed itself to have an edge over the Husky. The big difference was the power-to-weight ratio. The Husky had

In 1950 Austin Airways took over Nickel Belt Airways, a large Sudbury-based operator with several Huskies, Fleet Canucks and other types. This Nickel Belt Husky (left) is drawn up on a rocky beach at Old Factory River for repairs. (Above) Husky mishap: CF-EIL of Boreal, former Nickel Belt subsidiary, down in the bush well north of Roberval during 1955 while on a fur buying circuit. (Lloyd McTaggart, Don McIntyre)

a gross weight of 6400 lb; the Beaver 5100 lb. Yet the planes had the same engine, the versatile 450 hp Pratt and Whitney R-985. It provided ample power for the Beaver, but left the Husky short. Ontario's Lands and Forests looked closely at both designs but it seems to have been a hands-on flight given to Frank MacDougall, deputy minister of the Department of Lands and Forests, that turned opinion in favour of the Beaver. De Havilland's test pilot, George Neal, gave him a full demonstration of the Beaver's capabilities early on. MacDougall, one of the old-time bush pilots in Ontario, was convinced that this was the plane for his needs, and four were immediately ordered. This order was soon boosted and in time some 50 Beavers were delivered to Lands and Forests. The once-promising Husky was eclipsed forever and it was de Havilland, not Fairchild, that was almost buried in orders.

Even so, 12 Huskies had been delivered before Fairchild was forced to fold up. Of these, several went to Nickel Belt, where they were put to good use and were generally

well liked by pilots including Jim Bell and Jim Hobbs. In 1952 Nickel Belt, which had encountered operating setbacks including a serious fire, was bought out by Austin Airways. One Husky came with the deal, this being CF-EIQ. It had been purchased by Nickel Belt in April 1947 and to April 2, 1952, had piled up 2999 hours. In its first year with Austin it accumulated 772 hours, spending much of its time at work in northern Manitoba under command of A.J. "Kelly" Gibb. The DOT files for this particular Husky note its gross weight as 6500 lb on wheels or skis and 6800 lb on floats. CF-EIQ was to be lost at St. Jean, Quebec, when Aircraft Industries' hangar burned on December 8, 1954.

In 1952 Austin Airways acquired a second Husky when it bought CF-SAQ, a former Saskatchewan government plane. "Sad and Queer", as one pilot called it, was to be a reliable money-maker for Austin until sold in 1964.

Rusty Blakey, like most pilots, has favourable memories of the Husky. He notes that it was an excellent cargo airplane and he recalls one job moving drill equipment from Gogama to Rush Lake. The drilling operator wanted a Norseman for the job, but none was available. Rusty let him know that he'd use a Husky, but that the drilling boys would have to have each load weighed out to exactly 1400 lb. Rusty began shuttling back and forth, 1400 lb at a time, including one trip with a 1200-lb tractor transmission. The Husky performed perfectly, and a few weeks later the drilling company called back. They were moving camp again and insisted on the Husky to do the job.

George Charity had plenty of time on the Husky and described it as "a beautiful plane, strong and fast enough, but because of its small engine, you had to watch the size of your load carefully." He added that the Husky could carry a huge load inside that cavernous interior. Huge, that is, as long as you were carrying corn flakes! This sort of scene happened more than once with a Husky: George was at Paint Hills and had a charter to move a family of trappers. While he was busy with something else, the Indians started loading the plane. Before George knew what was going on, they had the Husky brim full, with about twice the payload stuffed aboard. They had to off-load quite a bit before George could take off. Just before he did, an Indian looked inside the Husky and commented, "Not much full yet!" It was at gross weight and that was plenty for George. J Pipe confirms that the Husky had its problems and admits that he would take his Norseman over a Husky any day. He recalls taking off downwind in the Norseman loaded with four 45-gallon drums; from the same lake on the same day Bill Davis, flying a Husky for Dome Mines, was using a full run of three miles into the wind with just two drums.

Another fan of the Husky was Don McIntyre. He had flown Halifaxes with 434 Squadron until shot down in August 1944. He then did his "tour" at Stalag Luft 3. After repatriation, he was serving in the post-war RCAF at Rockcliffe when a friend told him about Nickel Belt and suggested he call Jim Bell for a job. Don followed up the tip, but Jim didn't seem too interested. If there was a surplus of anything after the war, it was pilots, and thousands were vying for the few jobs available. Don persevered, though, and eventually had a meeting with Jim Bell in Toronto. Jim was there arranging for delivery of two new Fleet Canucks and was with a friend, Charlie Butchard. This was a break for Don as he and Charlie had been POW's together. In the end, Jim got Don to ferry one of the Fleets to Sudbury and, after some bargaining, hired him at $200 a month plus expenses.

Don was soon checked out on the Husky and flying it on jobs throughout the North, in northern Quebec, around James Bay and up into the Territories, primarily for Inco. His frequent companion was Inco geologist Hank Vuori and his summer students. Hank was surveying the Canadian Shield and there weren't enough hours in the day to get things done. The Husky was a real boon as it was reliable and rugged. With full tanks (135 gallons) and careful fuel management Don could coax nine hours range out of it so they could fly great distances. With canoes loaded in the cabin a 20-knot penalty was saved compared with lashing them on the floats. On the other hand, the float would accommodate a 22-foot freighter canoe, something a Beaver couldn't handle. Like all other Husky professionals, Don acknowledged the plane's slight power disadvantage and flew it accordingly. His appraisal of the Husky is succinct: "Be very polite when you speak about that airplane. It was the best bushplane I ever flew."

Classic Fairchild Husky photo. Nickel Belt's CF-EIP pulled up to the beach at Payne Lake near Chubb Crater in 1949. (Don McIntyre)

Hunting for Nickel

In the post-war years the International Nickel Company launched a major mineral exploration program in northern Manitoba and the Northwest Territories. Aerial surveying was to be used as never before and Austin Airways was to be the main contractor, though firms such as Nickel Belt Airways and Lambair were to share in the work.

Inco set up its first Manitoba camp on Cockeram Lake in 1947. Dr. C.E. Michener of Inco noted of the venture: "They didn't have adequate aircraft out there in those days. We needed this new type that looked quite good at the time and appeared to be a practical kind of bushplane." That airplane was the Fairchild Husky and Nickel Belt Airways of Sudbury supplied two under chief pilot Jim Bell. Jim's other pilot was Don McIntyre. The Huskies were

used to fly field crew around the country and keep the camps supplied with every need. The Husky's ability to accommodate canoes internally was much appreciated by the Inco people. Base camp for these operations was Wabowden on the Hudson Bay Railroad.

Lloyd McTaggart was an engineer on the Husky during this period and recalls: "It would hold eight passengers and was ideal as we could put two 16-foot canoes right inside the aircraft. We could run diamond drills right inside. We could load the aircraft in 15 minutes, whereas with the Norseman and Beaver any long articles had to be strapped to the floats. It was remarkable what you could carry in the Husky."

Other pilots were soon involved with the Husky opera-

Nickel-hunting Anson, CF-IVK, at Raleigh Lake near Ignace in northwestern Ontario, August 21, 1969. (Nick MacDonald-Wolochatiuk)

tion, though after 1952 they were no longer working for Nickel Belt, which had been bought out by Austin. New names included Kelly Gibb, Einar Kallio and Dave Brand.

Dave Brand spent part of his early flying career with Austin Airways in northern Manitoba. He learned to fly with the Wongs (Central Airways) at Toronto Island Airport in 1946, then got his first job flying with Great Northern Skyways at Algoma Mills. He did some work for Georgian Bay Airways at Parry Sound but soon joined the excitement at Sept Iles, flying for Hollinger Ungava Transport on the airlift along the railroad to Knob Lake.

While with HUT Dave met Jim Bell, and as the airlift subsided Jim steered Dave to Jack Austin. Jack appraised Dave's record of flying bushplanes and DC-3s, and promptly hired him. Thus, in 1953, Dave found himself flying one of Austin's Cessna 180s from Snow Lake, north of The Pas. It wasn't long before this venture ended, as the 180 went up on its nose one day when it lost a ski on takeoff. The plane was shipped off to Sudbury and Dave got a replacement, but he was moved up to Ferguson Lake where Jim Hobbs was also based with a Beaver purchased especially for the job.

In 1954 Dave again changed planes, this time taking over the Husky CF-EIQ. At first he operated on skis at Mystery Lake, then spent the summer at Ferguson with Hobbs. The role of the planes there was to service a number of small Inco drills throughout the countryside and to fly prospecting parties around on their exploration work. Dave recalls that the contract included the typical statement that the company was to have plane and pilot available for work throughout the hours of daylight. In summer, at Ferguson Lake, that meant some very long days in the air!

Dave was involved in the usual pranks that come up in

the bush or out on the tundra. One day while loading at Thicket Portage, Dave had the dock hands heave three 45-gallon drums aboard 'EIQ. Then, in full view of Kelly Gibb, he had them put a fourth drum on, and took off—something which left Kelly musing. Four 45s! He couldn't let this challenge slip by so he had his machine, 'SAQ, loaded with four drums for his next trip. But try as he might, Kelly couldn't get his Husky off the water. Finally he gave up and taxied back to the dock totally frustrated.

His frustration turned to real annoyance when he was told that it had all been a prank—Dave's fourth barrel had been an empty! Kelly had stayed up all night before sanding and polishing 'SAQ's wings, trying to clean it up to carry four. Kelly bided his time waiting to get even, then made his move. He conspired to get Dave's tongue loosened up one evening, using a jug of the best. He then got Dave to express some of his innermost feelings about the company and its employees. Later he asked Dave if he'd care to hear the conversation again. Kelly had taped the whole thing. In future Dave would refrain from playing unsportsmanlike tricks on the great Kelly Gibb or a certain tape might end up in the wrong hands.

Dave Brand has generally good memories of the Fairchild Husky, which he came to know so well with Austin Airways: "The Husky was a great old airplane. It was perhaps a bit underpowered, but it was nicely laid out and comfortable from a pilot's viewpoint. And it was very easy to load."

Another little incident that Dave remembers is the time that he had just arrived at The Pas with Lloyd McTaggart and Fred Knox; the three were still dressed in city clothes but were immediately sent out on a trip to collect a fellow from the wilds. They arrived at the camp and Fred tramped through the snow to the cabin. Never had the bushwhacker who opened the door been more surprised, for there, in the depths of northern Manitoba, stood a gentleman attired in camel hair coat, silk scarf and fedora.

Longtime Inco engineer McTaggart has his own memories of Kelly Gibb. He writes, "I first met Kelly in the summer of 1948 when he was flying a Fleet Canuck for Pineland Timber. Looking at Kelly, it was hard to tell his age. He may have been 35 to 40. He was a big man and probably weighed over 180 pounds. He was a first-rate pilot and engineer, very self-assured but also very gruff. What Kelly Gibb wanted to do, Kelly Gibb did. What Kelly Gibb wanted to say, Kelly Gibb said. And it didn't matter what, when or where.

"Kelly was a hard man to get to know and, like myself, you mightn't like him at first. But if you persevered, you couldn't help but like him in the end. And once he got to know you, and you passed muster, Kelly would do anything for you.

"In 1950 Kelly and I went out to Wabowden. We had a Nickel Belt Husky and were working for Inco. At the time I didn't have my engineer's licence, so Kelly was signing the aircraft out. We flew from daylight till dark, flying men and equipment out to Mystery Lake where the main bush camp was located, and to various field camps.

We all stayed at the Inco camp at Wabowden, living in tents. Wabowden wasn't so bad. At least it had a hotel and a fellow could get a beer.

"July 1, 1950, was a day I shall never forget. About twice a month the Inco geologists went to The Pas to phone Copper Cliff. At the time there were no phones at Wabowden. The trip suited us OK as it usually meant a couple of days in town. The seaplane base for The Pas was at Grassy Lake, another place without a phone. So the drill was to fly over the town and change pitch. This would signal a cab which would then come out and pick us up.

"On arrival over The Pas on this particular day Kelly changed pitch all right. He came across very low, maybe just a hundred feet, pulling 36½ inches of manifold pressure with the prop in fine pitch. That Pratt and Whitney was really screaming! The Indians at the Opasque Hotel thought the roof was caving in and they took off out the door carrying their beers. That was the first time in history that that men's beverage room was empty in the middle of the afternoon! Besides that near-calamity, Kelly's noisy arrival also caused at least one lady to faint. All this we later heard at the DOT inquiry.

"Anyway, we landed on the lake and taxied in as usual, but as we did, a car arrived at the dock. I tossed a rope to its driver, jumped onto the dock and proceeded to tie up. Then this fellow asked for our logbook. Kelly replied something to the effect of 'Jump in the lake,' after which our dockhand identified himself as a lawman. Not that that especially humbled Kelly!"

Another amusing Husky story involved a paint job. Kelly's machine had been sent out to Sudbury for maintenance and while it was there Frank Russell arranged to have it repainted in the black and red Austin scheme. When it got back to Manitoba, Kelly was rather ticked off. He didn't think the Husky looked right, so he personally undertook to strip all the paint off. Bit by bit he scraped away and when the paint remover ran out he resorted to bottles of nail polish remover. Eventually the job was done and Kelly was satisfied.

Kelly's more serious side shows in these comments from Inco's Cliff Alguire as recorded in an interview with Don Dunbar: "I can recall back at Thicket Portage when our third girl got very sick in the middle of the night. I went over and asked Kelly if he would mind flying into The Pas, and right at daybreak he was in the aircraft and had it ready. My wife took Katherine down and Kelly flew her into The Pas. When he got back I asked him how much I owed him and he said, 'Oh, that's all right, that's just part of our duty.' That's the type of person Kelly was.''

Fred Knox was an engineer with Austin Airways in northern Manitoba from 1953 to 1956. He had been an air gunner with the RCAF during the war, then spent several post-war years as an aero engine mechanic in the air force, serving at such places as Trenton and Summerside. In his spare time he and his brother flew their own Tiger Moths and were involved in gliding and parachuting. After his discharge, Fred flew bushplanes for Eastern Provincial Airways and worked for several other operators including Kenting, the Moncton Flying Club, and TCA at Dorval. One spring day in 1953 at Dorval the budworm spraying fleet came through—a flock of open cockpit Stearmans—and the sight was too much for Fred. He just had to get back flying. He arranged for an interview with Jack Austin in Toronto and was hired as a mechanic but with the hope of getting a flying job when an opening came up.

Two pictures of the Cessna 180, CF-HDX, damaged when a ski broke on takeoff. After salvage, it was trucked to the railroad and shipped out for repairs. (Fred Knox, Bruce Gowans)

Fred was sent to Sudbury, then out to Snow Lake as Dave Brand's mechanic. Dave had the Cessna 180 and Fred got to fly it from time to time on non-revenue trips. Jim Hobbs was out in Manitoba then and Fred remembers him as a thorough professional who always flew with a sextant and astro compass for navigating the barren lands. Tommy Nelson was Jim's mechanic at the time, keeping their Norseman in shape.

Fred remembers Dave's 180 prang. While he was taking off, a bolt sheared on a ski and totally ruined his plans for the day. The airplane was a mess and Fred had to organize its salvage. Normally he would have used a small Caterpillar tractor to haul in the wreck, but it was spring and the insurance was off the Cats for use on ice. So Fred hired a Bombardier. He, the Bombardier operator and a local RCMP officer teamed up in the sub-zero temperature to disassemble the 180 and move it 40 miles to the railroad. The airplane was shipped off by box car and for several days could not be located: the railroad had failed to note the number of the box car that it was travelling in.

Fred reports, ''Kelly Gibb was always pulling something on somebody. One day Dave and I were returning from Sudbury in a newly refurbished Husky. We were to use it all that summer at Ferguson Lake so were happy to have an overhauled machine. When we got to Mystery Lake, Kelly was there looking suspiciously at our nice Husky. 'Well, looks like this is where we change planes, fellows,' he says. This was news to us, but Kelly insisted that this was the information he had from Jack Austin. Always suspicious of Kelly, and realizing that he'd be glad to unload his tired-out Husky on us, we asked for proof. He said he had a letter with the instructions. Dave agreed that if Kelly could produce the letter he could have our Husky. The letter never appeared, so off we went to Ferguson as planned, in our own aircraft.''

Fred notes that the Husky was very critical as far as loading went. More than once he had to throw something like a 50-pound bag of onions off to give that little edge that allowed takeoff. Even bugs on the leading edge could be a noticeable drag on performance and would have to be scrubbed off whenever they built up.

One day Dave and Fred were flying a canoe in the back of the Husky. An Indian passenger was along and as it was a tight squeeze the passenger had to sit in the canoe. As they cruised along they weren't careful to watch the fuel and their tank ran dry. The engine sputtered and for some reason the crew both looked back, maybe because the fuel tanks were under the floorboards in the cabin. Just as they did, the Indian also felt the engine sputter and, as instinct would have it, he immediately grabbed a paddle and started to dig in. All three suddenly realized the humour of the moment and started laughing so hard that they could hardly get the tank switched over and the engine restarted.

Fred left Austin Airways in 1956 to work for the Lands and Forests, but soon went back to TCA. He remained there until 1981 when he left the business, at the time having all five Air Canada jets on his engineer's licence.

The Anson Years

In the post-war years, War Assets Corporation was disposing of thousands of surplus military aircraft. They were mainly sold as scrap, but many were also cleared for civil flying. Of these aircraft, Chuck Austin felt that the Anson V might be a useful freighter, so in December 1949 Austin Airways acquired two, CF-GRU (ex-RCAF 11990) and CF-GRV (ex-RCAF 11680). They were ferried to Sudbury where one was fitted with a set of Elliott Brothers skis, but once the airplane was weighed it was clear that the useful load would be negligible. It was decided to scrap the Ansons, salvaging whatever might be useful.

But just then Austin Airways was approached by International Nickel, which proposed using the Ansons as aerial surveying aircraft. Inco was developing a big exploration program on the Canadian Shield using airborne electromagnetic surveying, and the Anson, having a wooden airframe, would be ideal for EM work. The first contract was soon struck between Austin Airways and Inco's subsidiary, Canadian Nickel Co., to provide Ansons for mineral exploration. CF-GRV had already been scrapped, but CF-GRU was converted for EM work and a new era was launched in the Austin Airways story.

Before long a fleet of Ansons was at work on the Inco projects, these being CF-DTW, 'EJX, 'GRU, 'HQZ, 'IVK and 'JAW of Austin Airways, and Inco's own aircraft, CF-HOT. Spartan Air Services of Ottawa discovered the usefulness of the Anson at the same time and was also building up a fleet for EM work in Canada and internationally. Each aircraft was fitted with sensing equipment housed in a "bird" or "bomb" slung under the belly. It could be let out to fly behind the aircraft on about 350 feet of light cable. Surveying was done at low altitude, with the bird flying along 100-150 feet above the terrain. On board was equipment that would give magnetic anomaly readouts indicating the presence of mineral deposits in the rock below. Pilot, navigator and EM operator crewed the aircraft.

For over 20 years the Austin Airways Ansons were to operate in their EM capacity throughout Canada—in New Brunswick, northern Quebec and Ontario, across the top of the Prairie provinces, and up into the Northwest

Husky 'EIQ at Tavanni, N.W.T., during 1951. Few bushplanes could carry the load seen here—a massive freighter canoe. (Don McIntyre)

Anson CF-EJX, with its EM "bird" fitted, waits at Ferguson Lake, 1952. (R.L. Savage)

Territories. Occasional jobs were also done in the northern United States. Surveying was a distinctive aspect of the airline, unlike its VFR bushplane or Canso/DC-3 operations in the requirements placed on pilots and equipment. The initial Anson surveying was done for Inco in northern Manitoba from such places as The Pas, Flin Flon and Wabowden, with Prince Albert, Saskatchewan, as the base for special maintenance.

Ed Kenyon and Gil Hudson were two of Austin's early Anson pilots, working with a variety of Inco navigators and EM operators. Ed's aviation career began in 1926 when he used to help out as a kid at Jack Elliot's flying operation at Hamilton. He managed to do a bit of flying through the thirties but his break came in 1939 when the

Following the war Ed flew a bit with Peninsula Air Service at Mount Hope but in 1951 joined Austin Airways, where most of his flying was to be on the Anson. One of his first jobs resulted in a major lead-zinc-copper find in New Brunswick. As one might expect, the work was generally routine and unexciting. To fill in many of the long days waiting on the ground for weather to clear Ed busied himself with his hobby, painting the local scenery.

However, life was not always as dull as flying lines, or as relaxing as sitting at the easel. One day Ed took off from Flin Flon on a trip to Stony Rapids flying CF-EJX. This was an Anson he had picked up at St. Jean, Quebec, and from the outset it proved to be a clunker. On this trip everything seemed to be going wrong so Ed turned

Austin's first Anson, CF-GRU, parked by a Husky at Ennadai Lake; then seen on a murky day at Wabowden. (George Charity Collection, Ed Kenyon)

war started. He landed a job instructing at No. 10 EFTS, Hamilton, and later joined No. 124 (Ferry) Squadron at Rockcliffe. Towards the end of the war he checked out on the Mosquito at Greenwood and went to work for Harry Umphrey testing new Mossies for Central Aircraft at London, Ontario. This was the closest Ed figured he'd ever get to combat and he made the most of it. He relates how one day he, Moe Sears and another pilot put on a three-plane air show at London for the benefit of some military observers. They went far beyond what was expected of them, putting on a show that amazed everyone. At one point Ed recalls roaring down the runway to see another Mossie coming straight at him. That wasn't on the program. After scaring the daylights out of themselves and those on the ground, the three self-styled aerobatic pilots landed and climbed from their airplanes just as if the whole display had been planned in advance.

back. As he approached the airport both engines quit and he immediately aimed for a landing on nearby Ross Lake, the town sewage dump. As the gear was down, the Anson flipped when it touched the water and fell heavily onto its back. Ed later reported that getting clear of the wreck was a problem: "I was under water holding my breath but didn't realize we were upside down. I undid my safety belt and tried to find an emergency hatch which should have been above my head. Actually, it was smashed into the bottom of the lake. I was just about drowned by that time but I finally floated up and found there was about six inches of airspace around the cockpit floor."

He finally got free as did the other two aboard, engineer Fred Dryden and Inco geologist Jim Musselman. The three men spent a few hours in hospital getting over some minor bumps. CF-EJX was hauled from the lake, stripped for salvage, then doused with gasoline and burned.

In 1957 Ed decided to leave the frigid northland for good and bought a property in Florida, where he spent several years as a deputy sheriff and working for the county parks department before retiring in 1976. When

Anson swan song. The photo sequence shows CF-EJX submerged at Flin Flon after its forced landing; being hauled out; and being incinerated; and pilot Ed Kenyon, engineer Fred Dryden and Inco geologist Jim Musselman recuperating in hospital at The Pas after their prang. (via Ed Kenyon)

Ed decided to move south, Jack Austin hired an able replacement to head the Anson operation, Maurice L. "Moe" Sears. Moe had begun flying on August 4, 1942, with a familiarization ride in Tiger Moth 3977 of No. 7 EFTS at his home town of Windsor, Ontario. After getting his wings, he instructed on Harvards at Camp Borden, then went to No. 36 OTU, Greenwood, Nova Scotia, to convert to Mosquitos. His first Mossie ride was on November 4, 1943, and he soloed after two hours. Next stop was NO. 13 OTU, Bicester, England, then on to 418 Squadron and night fighter ops, commencing July 20, 1944. After a tour on Mossies and many an exciting trip (the worst two of which were being struck by lightning and being coned one night by enemy searchlights), Moe returned to Canada. At first it was more Harvard instructing, then a test pilot's job flying newly built Mossies at London that lasted till August 27, 1946.

Once back on civvy street, Moe returned to Windsor and a variety of commercial flying. He ran a two-Anson flying operation for Progressive Welders Corp. of Detroit, making many trips between there and Florida, then took over as chief pilot with Great Northern Skyways, based at Gore Bay where Bob Kerr was engineer. There he flew Ansons, Fox Moths, a Fairchild 24, a Fairchild 71 and a Seabee until joining Georgian Bay Airways. In July 1955 he began flying for Austin Airways, initially on the Cessna 180 (CF-FYQ), and soon after on another 180 (CF-IBQ) and Beavers (CF-FHE, CF-GQQ and CF-FHX).

A typical day's flying appears in Moe's log for September 17, 1955. The aircraft were CF-FYQ and CF-GQQ and all trips were from Sudbury and back: Koko Lake (40 min.), Bell Lake (40 min.), Koko Lake (40 min.), Venetian Lake (45 min.), Three Narrows (45 min.), Three Narrows (45 min.), Tyson Lake (40 min.) and Bell Lake (40 min.). Also during this period Moe flew Norsemen CF-BSJ, 'GMM, 'HZR and 'IGG and Beaver CF-GBC.

During his second year with Austin, Moe Sears began flying the survey Ansons. He always felt that he got railroaded into the job by Jim Bell. As he recalls, "Whenever something came up and the company was in a bit of a fix, Jim used to say, 'Where's Moe?' and I'd get the job." Not that he objected to flying the Anson, and Jim knew

(Left) Austin's trio of Jim Hall, Scotty Buchanan and Mark Nieminen change an engine on Anson CF-DTW at Earlton in Northern Ontario. (via Jim Hall)

(Right) Gil Hudson, left, and friend Ralph Shapland with their Husky prior to Gil joining Austin Airways. (via Ralph Shapland)

perfectly well that if there was a right man for the job it was Moe, with all his experience flying wooden wonders.

Moe's first trip in an Austin Anson was on March 1, 1957, in CF-JAW, hauling passengers between Timmins and Moosonee. On March 23 he took CF-DTW out on his first electromagnetic survey flight and on May 10 he set out for Esker Lake in the Ungava region of northern Quebec where he operated until June 18. Then word came that CF-GRU, conducting a survey from Desolation Lake in the Northwest Territories, had crashed. Moe was to get out there as quickly as his Anson would carry him and

complete the job. The log of the Esker Lake-Desolation Lake transit reads:

June 18	Esker Lake-Ft. Chimo	2:15 hours
	Ft. Chimo-Knob Lake	2:00
	Knob Lake-Seven Islands	2:40
19	Seven Islands-Forestville	2:00
20	Forestville-Roberval	1:30
	Roberval-Val d'Or	2:10
	Val d'Or-Sudbury	1:30
21	Sudbury-Nakina	3:10
	Nakina-Sioux Lookout	1:50
	Sioux Lookout-Winnipeg	1:45

Group portraits taken at Ennadai and Ferguson Lake showing local Eskimo families. (E.A. Kenyon)

Night fighter pilot Moe Sears, right, with his navigator, Frank Hill, pose by their Mosquito at Hunsdon near London in 1944. Moe was a top Anson pilot after the war. He died September 2, 1983. (via Moe Sears)

(Top) Distant view of the Inco camp at Ennadai. (Above) Fun time. Members of the Inco crew roll barrels in this macho display at the company's Ennadai camp. What else for a fellow to do in the middle of nowhere! (Ed Kenyon)

Two of Austin's Beavers. CF-FHE (left) was bought from a Quebec lumber company to replace the Husky burned at St. Jean. CF-JKT (below), one of Austin's longest-serving Beavers, was bought new from de Havilland and over the years wore a variety of colour schemes. It appears here on floats in the Gogama region. (Jeff Wyborn, Ontario Government)

(Left) Ray Lejeune during his days flying EM Ansons for Austin Airways. (via Ray Lejeune)

(Right) CF-DTW being gassed up at Ramsey Lake. (Ed Kenyon)

Two of the Ansons frequently under Moe Sears' command: CF-IVK with bomb installed at Fort William on July 5, 1962; and Inco's CF-HOT at Malton, August 16, 1959. In 1983 'HOT was Canada's only airworthy Anson, being part of the Canadian Warplane Heritage Collection. (Jack McNulty, Larry Milberry)

22	Winnipeg-Yorkton	1:58
	Yorkton-Saskatoon	1:30
	Saskatoon-Edmonton	2:15
	Edmonton-Ft. McMurray	2:05
	Ft. McMurray-Ft. Simpson	1:45
	Ft. Simpson-Yellowknife	1:20
23	Yellowknife-Desolation Lake	2:30

Total time for the gruelling 17-leg trip was 34:13 hours in six flying days at about 130mph average speed. And the job at the other end? Moe finished it in less than two days, or 7:15 hours of line flying, then headed back to Esker Lake. Check an atlas of Canada to see what passed for "routine" on the Anson operation.

Moe reported that out in the field the party leader called the shots, including flight scheduling, though the pilot always had the last word if the weather was marginal. Navigators and EM operators were always Inco employees, and Moe remembered Frank Gibson as the navigator he worked best with. Moe and Frank were usually able to complete a job ahead of schedule.

Exciting happenings rarely interrupted the dull routine of flying survey lines, but Moe recalled one that still got him steamed up years later. CF-DTW was just out of the shop all checked over and freshly painted. Moe had briefed one of the pilots about landing on the Severn strip: there was a hump midway down the runway and the tail must be kept up until the Anson passed the hump. Nonetheless the pilot let the tail down too early and lost control after rolling over the hump. He swerved into a snowbank and the Anson was wrecked.

One place not to be stationed too long, claimed Moe Sears, was Wabowden on the Hudson Bay railroad in northern Manitoba. There the Anson crew put up in the local hotel. Its sanitation system consisted of a 5-gallon bucket that used to overflow and run down the stairs. As for meals, no problem, as long as you were happy with the only meal in town—sausages and eggs. His only really dicy flight involved a landing at Flin Flon. Ground fog had moved in just as the Anson returned. The plane was low on fuel so there was no hope of reaching an alternate. Moe made a pass where he thought the runway ought to be and to his delight found on coming around that his prop and wake turbulence cleared enough of the light fog to give him a glimpse of the runway and enable him to get down.

Year after year Moe continued as Austin's "chief pilot" on the Anson. Time through 1968 on CF-IVK and CF-HOT was: March, 41:25 hrs; April, 36:45 hrs; May, 64:15 hrs; June, 37:50 hrs; July, 43:45 hrs; August, 44:30 hrs; September, 35:05 hrs; and October, 44:30 hrs. He logged his final Anson flying between June and September 1976 when Inco called him in to fly a survey in New Brunswick. After 130 hours of flying on CF-HOT, Moe brought the Anson back to Sudbury where it was retired from service. It was later handed over to the Canadian Warplane Heritage, which restored it to its wartime colours and operates it at airshows around the continent. Moe continued flying for several years, his affair with the Anson over after some 8000 hours on type.

J.R. "Ray" Lejeune was another of Austin's longtime Anson pilots. He had started flying at No. 9 EFTS, St. Catharines, in January 1941 and in October of that year completed his training on Spitfires at an Operational Training Unit in England. He went to Malta in February 1942 with 126 Squadron and for much of the war was flying in the combat zone, making his last flight in the Spit from Eindhoven on July 24, 1945.

Ray resumed flying in December 1948 with 417 Squadron at Rivers, Manitoba, and spent some busy years on Cansos, Lancasters, Dakotas and other types until he left the RCAF in early 1953. In February that year he decided to take some instruction at Toronto Island Airport and qualify for a civilian instructor's permit. No sooner had he begun than Bob Wong of Central Airways steered him over to Jack Austin's Island Airport office where he was hired on the spot. On February 24, he made his first trip with Austin Airways, flying with Jim Bell in a DC-3, CF-FAX, from Churchill to Ferguson Lake return. By the end of March he had logged a respectable 165:10 hours on the Dak and on Canso CF-FAR.

Aircraft checklist for the Anson V as it appeared in the Austin Airways operations manual.

START	AFTER TAKEOFF
Parking brake on	U/C up
Gas on outer tanks	Power 2000 RPM 30"
Gear Select (Down)	Initial climb 100 MPH
Carb. Cold	Continuous climb 110 MPH
Mixtures rich	Carb. heat as req'd.
Props fine pitch	Cockpit check
Wobble gas to 3 lbs.	
Prime	CRUISE
Switches on	1800 RPM 27"
Starboard then port	Max. 2000 RPM 28"
	Max. cont. 2200 RPM 33"
RUN UP	Cockpit check
Oil temp. 40°C	
Cyl temp. 150°C	LANDING
Gas inner tanks	Speed 120 MPH
Mixture rich	Best tanks
Carb. cold	Cockpit check as in T/C
RPM 1500 work props.	Check warning horn
Mag. check at 30"	Lower U/C
	Speed final 90 MPH
	Check warning horn
T/O CHECK	Flaps 20 to 40 deg. as req'd.
Rudder trim neutral	
Elevator trim as req'd.	AFTER LANDING
Radio panel R to L	Flaps up
Inst. panel L to R	Pitot heat off
Pitch fine	Cockpit check for switches,
Mixture rich (back)	gyros, etc.
Carb. cold	Leave A/H uncaged
Oil coolers as req'd.	
Flaps up or as req'd.	CAUTION
Gas on outers	Parking cold weather brakes off,
Cross feed normal	wheels checked.
Controls free	Leave engine controls in start
	position in cold
T/O POWER	weather.
2300 RPM, 36.5"	

Norm Kern thaws out the tail of his Anson at Gods Lake, Manitoba, 1958. (James R. Lee)

On April 15, 1953, Ray began his 20-year involvement with the Anson, after a short check flight with Jim Hobbs in charge. The same day he flew from Prince Albert to Lac la Ronge then Stony Rapids in northern Saskatchewan to begin survey work flying CF-GRU. By April 24 he had made 20 flights when a mishap interrupted things. He was returning to Ennadai Lake after a 4:20 hour flight but found the strip fogged in. As he was low on fuel he was forced to make a wheels-up landing on the snow. The Anson was undamaged and within a few days Jim Bell and engineer Chuck Rose had flown in with a set of skis from Prince Albert. They dug the snow from under the wings, lowered the wheels, fitted the skis and away went 'GRU. Ray worked on the Ennadai Lake survey until June 23, logging 80 flights and 170:20 hours, then returned to the Canso for two months, working from Churchill and Ferguson Lake with pilots Jim Bell, Gil Hudson, Doug Mackie and Paul Hayes.

On August 29 Ray ferried CF-GRU from Sudbury to Bathurst, New Brunswick for a two-month electromagnetic survey involving just over 100 hours of flying. Most of his next two years were spent on CF-GRU and CF-DTW, flying in the Snow Lake, Mystery Lake, Lynn Lake and Flin Flon regions. Ray's Anson time for 1954 totalled 333:40 hours but he also logged time that year on the Canso, Norseman and Cessna 180.

The flurry of air freighting brought on by the Mid Canada Line construction project took Ray away from the Ansons in 1955 to fly the Canso and DC-3, but he returned to EM flying in February 1959, working out of Wabowden on the Hudson Bay Railroad that month with CF-IVK. A two-month job flying from Pat Lake in northern Quebec followed, then further surveys from Hay River and The Pas. Hereafter, places like Gillam, Moak Lake, Red Lake, Timmins, Kapuskasing, Rouyn, Horden Lake, Senneterre, Sioux Lookout, Dryden and Kenora are regularly noted in his log, all located in that huge shield-shaped mass of precambrian rock that sweeps around Hudson and James Bay. Thanks in large part to the Austin Airways Ansons, the region was to be developed into one of the world's greatest sources of mineral wealth.

Ray continued Anson flying, but interspersed plenty of DC-3 and Canso time, including ice patrol in the Arctic. He also spent a season flying Canso water bombers for the Quebec government. He wrapped up his commercial flying career in 1973. His last flight with Austin was a short EM trip from Sudbury on August 8, 1973, aboard CF-IVK.

Anecdotes are related about all the Anson pilots, Ray Lejeune not excepted. One day at Devil's Lake two Ansons were on final from opposite ends of the runway at the same time! Ray was flying one and Norm Kern the other. Good sense prevailed at some point during this dicy few moments and everyone survived. Another day, Ray took off from Severn Lake and lost his tail wheel. It bounced along and came to rest about half way down the strip. Ray carried on to fly his lines for the day but couldn't be reached as his radio was off. To alert him, the party leader had some vehicles parked at each end of the runway. When he returned, Ray noticed them—and the tail wheel! At this point he was heard over the radio chuckling to himself, "Ha! Norm's lost his tail wheel." Then he called up the camp and got the bad news. "No, Ray, it's not Norm's tail wheel. It's yours." Not so funny, but fortunately Ray set down without causing any damage.

Ray is also noted as the pilot who brought an Anson back to Sudbury from Gimli, where it had been purchased from a fish hauler: he arrived to find that the Anson he was due to collect was unserviceable but, undaunted, he simply returned to Sudbury with a rather beat-up machine, reeking of fish, that had been parked beside the intended one. Thus Austin Airways acquired CF-HQZ. Never anyone's favourite Anson, 'HQZ was eventually written off by another pilot at Sioux Lookout when it landed with one tire flat. Navigator Don Taylor recalls it all happening—the Anson careening down the runway and coming to rest, a sorry looking pile of scrap.

Another day Ray was taking off from Wabowden with

Fred Knox aboard as engineer. Part way down the runway the Anson dropped into a mud hole and swung violently. Ray brought the plane to a stop and taxied back for another go, saying to Fred, "Remember where that hole is." He again started his takeoff roll, but as the plane was heavily loaded it was slow getting up. Fred remembers that as soon as they ran out of runway and he saw ugly-looking stumps right under the nose, he selected gear up. The Anson kept going and gained height, having cleared the stumps by inches.

Norm Kern of Winnipeg was another of Austin's Anson pilots, a member of the famous trio of Sears, Lejeune and Kern. Norm had learned to fly with Konnie Johannesson at Winnipeg in the late thirties. He flew with the Air Observers School at Winnipeg and late in the war worked for CPA at Sioux Lookout. After the war he was bush flying in northwestern Ontario before joining Austin around 1956.

The Anson "trio" gained quite a reputation as top pilots. They were a rugged bunch who could endure months of isolation and boredom. They were hardly the world's most genteel characters, but as time has proven they were the men for the job. Very little could faze them. Doug Taylor tells of being out one day with Norm Kern when they got into some poor weather. The hours went by and there was no sign of the ground. Finally Norm spotted a hole in the cloud, dropped through it, got his bearings and made it into The Pas. As his friend Cliff Larry has remarked, "Norm had a vast knowledge of the country, especially of Saskatchewan, Manitoba and Ontario." The flight that day had been 5:25 hours. Next day Norm and Doug went out and lost an engine!

Many other pilots flew the Ansons for Austin Airways. One was Bill Gwynn, who started on Ansons in 1963. Bill tells that in summer survey flying generally started at first light in order to avoid the thermals that developed as the day wore on. Lines were only ¼ mile apart, yet turns had to be kept flat as the EM bird was flying below, skimming over the surface at 150 feet. Anson flying was usually curtailed by midday, then, once turbulence subsided towards evening, another flight was generally conducted.

On April 13, 1963, Bill was flying CF-IVK over northern Quebec when the bird struck the ground. Writing off the bird was not uncommon, and did little to endear pilots to the Inco party chiefs. On another occasion, while flying off Levac Lake in Quebec, the ice began melting. It became too soft to use during the day, but in the evening it firmed up. They pushed the Anson down to the end of the ice strip and set it on two big makeshift skis (actually the ply-

Anson CF-GRU after she slithered into the lake at Flin Flon in June 1956. (Bruce Gowans)

(Below) Anson CF-GRU after its accident at McGregor Lake. The decision was made to torch the Anson after stripping it of useful equipment. Being of wood, fabric and who knows how many layers of paint, she went up in a beautiful flash! (R.L. Savage)

Constructing a drag for use in clearing the runway at Severn Lake in 1969. (James R. Lee)

A Beech 18 of Severn Enterprises delivers 45s to the Inco camp at Severn Lake. (James R. Lee)

Inco data man Gary Michalak logs a flight in the "office" at Severn Lake during the 1969 season. (James R. Lee)

wood doors from tents). Early the next morning the Anson took off. The skis had been rigged to drop away as soon as the wheels lifted, and the scheme worked.

As soon as Bill was airborne he called Timmins, his destination. He found out that Timmins was down with weather so he changed course for Moosonee. There he was greeted by freezing rain and a mushy runway, and as soon as he touched down the Anson sank into slush and mud, though it came to rest in one piece. A typical month of Anson flying appears in Bill's log: April 12 to May 14, 1963, 57:05 hours.

Bill describes the Anson as a beautiful flying airplane. It had its idiosyncrasies, but minor ones. Landings took some getting used to, as the bladder-operated brakes had to be pumped several times before they would start to grab. And with experience one learned the knack of effectively steering down the runway using aileron and rudder. Of course, the Anson was a tired old bird at the time. Someone commented to Bill one day, "This old Anson will be OK, as long as the termites keep holding hands!"

The career of each of Austin's Ansons was to be unique. CF-EJX ended up in the sewage pond; CF-HQZ doesn't seem to have been anyone's favorite; but others like CF-DTW and CF-IVK were. CF-GRU seems to have been a reliable and hard-working airplane, spending a lot of time in Manitoba. During this period someone had christened it the Graphite Queen, because of its work in mineral exploration, and its black paint scheme. CF-GRU operated for over 2500 mainly trouble-free hours with Austin. It had one incident at Flin Flon on June 25, 1956, when it ran off the runway and slipped into Schist Lake. Hauled out and checked over, it was found only slightly damaged and was soon back to work. The reliable Anson, though, was in for a second and final embarrassment. On June 14, 1957, it was operating from an ice strip at Desolation Lake in the Coppermine River region of the Northwest Territories. Pilot A.J.C. Hamilton had taken off on a survey flight but had to return when some of the electronic gear acted up. Coming in to land, he flew into a whiteout and crash landed on the overshoot. There was enough damage to render the aircraft a total loss. Just where she lay, the once-lovely Graphite Queen became her own funeral pyre. In some 8mm colour movie footage kept by Moe Sears, she can be seen erupting in a great billow of flame and smoke, put deliberately to the torch to get the broken hulk out of the way. This certainly saved engineer Chuck Rose a lot of trouble patching up the old veteran.

As much of the Anson work was done from remote sites, it was usual for Inco to send a crew into a region, often hundreds of miles from "civilization," to build a camp and put in an airstrip. As the easiest way of coping with the need for an airstrip was to operate off the ice, the surveying cycle revolved on a seasonal basis—do the flying in winter and spend the summer analyzing the data. Thus names like Desolation Lake, Esker Lake, Levac Lake, Horden Lake and Severn Lake came to be burned into the memories of some of the old timers at Austin and Inco. Few other Canadians had ever heard of such places!

Jim Lee was party leader at many of the Inco camps. The biggest he managed was at Severn Lake in remote northwestern Ontario. He flew in there with a crew to start laying out the camp in November 1968. Forest was cleared and a long row of big plywood-floor tents was set up. An ice strip was prepared and in January operations began. The camp population included party leader, cook, helper, handyman, tractor operator and two data men. For each Anson there was a pilot, navigator, operator and engineer. The tractor operator had the vital job of dragging the strip to keep it constantly operational. The camp became a real showplace in the region and one day 11 aircraft could be counted there.

Part of Inco's interim report of 1969 covering the Severn Lake operation reads: "For the survey of this area a tent camp was constructed on an island in Severn Lake 170 miles northwest of Pickle Lake. Aviation gasoline, groceries, building supplies and enough fuel oil to start the operation were air-freighted from Pickle Lake by Severn Enterprises. The remainder of the fuel oil was hauled by tractor trains operated by Sigfussion's Transport from Pickle Lake. Electricity was supplied by a 15Kw Onan diesel lighting plant. A 2000-gallon gasoline storage tank and electric pump for aircraft refuelling were supplied from Big Trout Lake by Severn Enterprises.

"A runway 5000 feet long and 200 feet wide was packed on the lake ice. A TD-5 tractor was used until a heavier D-4 could be driven in from Pickle Lake. The tractors were rented from Koval Brothers of Pickle Lake but a Canico employee was employed as operator. A drag constructed from 15-foot timbers (the maximum allowable length for air-freighting with Otter or Beechcraft) was found to be too short, resulting in a wavy surface. To correct this, two 25-foot timbers were cut from the bush and using three of the 15-foot timbers as cross pieces, a very satisfactory drag was constructed."

The report notes that three Ansons were used on the job, with CF-DTW arriving first on January 17, 1969. It flew its first survey two days later but was wrecked on March 3.

Inco's EM operator Vic Kanerva in winter flying suit poses arm in arm with one of the bombs. (Ed Kenyon)

(Below) Austin mechanic Mark Nieminen checks the final installation of an EM "bird" fitted snuggly under an Anson. (via Jim Hall)

Life with Austin's survey operations was demanding. Crews could generally expect long periods of isolation, something that wasn't to everyone's liking. Requests like "Get me out of here!" were not uncommon from crewmen who had had enough. One of Austin's seasoned engineers found himself on one job trapped in the boondocks with a mechanic who simply was not cooperating. The engineer's letter to home base in Sudbury could have been signed "Desperate":

"I don't believe he has the necessary ambition or atti-

Inco's Horden Lake camp in northern Quebec during 1965. (James R. Lee)

Moe Sears always got very annoyed when someone bent a fine old airplane and could have cried when someone "did a number" on his favourite Anson at Severn Lake. The upper photo shows Anson CF-DTW after its wheels-up landing in northern Manitoba. Norm Kern works on the starboard prop. The plane was successfully salvaged but was not so fortunate in the later incident at Severn Lake. In the lower photo local inhabitants "recycle" the plane. Old Ansons never die, they just get towed away. (Terry Monk, James R. Lee)

94

Severn Lake in 1969, with the full crews for three planes. In the back row are: J. Munroe, B. Caughill, Bill Henderson, R. Dutchburn, Ray Lejeune, W. Evershed, Moe Sears, J. Murphy, H. Tucker, Gary Cook, Alex Fiddler. In front are: Paul Wesser, G. Michalak, T. Blatchfor, S. Wojnas, Alex Grzelak, John Wenham. Absent were Hans Prass and Bruce Edsel. (James R. Lee)

One of Survair's "flying clothes line" Twin Otters, CF-INB, visiting Severn Lake in March 1969. To the left is an Austin Anson. (James R. Lee)

The big Inco smelter at Thompson, Manitoba, seen below in July 1972. The nickel deposits worked here, along with other major mineral finds in Canada, were located using EM Ansons from Austin's fleet. (Larry Milberry)

A mixed Inco/Austin crew at Gauer Lake, Manitoba, in 1963. Seen here are Ed Morrison, Cat driver Charlie Spencer, pilot Rudy Hoffman, cook Lee Rogers, John Lahti, air engineer Jim Leblanc and data man Ray Parisotto. (R.L. Savage)

Some of the boys at Lac La Ronge, where Inco was surveying in 1955: Larry Coddere sits on the big rock while the others from the left are Vic Kanerva, Joe Mihelchuk, air engineer Chuck Rose, pilot Ray Lejeune and Fred Carter. (R.L. Savage)

tude for a job like this. He tomcats all night then expects to sleep all day...It's a 10 minute walk from town to the airstrip yet he'll sit and wait for someone to drive him out with the result that we often miss part of our a.m. flight. After having difficulty getting away at daylight a number of times I concluded that the only way to make it was to sleep in the shack at the airstrip on nights when it looked

good for an early flight. I'd light the Herman Nelson at 4 a.m., walk into town, and if he hadn't made any move, put the pressure on to get him out there. Last Sunday a.m. I arrived in town at 4:30 having left the Herman Nelson running. There he was, sitting in the lobby of the hotel waiting for a miracle to happen to get him to the strip! He had borrowed the truck for his personal project that night and left it sitting too long so it froze up. He was sitting there in a daze. I don't believe he had any sleep. I told him to start walking which he did reluctantly.

"I walked out to the strip at 5:30. There was no sign of him, but the Herman Nelson was running with the burner out. No gas! He was sitting in the heated shack, fast asleep! Lucky I was there in time to start the engines and get a reasonably early takeoff. We got 6:15 hours of good record that day."

Austin engineer Spencer Woods has a few special memories from Anson days. He remembers that on March 9, 1965, while flying from Lynn Lake, pilot Terry Monk had an engine quit. The Anson could not hold altitude so Terry picked out a frozen lake and made a wheels-up landing. He was able to raise help over the radio and soon Norm Kern had shown up in an Otter. He flew the four-man Anson crew to Thompson, where Spence and Terry organized for salvage. They borrowed two propellers and a set of skis from a local fellow who used an Anson to haul fish, then returned to their plane. The Anson was jacked up and repaired as necessary, then flown out to Prince Albert on March 18 for further work. By March 29 it was back in business. Another Anson incident that Spence mentions concerns a pilot who was a notorious chain smoker. One of Spence's frequent duties was to sweep up around the cockpit. It was always littered with butts, which annoyed the sweeper, a non-smoker. Eventually, Spence was recompensed for all the aggravation. One day as he cruised along, puffing away as usual, the pilot noticed an aroma that didn't belong. Then there came a trail of smoke drifting up from the floor. A sudden flurry of activity followed, and the emergency was quelled. The pilot's seat was on fire —careless smoking!

During the whole Austin Airways/Inco association, one matter of policy was never compromised by Austin. That concerned confidentiality. Employees on the survey program were expected to maintain absolute secrecy regarding mineral data. The fact that pilots and other Austin employees proved themselves trustworthy in Inco's eyes assured excellent working relations between the two companies. As Jack Austin expressed it, "We stuck to our business, and that was flying".

More of the Bush

Flying from Nakina

Bill Gwynn flew from Nakina long after Gord Mitchell and Elmer Ruddick first knew the place. Bill had started flying with Lorne Airways at Toronto Island in 1951. He took his first job with Superior Airways in 1953, O.J. Weiben's Lakehead operation. He flew a Cessna 180 and a Skyrocket for Superior from Sioux Lookout and Geraldton, spent two years flying for Stan Deluce at White River, then went back to Superior. In 1959 he was hauling fish from Nakina when Elmer Ruddick called him to ask a favour. Austin had a medevac emergency which it couldn't handle at the moment. Could Bill help? He did and before long, found himself working for Austin and living at Nakina, flying a 180 (CF-IBQ) and Norsemen (CF-IGG and CF-GMM). Engineers at the time were Bill Montgomery and Frank Krochel.

Flying from Nakina, Bill recalls, basically involved three mail runs, taking in Nakina, Ogoki Post, Lansdowne House and Fort Hope. There was also plenty of staple hauling for the Hudson's Bay Co., Indian Affairs, and co-ops. Routine charters served the usual assortment of trappers, prospectors, sportsmen and so on.

Fish hauling was still big business at Nakina in 1959 and Indian Affairs had implemented a program to keep that activity going. They chartered Austin aircraft to fly mostly pickerel and whitefish to Nakina from Lansdowne House and Fort Hope. Until the fish were picked up by Norseman, sometimes cleaned, sometimes not, they were kept on ice. When the Norseman came in, the fish, less ice, were dumped into big galvanized washtubs and loaded onto the plane. Boards were laid across one row of tubs and the second row was added. Later on, canvas bags hung end to end in the Norseman were used. As the old Norseman would heat up like an oven in summer, wet burlap bags were spread over the tubs to keep the fish moist.

On these flights, Indian Affairs usually provided a back haul. During Bill's time, this often took the form of a local delicacy called "Diefenbaker pork"—canned pork produced by the ton at the instigation of the Diefenbaker government as a concession to pig farmers who, at the time, were suffering from a slump in the pork market. Large quantities of canned pork were distributed among the reserves north of Nakina.

Bill's cohort in the sturgeon hauling business was Emile Coté, a trapper and guide by profession. Usually once a week in summer, the pair would head out from Nakina and begin a series of six or more stops at fish camps along

(Left) Bill Gwynn captains an Austin DC-3. (Right) Nakina regulars: Emile Coté and Norseman CF-BSJ. Emile was a top guide who spoke fluent Ojibway. He took expert care of any tourists in his charge. All his gear was kept in perfect shape and his camps were immaculate. Weathered in alone at a camp one time, Emile went several days without so much as touching the grub that had been laid in for his customers. (Austin Airways, Fred Knox)

the Albany River where sturgeon was still being taken. Mid-stream cribs were no longer in use by this time, the fish being kept alive on ropes let out from shore. When Bill and Emile arrived, the fish would be pulled in and immediately killed, weighed and gutted. Emile would then pay for them in cash or would barter them for flour, lard or other staples. A good day saw the Norseman back in Nakina with ¾ ton of sturgeon. At Nakina the task of processing the day's haul fell to Emile, and that was a job he was very good at. To retrieve the caviar Emile had to remove the sacs of roe, soak them in brine, then screen the eggs out without breaking them.

One day Bill was watching the proceedings at one of the fishing camps when an Indian invited him to give a tug on one of the lines. Bill picked it up and started to pull the fish in. Suddenly there was a great fuss and Bill was nearly pulled into the river. At the end of the line was the champion sturgeon of the day—a 125-pound whopper. Besides its commercial fishery, Nakina was an important sport fishing hub. The main camp was at Esnagami, run by Hugh and Mary Campbell. Pickerel, pike and trout were the common sport fish in the area.

Frank Krochel, Austin's engineer at Nakina for several years in the 1960's is remembered by pilot Bill Gwynn as a mechanical genius who once hand-ground from raw steel the three bolts needed in the tail gear assembly. The bolts worked perfectly. On March 6, 1961, Krochel wrote a letter to Frank Russell in Sudbury and the letter, along with Frank Russell's reply, provides a revealing glimpse into the engineer's world. From Nakina Frank Krochel writes:

"Enclosed are inspection sheets for GSR. I'm sending some metal which was in the plug of the oil screen. It seems to be bearing metal. The only think I can do is to keep it under close observation and drop the oil screen more often. There is another unpleasant feature on GSR: the oil tank is leaking. On the bottom of the weld where the elbow for the return line is attached, there is a slight crack. The crack has been there a long time, but it is so fine that I could not locate it. Since it is in a vertical position I don't think I can repair it with aluminum solder, but as soon as I get a chance I will try to get some metal mender in Geraldton that's recommended for leaking gas tanks.

"Concerning the metal in the sump pump, the engine runs very well and has low oil consumption. Oil pressure is the same as usual. Oil temperature 450 RPM is 28 lbs., 800 RPM 65 lbs., 1200 RPM 75 lbs., 1500 RPM 80 lbs. Please send an artificial horizon for GSR. The one which

April 3	Moosonee-Ft. George-Paint Hills -Eastmain-Moosonee	7:05 hrs.
4	Moosonee-Eastmain-Ft. George- Great Whale-Moosonee	3:05
5	Moosonee-Ft. George-Clearwater Lake-Rupert House-Moosonee	4:50
6	Moosonee-Ft. Albany-Attawapiskat -Ft. Albany-Moosonee	4:50
9	Moosonee-Rupert House-Moosonee -Ft. Albany	4:15
10	Ft. Albany-Moosonee	4:20
11	Moosonee-Winisk	5:30
12	Winisk-Ft. Severn-Winisk-Nakina	8:50
13	Nakina-Lansdowne House-Nakina	3:00
14	Nakina-Ft. Hope-Nakina	2:20
15	Nakina-Ft. Hope-Lansdowne House -Nakina	7:25
18	Nakina-Ft. Hope-Nakina	2:20
20	Nakina-Lansdowne House-Nakina -Ogoki-Nakina	5:20
23	Nakina-Ft. Hope-Nakina	2:15
24	Nakina-Ogoki-Raven Lake-Nakina	1:45
27	Nakina-Ft. Hope-Lansdowne House	3:20

A typical month's flying was recorded in Bill Gwynn's log for April 1962. The flying was split between Moosonee and Nakina aboard Beaver CF-DJI, and Norsemen CF-GSR and CF-OBN. Not all intermediate stops were shown.

is in now doesn't work properly and has to be replaced. IBQ is alright so far."

To this, Frank Russell replies: "Regarding the metal particles in the oil screen of GSR, I have checked your sample and it is not bearing metal but appears to be solder. It could be assumed that it came from either an oil can or funnel, possibly out of a generator. I would not worry too much about it unless you find more.

Date	Total Time	Hours Between Annual C of A
June 4, 1958	6397:40	780:55
June 10, 1959	7178:35	780:55
May 25, 1960	7609:20	430:45
May 16, 1961	7955:10	343:50
September 17, 1962	8507:05	551:55
August 29, 1963	9136:00	628:55
September 2, 1964	9918:20	782:20
August 27, 1965	10578:15	659:55
August 17, 1966	10993:05	414:50
August 1, 1967	11256:10	263:05

Norseman 10-year utilization log, CF-OBN of Austin Airways.

"As to the oil tank, we do not have a spare here, so if you can keep it going until breakup it would be welded then. I am happy to hear that IBQ is going OK after so much trouble.

"Sorry that letter got out from Toronto office regarding the ski axles. That modification was carried out on our aircraft five years ago. They originally had Dural axles and the new type are steel. The eight-bolt axle is an improvement but I don't think it would be worth our while to change.

"We do not have an artificial horizon back from overhaul as yet, but will send one as soon as possible. We are shipping the floats for IBQ tomorrow. Thought it best to crate them. Regarding the pulleys for cables on these floats, I am waiting on a new type of pulley to come in and then we will modify the complete set-up with larger pulleys. So if you can start off with these they will do for the time until we can get the other type.

"We have had a bit of snow here and it is a little colder; but it's been a very easy winter otherwise. Hope your cold has cleared up and everything else is OK."

Hard Times at Nakina

One of Nakina's hard-working bushplanes was Norseman CF-BSJ. Built in 1946, it was first used by USCAN Engineering in the Northwest Territories. Austin bought it in 1948 for $30,000 including floats, skis, wheels and a spare engine. Over the following years it piled up hours at the rate of nearly 1000 a year.

Misfortune struck CF-BSJ on September 15, 1958. Ab Dinnin took off from Nakina that day, dropped a passenger off at Kaedon Lake, then headed for Fort Hope with

Beaver CF-JKT overflies the vast Inco smelters at Copper Cliff (via Hal McCracken)

a load of freight. But the weather ahead closed in and he turned back for Nakina. As he came in over town, people saw him bank. Suddenly his Norseman literally fell apart, crashed to earth and burned, killing the pilot.

An exhaustive investigation determined that the plane had disintegrated when the front eyebolt attaching the wing strut to the front spar had failed due to fatigue, causing the wing to fold upwards. Tests at the National Research Council verified that the eyebolts in use generally had lives that would far exceed the life of the Norseman airframe. Only two of the many examined were found with fatigue cracks! The failure in CF-BSJ was an unpredictable fluke.

Records show another case like that of CF-BSJ. On January 22, 1963, Norseman CF-BHW of Transair was on a circuit from Pickle Lake to Round Lake, Bear Skin Lake and Trout Lake. It failed to turn up at its first destination and was found the following May 30, crashed northwest of Pickle Lake. Wreckage was widely spread, indicating in-flight breakup, and the DOT investigation concluded, "Fatigue failure of the front eyebolt on the left wing strut."

Beavers and Otters

Austin Airways stepped up to a new bushplane in 1949 when it purchased a Beaver from de Havilland. The airplane was CF-FHX, Beaver No. 60, and it was to spend many of the years that followed operating from South Porcupine flown by Hal McCracken. A string of

other Beavers followed as demand increased and the tough bushplane proved its worth. One was bought especially to serve Inco's needs in northern Manitoba and the Northwest Territories. Inevitably the legendary Norseman was to be edged to the sidelines by the more practical Beaver.

The Beaver served with Austin Airways until 1981 when the last one was sold, although it continues serving at several historic Austin bases such as Sudbury, Gogama and Temiskaming (now under new management). It will be decades before the ubiquitous Beaver fades from the scene.

As usual with all bushplane operations, 99.9% of Beaver flying was strictly routine. Only occasionally did anything dramatic happen, thank goodness! But one day there was drama, the kind nobody needs. Austin pilot Brian Steed tells what happened on a day he would rather have not gone flying. It was October 5, 1968:

Just that morning I had warned a passenger, "Watch out for that propeller." I was helping him onto the pontoon and up the five-rung ladder on the side of the light Beaver aircraft we use to haul supplies and personnel to isolated campsites in northern Canada for the International Nickel Company. The plane was idling, warming up for takeoff across the lake, and its whirling prop was only four feet from the ladder. If you should ever happen to slip. . . .

Now, however, my mind was on other things. The

company had sent me to this uninhabited lake to scout it out as a possible supply base. I was alone. There had been no problem with the landing and no difficulty taxiing the Beaver plane around the lake looking for snags and obstructions. None that should give any trouble. The lake would do admirably as a landing site. Now it was time to head back to the company base, 20 miles away.

I brought the plane downwind and nosed her around, heading into the breeze for takeoff when suddenly a sharp gust of wind snatched my pilot's cap off my head and threw it into the water. Drat the luck! Every flyer seems to have a favourite hat. Mine was tan canvas with an extra long bill, lined against the bitter Canadian cold. I really didn't want to lose that hat. I could see it, all right, floating in the water behind the slowly moving aircraft.

One of the things a bush pilot learns early is how to pick objects out of the water from a moving plane. You have to climb out of the cockpit down onto the float, reach in the cockpit door and steer with your hands on rudder pedals until you have manoeuvred the plane where you want it. Then you reach down and grab. It's sort of fun, requiring balance and coordination. I decided to get my hat.

I swung the plane around again and headed it in the right direction, then throttled way down so that I was moving through the water at about the speed of a rowboat. Then I climbed out of the pilot's seat and started down the ladder to the float.

"Careful of that oil spill," I said to myself. I'd been carrying oil drums that morning and a little had got onto both my bush boots and the pontoon. It seemed to be a permanent condition when you were hauling supplies for a mining company. But then, every type of flying has its special hazards. This job was the way I earned my living, but my "real" job—as a flying missionary to the isolated Indian tribes of these far-north woods—put me daily into situations no pilot's manual ever mentioned. You learn a lot about planes and a lot about prayer in the forest.

I was down on the pontoon now, steering the plane around to the hat, still bobbing in the water, when a slight pitch caught me off balance. My feet slipped on the slick canvas, and I plunged toward that prop. I felt a whack on my shoulder, as if someone had hit me with a leather riding crop, and the next thing I knew I was thrashing around in the lake.

Must have hit a strut, I thought. It didn't hurt and I didn't think a thing about it. I was just lucky that old propeller hadn't hit me, that's all. My job right now was

to get back to that aircraft before it taxied right away from me. The pontoon floats are some 20 feet long, and they were almost past me. If I wanted to grab even the stern, I'd better get swimming.

Something was wrong with my right arm, though. Nothing serious, I was sure, because there was no pain, it just felt numb like an arm that's gone to sleep. Well, I'd swim with my left arm.

Keeping my eye fixed on that pontoon slowly moving by, I half dog paddled, half kicked my way through the water. At the last possible moment I lunged forward; my left hand closed on the rudder cable. "Thank you, Lord," I whispered. Another tenth of a second and it would have been out of reach. Now all I had to do was hoist myself aboard and I'd be off.

Brian Steed (on the right), Bob Gauthier and Beaver CF-FHX at Shebandowan Lake in October 1968, not long before Brian's accident. He still flies his own airplane as a Pentecostal missionary in the North. (via Brian Steed)

I tried. But the circulation still didn't seem to have returned to that right arm. I couldn't even lift it out of the water. I tried again, and then again, as I was dragged along behind the plane. At last, for the first time, I looked down and saw the blood. Not much; the water was carrying it away fast. But I was bleeding all right. I'd better see what the trouble was. I raised my right shoulder.

There was no arm there.

Just the shoulder of my leather pilot's jacket. Beneath it, nothing. No sleeve. No arm.

Austin's veteran Beaver CF-FHP alongside Otter CF-MIT at Nakina on March 3, 1975. (Larry Milberry)

In that first moment of horror, I almost let go my grip of the cable. And in the second moment I thought, why not? How do you live without your right arm? Why not let the sudden dizziness and roaring in my head take over, and just sink down under the black water.

And then I thought of Norah and our two little children, waiting for me at home. Tomorrow was our little girl's first birthday. I thought of the Indians who had given me their friendship and trust. I thought of the work God had given me to do. And I suddenly knew that I wanted very much to live.

But how could I get back to the base before I bled to death? I couldn't even get up on the float. I had to act fast. Not only was I losing blood every second, but the aircraft was moving closer and closer to the shore where it would crash and I'd bleed to death long before anyone came to look for me.

"God is our refuge and strength, a very present help in trouble," I said aloud. Even as I repeated the psalmist's promise, I felt God beside me in the water. I could feel His sure presence and, miraculously, I could feel his strength. "Lord Jesus, I'm in trouble all right. I need Your help now." And I gave one last lunge.

It was enough. I hitched my stomach up onto the float, rested, pulled, wiggled, slid until at last I lay full-length on the pontoon. After a bit I crawled forward, my arm spurting blood, reached the ladder, struggled up it and threw myself into the cockpit. I reached for the ignition key.

The engine slowed and died. There. At least the plane had stopped plowing toward shore. At least I was out of the water.

The arm still didn't hurt. Shock. Praise God for shock. But if I didn't stanch the blood. It was coming faster now; I could count my heartbeats. How was I going to make a tourniquet? I looked around the cockpit. There was a line, the one I used to tie the plane up to dockside. I reached for it and tried to wrap it around that slippery stub, but it kept coming off. "What am I going to do? I'm getting fainter, Lord. What should I do?"

The prayer was hardly out of my mouth when the idea came that I could loop the rope loosely around my arm stump and then wind the rest of the rope around my neck. I did just that, then leaned my head hard to the left and looked down. The bleeding was slowing. *Oh, man, that's it. Let's get out of here.*

I turned the switch and the roar of the engine answered reassuringly. I steered the craft downwind, toward the centre of the lake. Flaps, carburetor heat, pitch, trim, water rudders; all okay. Instinctively I reached for the seat belt; of course only the left strap came up. With my left hand I eased the little plane forward and within a minute there were the tops of the spruce trees slipping away beneath me. The trip back to base camp took only 12 minutes, but they were 12 long minutes.

Shebandowan Lake at last came into view—and what a beautiful sight it was! I circled the lake, then came down with a shuddering bump. I steered for the dock, pulled

Austin's long-serving Beaver, CF-JKT, and a leased Otter, both circa 1965.

Illustrations by Peter Mossman

alongside and cut the engine.

Bob Gauthier and Jim Fennel happened to be at the dock then. When they saw my blood-covered figure stepping out, they rushed to my side.

"I've had an accident, fellows, and I guess we had better find a hospital," was all I could say.

We decided to get back in the plane and fly the 65 miles to the hospital. Bob was only qualified to fly on wheels, but this was no time to quibble. We refuelled and then the three of us were airborne.

After a smooth landing on the shoreline of Lake Sup-

erior, I was whisked off to Port Arthur General Hospital where I was to spend many days of recovery—days filled with moments of gratitude for being alive, thanks to Almighty God.

Many people have told me that most bush pilots would have panicked had they found themselves in my predicament. Perhaps I would have too, had not Psalm 46:1 been tested and found true in every way: "God is our refuge and strength, a very present help in trouble."

Brian Steed

Unlike the smaller Beaver, the DHC-3 Otter was not to see such wide use with Austin Airways. For many daily jobs it was just a bit too big, and hence not economical. Beaver, Norseman and Husky were able to meet most company needs through the fifties and sixties; and where needed, an Otter could be leased from another operator. Austin pilot Moe Sears recorded considerable Otter time with the company. In 1972 he flew Otter CF-QEI, on lease from Bradley Air Service. His log shows the following for that September, including goose hunt charters to camps at Hannah Bay and Cabbage Willows:

Route/Destination	Time	Miles
Sept. 1 Albany-Attawapiskat-Albany	5:45	490
2 Albany-Attawapiskat-Kashechewan	5:30	660
3 Albany-Attawapiskat	3:00	300
5 Albany-Attawapiskat-Kashechewan	3:50	365
6 Rupert House-Paint Hills-Ft. George	5:45	530
7 Albany-Kashechewan	1:50	185
8 Rupert House-Paint Hills-Ft. George	5:05	510
9 Hughes Camp	1:40	90
10 Hannah Bay (3x)	2:45	264
11 Cabbage Willows	1:05	88
12 East coast sked	7:00	690
13 East coast sked	7:10	690
14 Attawapiskat	4:40	500
16 East coast sked	3:55	390
18 Cabbage Willows	1:10	130
19 Kashechewan-Attawapiskat-Cabbage Willows	5:45	610
20 East coast sked	4:10	396
21 Attawapiskat-Kashechewan-Albany	4:35	480
23 West coast	2:50	300
26 Albany-Attawapiskat-Kashechewan	6:35	680
27 East coast	6:05	620
29 West coast	3:45	400
30 East coast	5:05	530

Austin Airways did not make extensive use of the Otter, a type generally a bit too big for the company's day to day needs. Two examples that did serve in the company's pre-1974 years are shown. CF-EYY (leased from Ray McLeod of Montreal) is seen in the photo below at Ramsey Lake. This Otter now serves with Quebec operator Propair. CF-HXY, seen at Toronto Island Airport while still owned by de Havilland, joined Austin in 1971. (Hal McCracken, Larry Milberry)

Norseman CF-IGG, photographed as hunters load moose meat aboard near Cochrane. (Ontario Government)

Otter flying days gave Moe Sears his closest brush with bush flying danger. A Beaver had taken off from Attawapiskat for Winisk. The weather was bad with stiff headwinds, and the pilot had been warned not to try for Winisk. Nonetheless he took off and was eventually forced to make an emergency landing just before dark. Next day, an Austin DC-3 and an Otter flown by Moe took off to search for the downed Beaver with its five souls.

The DC-3 spotted the Beaver and called in Moe who, incidentally, was suffering from an intense toothache. Moe landed in a very confined area on a narrow, winding river. He found the five stranded survivors in grim shape. They were stuck in minus 40 degree weather in howling winds, and had only one sleeping bag along. Moe realized that they had to get out of there promptly or someone was going to die. He mustered everyone to the Otter and got them to swing his tail around as there was no room to manoeuvre. This done, everyone crowded into the plane and Moe took off in the tracks he had made landing. There was some dicy steering around river meanders with trees at each wingtip, but the Otter got off safely and the story had a happy ending.

July 1974 was noteworthy for Moe and his Otter. That month he flew some 160 hours and logged a record 16,251 miles flying CF-HXY on James Bay. About this time he left Austin and began flying Aztecs seasonally with Geor-

gian Bay Airways on their fire patrol operation. Moe continued with GBA until he retired from flying in 1981. He died in September two years later.

Blazing Norseman!

Norseman CF-IGG had gone to work for Austin Airways in August 1955 and was a reliable old Trojan for the company until one fateful night at Moosonee in October 1969. All was quiet. Only John der Weduwen was in the staff house. Outside, several aircraft were tied down. Suddenly John spotted a glow. He rushed out to find CF-IGG ablaze and grabbed a fire extinguisher to quell the flames. But a brisk wind had already fanned up a good fire and all John could do was phone for help. Soon Steve Hyrniuk, Ray McLean and others were on the scene but they soon gave up on 'IGG, concentrating their efforts on the company's Husky.

CF-IGG was totally burned out that night because of a freak occurence. The windsock had been set on fire by contacting a broken light bulb. A piece of flaming material from the sock then blew onto the Norseman, setting it alight. As had so often happened, a minor incident led to disaster for another bushplane.

Native Talent

Rusty Blakey relates a little incident that occurred near Nakina. For him it was another example of the instinct and local knowledge of the native contrasting nicely with the frequent lack of good judgement of the white man. A

Norseman CF-IGG burns furiously at Moosonee in this dramatic photo taken by Austin's Neil O'Brien. Dave Russell photographed the burned-out wreck the next morning.

party of Indians had trudged out through the snow from their camp and requested a plane to bring in supplies. A Cessna 180 was dispatched from Nakina, and upon arrival at the designated lake the pilot noticed that a strip had been marked on the ice. He landed, but wondered why the runway was so far from the camp. He decided to taxi over to the shore rather than walk it, but as soon as the 180 left the marked out area, it broke through the ice. The usual costly and time-consuming salvage operation followed. Somewhere along the line the pilot was questioned about his decision: "I couldn't figure out why the strip was marked so far from the camp," he reported. "Do you think an Indian likes a long walk across a frozen lake any more than anybody else?" was the reply.

Another time Rusty landed at Port Harrison to hear that a party of seal hunters was missing. The local Eskimos asked if he would go searching for them and said he

should fly north. This seemed wrong to Rusty as there was a stiff north wind blowing that would seem right for driving ice floes south. However, he flew north and soon located the missing hunters. Explanation? The Eskimos knew there was a powerful easterly tide at the time that would move ice northward in spite of the wind.

Austin's crews had many a light-hearted experience with the natives. One day Rusty was over at Hannah Bay during the goose hunt. One of the Indians there, Eddie Faires, asked him to bring him an axe next time he was coming back from Moosonee. So Rusty went into the post, picked out a good solid axe and brought it over on his next trip. But Rusty was surprised when he next saw Eddie. "This axe is no good, Rusty," complained Eddie. "How do you expect my little wife to chop wood with that big thing!" Needless to say, Rusty took the axe back and, realizing Eddie's little wife, Kathleen, was the wood chopper, later came back with a suitable axe.

Rusty's experience was that, contrary to the traditional viewpoint, the native people were well treated and highly regarded by the HBC factors. He remembers their concern for the Indians or Eskimos as far as business dealings, health, education and such things went. They would usually try to make sure that the kids got out to school, or down to Moose Factory if they were sick, and so on. At first Rusty wasn't sure that sending the kids out to school was a good idea, but he gradually changed his mind as he realized what a harsh life it was for the kids out with their family on the trap line compared to life at the residential school. On one occasion Doc Harper had to have one of Tommy Nacappo's daughters flown out from the interior to have an injured fool tended, but Tommy needed her help. To make up, he asked for another daughter to be sent back from school in Fort George. Rusty recalls how little Mina cried at the thought of leaving school and going back to the difficult life of living off the land. Another time Rusty flew a load of kids back to the reserve and was saddened to hear one of them cry with dismay, "Oh my, what a place!"

On one charter Rusty was to fly a big load inland for some trappers. He landed at the designated lake but got bogged down. As he was a day early, the Indians had not yet arrived, so Rusty settled in for the night. Bright and early next morning one of the trappers showed up and helped Rusty get his Norseman unstuck and away. This fellow had heard the plane coming in but when he didn't hear it leave he knew that there was some problem. Knowing the country well, he trudged overnight through the forest, certain that Rusty must be needing his help. Whenever there was trouble, the Austin crews were sure of help from the local people.

The early bush pilots have freqently been noted for their own "sixth sense." Not all white men in the North were foolish. In fact, most have been quite capable people.

Inco boys prepare to set up their field camp, with all the necessities being flown in by Norseman. The site is Ministic Lake in Northern Ontario. (R.L. Savage)

Beaver CF-JKT picks up passengers from an isolated cabin. (Rusty Blakey)

An Eskimo fishing party displays its catch of speckled trout. In another photo from the early fifties, a soapstone carver is seen at work. (Rusty Blakey)

Men of the old ways. These Eskimos at Great Whale display a beluga whale just towed ashore, a scene from 1951. (George Charity Collection)

This simple example may illustrate the point. Dick Blakey, Rusty's son, tells the story: "On Friday, October 19, 1956, Frank Russell mentioned to me that he had to go up to Moosonee to inspect an airplane. If I wanted to come along, there would be room, and I could come back Sunday with Dad. He had been out at the goose camp for a month and was due to fly home.

"On Saturday Jim Keane flew us north, where we enjoyed a lovely autumn weekend. We stayed overnight at the Hudson's Bay staff house at Moose Factory and at noon sat down for a hearty lunch before heading home. Frank Russell and I dug in and really enjoyed a delicious meal of roast pork prepared by Mrs. Christianson. Soon Dad and I were off in the Norseman with Jeff Wyborn and Frank tailing along behind in another aircraft.

"About an hour after we took off, I began feeling ill. I told Dad and sat patiently, hoping to make South Porcupine, still an hour off. Well, I didn't make it. Just as Nighthawk Lake appeared in the distance I became very ill indeed. We landed, and several more times in the next while the illness hit.

"Then we realized that Jeff was overdue. That caused some concern, but meanwhile Dad had had me looked at by a doctor. Diagnosis—food poisoning. That pork seemed the likely culprit. Eventually Jeff arrived. He was late as Frank had become so ill that he had had to land to give him some relief. But why hadn't Dad and Jeff also been sick? The answer was simple. Both had somehow suspected the pork and had chosen something else to eat. No special reason, just a hunch. That's something that made pilots like Dad, Jeff, George and Hal so remarkable. No matter what the predicament (even if no predicament was apparent at the time) they had the natural ability to size things up and make the right decision."

Dick remembers another incident that shows the professional bush pilot's ability to judge prudently. He and his father were flying from Timmins to Sudbury. En route Rusty heard that Sudbury was fogged in. Sure enough, about 40 miles out he ran into the fog. At first he turned west and flew down Scotia Lake looking for a way through. Nothing. Next he turned north and intersected the CN line that runs south into Capreol. Now he looked for a convenient place to land where he could tie up and they could catch a train. He landed at La Forest, where the trains stopped to take on water. They waited overnight until one of the regular freights arrived. As it began watering up Rusty and Dick had to hurry down to the caboose before they missed their ride. That evening they reached Capreol, then had to get a drive to Sudbury through the fog. Later

Rusty had to return to La Forest to retrieve the plane. This may seem to have been a roundabout way of getting from Sudbury to Timmins, but for a prudent bush pilot it was the best way by far. Someone else may have made it through in spite of the fog, but pilots like that don't always live too long.

In the late forties it was clear that tuberculosis was sweeping the native settlements in northern Canada. To meet this crisis along James and Hudson Bays, the big hospital was built at Moose Factory and patients by the hundred were flown in by Austin Airways. A portable X-ray machine was flown around to the coastal settlements. Rusty Blakey was amazed at just how bad the epidemic was. One year over 100 people from Fort Albany were brought in, but as conditions improved numbers dwindled and Rusty notes that 10 years later only three cases were flown in from the same place.

Of course, TB was greatly feared by the natives. One old trapper was so frightened of going to hospital (many never returned!) that for years he headed for the bush upon arrival of the TB medical team. One year Jeff Wyborn flew a young sufferer to Moose Factory. This lad spent many a day sitting outside in the sun, whittling two fine big models of the Norseman. He painted them in Austin's black and red scheme and gave them to Jeff as a present. Sadly the young carver never returned home. Other stories were happier. One day Rusty and HBC factor Roy Jeffreys had to go out looking for two women with TB. They found them on an island near Fort George and persuaded them to come along to Moose Factory. As they were boarding the Norseman, the husbands of the women said to Rusty, "You bring our wives back as soon as possible. We need them." In time, the ladies were healed and did indeed go home.

"The Best Pilot I Ever Flew With"

Jim Bell's contributions to northern flying have always been admired by those who knew him. His whole life was dedicated to aviation and could easily fill a book of its own. After his early exploits flying his home-built plane around Sudbury, then flying for Austin in the late thirties, Jim entered the RCAF early in the war. But as he and the air force didn't see eye to eye, F/L Bell was soon a civilian again, flying in northern Quebec for CPA. After the war he was part of the Nickel Belt Airways organization, then went down the St. Lawrence with Hollinger Ungava Air Transport during the big airlift between Sept Iles and Knob Lake. Finally in 1952 he rejoined Austin Airways on their new Canso operation.

Norseman CF-GSR offloads sportsmen's gear along the Albany River. 'GSR has most recently been operating with Bearskin Lake Air Service in northwestern Ontario. (Ontario Government)

(Above) Rusty Blakey and 'BSC at the moment of liftoff from Ramsey Lake. Minutes later the engine quit and he had to make a forced landing. (Left) Charlie Kohls, veteran Austin mechanic, on the float of a Norseman at Sudbury, August 16, 1948. (M.L. McIntyre, via Rusty Blakey)

During one of the Chubb Crater surveys conducted by the
federal government, Austin's Norseman CF-JIN and Beaver
CF-MAP form a lineup with CF-FOX, a visiting Norseman
flown in by Ron Shirdown. (George Charity Collection)

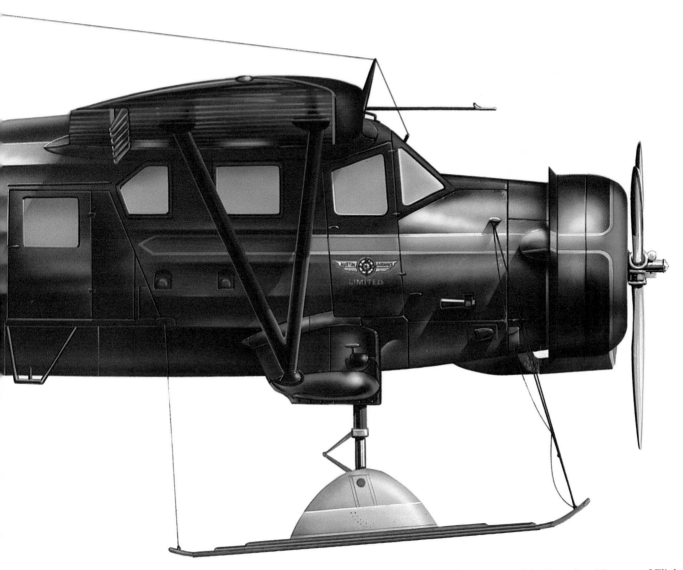

Norseman CF-BSC, probably Austin Airways' most famous and beloved aircraft. It is now part of the Canadian Museum of Flight and Transportation collection in Vancouver.

In the following years Jim was to be an important figure in the Austin story. He guided installation of the airstrip at Moosonee and, later on, development of the strip at Povungnituk. With Bob Moore and Bill Anderson he promoted the goose hunt with Austin, becoming the major supplier of transportation for the annual influx of hunters. Along with Joe Lucas he conceived the first Canso water bomber conversion and saw it through to service. Through-

out this period he was the company's chief multi-engine pilot and, simply by doing what he naturally did best, was a model of professional airmanship to many young pilots passing through the Austin organization.

Dusey Kearns recalls one trip with Jim Bell: "One day Jimmy Bell and I left Sudbury for Timmins. After a while the weather began closing in and Jimmy asked if I really wanted to go to Timmins. We were at the point of no re-

Alex Gunner is up on the Norseman's wing taking off the canvas wing covers which were vital in keeping snow, ice and that always-lethal frost off the wings. (Right) Plugging away: Johnny der Weduwen services a Norseman at Moosonee, 1963. (via John der Weduwen)

The last Norseman bought by Austin Airways was this Mk. VI. It was operating with Air Park Aviation in Manitoba as recently as 1983. (via Hal McCracken)

turn and just then the engine started acting up, and we began losing altitude. We kept on going, following the Mattagami River, then cut across to Timmins and landed on Porcupine Lake, where Ed Ahr was very surprised to see us coming in out of a snow storm. At the time I thought that Jim Bell was the best pilot. He was a natural." Many shared his view, including Holly Parsons who has written, "It is my own belief that Jimmy Bell was probably the best bush pilot I ever flew with, and there were some real fine ones."

After an eminent flying career, Jim Bell had to give up flying for medical reasons. He continued sharing his know-how with Austin Airways for several more years before retiring to his home in North Bay. Over the winter of 1982 he went to Arizona for a rest and on February 4, 1983, he died there.

The Chaputs'—A Special Place

An important focal point in Austin Airways history was the rooming house run by Sybil and Fred Chaput on McNaughton Terrace in Sudbury. Here assembled so many of the people that this book is about, men like Moe Sears, Norm Kern, Dunc Robinson, Ab Dinnin, Jim Keane, Jim Millard, Steve Hyrniuk, Hal McCracken, Eric Blackwood, Harry Metzloff and many others. Here a pilot could lay his tired body down after a month of gruelling work up north, enjoy Mrs. Chaput's home cooking, play cards, and sit at the round table to gossip or discuss his problems. The topics were often ones that didn't arise on the job—a very different atmosphere prevailed at the Chaputs'.

Who, for example, would ever suspect that Moe Sears, one of the rugged, ex-fighter pilot Anson drivers had a hobby that would capture a child's attention? From time to time Moe would ask Mrs. Chaput to accompany him on the piano as he put on a puppet show. He had a set of puppets and when he put them to work what usually developed was an evening of real fun at the rooming house. At one time an engineer was also staying at Chaputs', working on a job for Inco. He was somewhat relieved to discover that Moe was a puppeteer. Before he saw one of Moe's plays he had been a bit concerned: "Before tonight," he told Moe, "I was having trouble understanding what a tough old bush pilot would be doing with a bunch of dolls!"

A few of Austin's young married couples also lived at Chaputs, some with their young children. One Hallowe'en, as everyone was sitting at the round table, a rowdy teenager burst into the room wearing a mask. He teased the girls, pounded on the piano and generally made a nuisance of himself. Mrs. Chaput says, "I followed this creature right out to the porch as he left, then grabbed him by the collar. I tore off his mask in my anger. What a surprise to find that the obnoxious visitor was Jim Keane's young (and pregnant) wife Ruby!" Such was life at Chaputs. It was a vital and much loved centre for Austin Airways people for many years. For the fellows at Austin, the Chaputs were family and vice versa.

One of the Chaput children, their son Kipp, was attracted to airplanes from an early age. One day he asked his mother, "Mom, did you hear an airplane go over a little while ago?" "Yes," she replied. "Well, Mom, I was on that plane." Of course, Kipp's mother was a bit surprised, and he soon explained what had happened. He had been hanging around the dock down at "the Airways." Hundreds of young lads had done this for years (they still do). Rusty was loading his plane and invited young Kipp along. It was Kipp's first airplane ride and thereafter Rusty Blakey was his idol. An old story!

Inevitably Kipp Chaput became a pilot and eventually joined Air Canada. When he flew into Sudbury in the DC-9, he would always dial in "the Airways" and say hello as he came or went. Later on, Kipp went on to 747s, flying the global routes. This didn't change his eagerness to keep in touch with his good friends on Ramsey Lake, and whenever his routing takes him to Sudbury, he still calls in.

Satisfied Customers

Over the decades, Austin Airways won countless friends. Customers were generally so pleased with the service they received that they came back year after year. In time, some of these relationships were to extend across four generations. John Munger, a constructon man from Harrow, Ontario, started flying with the Austins many years ago. When he built his camp 32 miles northwest of Sudbury, Austin flew in the building material. John is remembered by Rusty Blakey for the delicious treat of canteloupes he liked to share with the Austin staff at Sudbury. Later on his son, Jack, then his grandson, Mike, were regulars at the Austin dock.

The Andersons were another family that came up to vacation each year. Before the highway was completed into Sudbury from Toronto, the Andersons would be picked up at Tobermory and flown across 50 miles of water to their camp in the Killarney Mountains. Now, of course, the family can drive to Sudbury directly and take the plane for the short hop to their summer place. Other

Norseman CF-OBN submerged at Moosonee. 'OBN finally met its end on August 10, 1968. That day it stalled and crashed near Winisk in the hands of pilot Don Plaunt. It had flown some 12,000 hours since new. (Dave Russell)

Bill Pullen (left) sits happily in 'BSC. His first airplane ride as a kid had been with Rusty Blakey in 'BSC. Years later he was as proud as a young pilot can be when Rusty cleared him as "captain" on the famous black Norseman. (via Bill Pullen)

(Below) A 1960s view of Austin's Ramsey Lake seaplane base. (via Hal McCracken)

clients for several generations include the Kimmels of Upper Sandusky, Ohio, and numerous other American families.

These days, families still come to the dock at Ramsey Lake for a flight into their camps, though the trip is with Ramsey Airways. However, odds are good that the pilot will be the same one their grandfathers knew and respected 40 years earlier—Rusty Blakey.

Jack Austin and Rusty Blakey at a celebration in honour of Rusty's 25th year with the company. (via Jack Austin)

(Below) Photo survey view of Moosonee, at top left, and Moose Factory, lower right, on the island. The Ontario Northland Railway tracks can be seen near Moosonee. Compare this high-level view of Moose Factory with the low-level view on the facing page. (via Austin Airways)

Moose Factory in the fifties. In the foreground is the hospital complex. (via Austin Airways)

Springtime follies at Moosonee. Ice crushed Austin's main dock in this 1963 episode. (John der Weduwen)

(Right) Fort George, another important community on the East Coast, seen in the early fifties. (via Austin Airways)

History from the photo album. Rusty Blakey's son, Dick, took these snaps as a boy, as he travelled the North with his father.

Norseman CF-BSC tied up at Winisk during June 1955.

Everybody came down to meet the Austin Norseman. This is a scene at Fort George in June 1955.

(Left) A local family at Fort George. (Above) Indians at Moose Factory in July 1956 paddle by with a curious looking load.

The Hudson's Bay Co. staff house (above) at Moose Factory where Austin Airways personnel bunked and had their meals. (Right) Belcher Islanders assemble to watch Austin Airways proceedings, July 18, 1955.

Of Cansos and DC-3s

In the early fifties Austin Airways reached another milestone by acquiring its first large aircraft. Inco was conducting a major exploration program in the Ferguson Lake region, some 305 miles northwest of Churchill. Bushplanes were being used to support local efforts there, but a greater air freight capacity was required. Inco again approached Austin with a proposition, this time that it provide a Canso for the job. Jack Austin explains how the deal was made: "Canadian Nickel Company, the exploration arm of International Nickel Company of Canada, approached us advising of their require-

ment for a Canso, for their exclusive use, serving the area north of Churchill, particularly Ferguson Lake.

"We purchased the aircraft on their behalf and had it brought up to the standards required. CNC then sold the aircraft to us and entered into a contract to purchase the flying required, giving a yearly minimum number of hours and for a limited period. The aircraft was financed through the payments on the flying involved so that when the contract was finished we had fully paid for it.

"We are much beholden to Mr. R.D. Parker, president of CNC and senior vice-president of Inco, for giving us

A crowd of Eskimos gathers around Canso CF-FAR to be photographed at Ferguson Lake. Note the cargo door modification which replaced the wartime observation blister, but the unmodified nose turret. Austin's first Canso, CF-FAR, was originally RCAF No. 11083. It was struck off strength in October 1946 and in 1951 was civilianized for Austin by Aircraft Industries of St. Jean, Quebec, under the supervision of Joe Lucas. (Bruce Gowans)

The unique non-retractable nose ski mod devised for the Canso by Austin Airways (Jim Bell Collection)

Austin's Canso has just brought fuel into Ferguson Lake and ground crew are draining it into 45-gallon drums. The Canso would routinely tanker 700 gallons to Ferguson on one side of its big main wing tanks. (Jim Bell Collection)

this opportunity of entering into the heavier aircraft field.

"Another plus in this development was that the Canso brought Jim Bell back to the company."

The Canso was delivered March 26, 1952, and put straight into service, Jim Bell and Gil Hudson being the main pilots. Freight was shipped up the Hudson Bay Railway from The Pas to Churchill, where it was assembled and loaded aboard the Canso, which would then drone up the Hudson Bay coast towards Ferguson at its steady 134 mph. It could home in on the beacon which Inco had installed at Ferguson, the only beacon in that part of the Arctic. The Canso was used to carry all sorts of loads: food, construction supplies, field equipment such as drill rods, fuel and so on. Fuel would be tankered from Churchill in one wing (700 gallons), much of it diesel fuel, or avgas for the bush planes. The Canso could make the trip both ways drawing fuel from the other side, though extra

drums were sometimes carried in case some refuelling was required at Ferguson.

Captain on the Canso's first operational trip was Winnipegger Gil Hudson, who had started flying with Austin in 1951. He too was a wartime type, having joined the RCAF in 1940 as a mechanic. He remustered to aircrew in 1943 and ended up on Cansos, flying from Yarmouth and Iceland with 162 Squadron. After the war he started medical studies at the University of Manitoba, but Konnie Johannesson enticed him back into flying before he became too deeply engrossed in his books. He flew an Anson for Konnie at Flin Flon, then worked for Sherritt Gordon, flying their Fox Moth, then their Husky. When the Husky was wrecked in August 1950 in a storm, he was hired by Austin, who was looking for a pilot to fly Anson CF-GRU on EM work. Though he only stayed with Austin a short time, Gil was to earn a reputation as one of its most skillful pilots. He left the company in 1954 to fly a Mallard for Fruehauf trailers and as late as 1984 was still in the corporate field, captaining a Florida-based BAC 111.

Austin's first money-making Canso trip was not to be a shining example of how to impress the client. The date was March 28 and pilots Gil Hudson and Ed Kenyon were aboard. The flight went along smoothly until near Ferguson low cloud and rime ice were encountered. As darkness had fallen, Gil elected to turn around but as they neared Churchill both engines began running intermittently, then quit altogether. The pilots knew they were going down. Gil flicked on the landing lights. Rough ice

Canso CF-FAR ran into trouble after just two days in service! Jim Bell later flew it off the ice "as is" and ferried it to St. Jean for repairs. (Jim Bell Collection)

More supplies, as DC-3 CF-FAX arrives at Ferguson with three tons of essentials. (R.L. Savage)

dead ahead! He snapped the Canso around and set it down on the only patch of level ice around. Ed Kenyon remembers his reactions at the time: "When the engines quit I just sat there calmly with my arms folded, thinking, 'Let Gil do all the work.' Once he set her down, Gil started to scramble like mad to get out till I reminded him, 'Don't worry, this thing won't burn. There's not a drop of gas in the tanks!' " CF-FAR sustained little damage in the night escapade. The cause of the event turned out to be a faulty mixture control lever.

The salvage work proved straightforward. The cargo was stacked on the ice for Don McIntyre to fly back to Churchill with the Husky. Tom Lamb flew in three barrels of gas for the Canso and Jim Bell took the plane into the air in a wheels-up takeoff from the ice. He flew to Churchill and made a landing on the main gear only, as the nose wheel was stuck up. Minor repairs were made and the plane was ferried down to Aircraft Industries for a good going over. As there was still a big job to do out of Churchill, Austin immediately leased a DC-3, CF-FAX, to carry on with the work. This was the company's first experience with the DC-3.

In charge of Austin's multi-engine operations was Jim Bell. One of his tasks was to organize the flying boat end of things and this meant writing a detailed manual for the pilots. For this job, nobody would argue that a company could have had any more qualified pilot than Jim. The excerpts noted here from Jim's manual reflect not only his knowledge but also something of his philosophy of flying:

Particular emphasis will be paid to ability to fasten lines and arrange knots.

On PBYs with the unbalanced rudder, there is a marked tendency to over-control and it will be noticed that directional control is difficult to maintain within close tolerances until some practice has been had and some judgement acquired.

It is a cardinal rule that aircraft proceeding down wind will have the right of way, and it is the responsibility of all others to keep clear. There are two acceptable speeds for manoeuvring on the water: either dead slow, or at high speed on the step. Anything in between may cause a good deal of water damage to the propellers.

Whether moored at a buoy or secured to a dock the engines are to be started in a sequence giving due consideration to your physical surroundings, and allowance for immediate forward movement. Remember, you have no brakes. At a buoy, the lines will be cast off at the captain's discretion either before or after starts, and at a dock, the moorings are generally loosened, but held in place by dock hands until signalled by the captain.

Taxiing this aircraft requires a bit of practice on the water as it is most unstable in direction. One must learn to anticipate rather than wait, and apply minimum corrections as required. It will require judicious use of all controls and engines. Should any wind condition exist, the ailerons are most useful in maintaining direction. The aircraft is normally manoeuvred on the water with the main gear extended, and the nose gear in the retracted

This Canso travelled the world with Kenting for many years before joining the Austin fleet in 1971. It's seen at Mount Hope on April 8, 1973. In passenger configuration the Canso carried 24 passengers. Its freight load was 6000 pounds, the same as the DC-3 (Jack McNulty)

Austin's famous DC-3, CF-ILQ, takes off at Moosonee in Mid Canada days. It was bought by the company in 1956 and served for over 6000 hours. Its big Federal skis weighed 1000 pounds. (via Hal McCracken)

position. With the main gear out, a good deal of drag is brought into play and consequently more power can be used with the resulting improved control.

Approaching moorings whether docks or buoys is done into wind wherever possible and at a minimum forward speed, due consideration being given to currents or wind drift, and the shut down effected far enough back so that the speed is reduced to zero at contact. Here again, a good deal of practice is necessary in order to acquire sufficient judgement. Remember, this craft weighs 15 tons and has a great deal of latent inertia.

Takeoffs, under normal conditions of light wind, are similar to any sea plane. Once the takeoff path has been selected and cockpit checks completed, the aircraft is driven into the wind (it will weather cock to a certain extent) and with the wheel fully back, the captain will run the power up to approximately takeoff figures. The co-pilot will settle them exactly and observe engine performance throughout the run.

When the nose has risen to its maximum nose high position, and here you will notice that it wants to drop by itself, bring the wheel forward and allow the aircraft to settle down to its step planing attitude. Keep straight with rudder. Elevator trim may be used to take the weight off the wheel at all times. Hold the aircraft in the planing attitude until flying speed has been reached and the aircraft flies off. The important phase here is to establish where this proper planing attitude is and it will take a number of runs to definitely establish this position. Once the aircraft is at a reasonable speed on the step, it is permissible to reduce power and slowly depress the nose. At once you will notice an increase in drag and the aircraft becomes unstable in direction and wants to dig in. Now,

as the nose is slowly elevated, you will notice a free acceleration as the aircraft goes through the proper attitude, and if you continue to bring it up, you will again notice a good deal of drag and a tendency to porpoise as it reaches a nose high position. Somewhere in between is your correct planing attitude. Once firm aileron control is established on your takeoff run, the wing tip floats can be selected up.

Jim Bell

The Mid Canada Line

Together, the durable Canso and DC-3 were to be the backbone of Austin's multi-engine passenger/freight operation for decades following the purchase of CF-FAR: 25 years for the Canso, over 30 for the DC-3. A new lease on life for these wartime veterans came in the mid-1950s when Canada and the United States decided to install a continental air defence network to guard against bomber attack from the USSR. There would be three radar/electronic defence lines strung out across the land and their construction required a huge civilian airlift operation that involved all Canada's regional airlines and a fleet of dozens of freight planes, including the DC-3, Canso, C-46, Avro York, Bristol Freighter and DC-4. The DC-3 and Canso were the most widely used.

For Austin Airways the most important of the defence lines was the Mid Canada Line, a series of stations strung across the 55th parallel, and Jack Austin was a key participant in this story. The Mid Canada Airlift Coordinating Committee was set up in 1956 by the Air Industries and Transport Association to organize the smooth operation of the commercial air transport side of the airlift. The

Austin's Canso is offloaded at Ferguson Lake in 1953. Note the kind of heavy equipment available. (R.L. Savage)

(Below) Mid Canada days at Moosonee. An Austin DC-3, Norseman, Anson and Beaver are awaiting their next trips as Dorval Air Transport's C-46 sits forlornly in the background after a mishap. (Jim Bell Collection)

committee included a virtual who's who of civil aviation: Jack Austin, J.H. "Red" Lymburner (Arctic Wings), W.G. McElrea (Dorval Air Transport), P. Lapointe (Quebecair), R. Rychlicki (Wheeler Airlines), C.F. Burke (Maritime Central Airways), Don McVicar (World Wide Airways), R.N. Redmayne and A.C. Morrison (AITA) and G.E. Hollinsworth (Airlift Coordinator) among others.

Basic aims of the committee were to provide a central source for the dissemination of information relating to the airlift; to act as an administrative body to coordinate the airlift; to discuss and attempt to solve contractual, administrative and operational problems; and to negotiate agreements with the Department of Defence Production. Chairman of the committee was Jack Austin.

To cut the time involved in servicing aircraft, the committee established an extensive store of spares and shop equipment at Knob Lake and St. Jean, Quebec. Supplier of the stores was the Babb Company of St. Jean, J.H. Lucas, president. Separate inventories were established for summer (Canso) and winter (DC-3) operations. The

Canso season was designated as May 1 - October 31, and the DC-3 season November 1 - April 30.

To ensure efficiency and safety during the airlift, the committee devised an operations manual "to provide the most accurate route and terminal information, together with rules and regulations, for flight crews, dispatchers and other personnel engaged in these operations. Also, it is desired to set forth the basic policies required to conduct a safe and efficient airlift in the best interests of all concerned."

Some of the limitations and hazards of Mid Canada flying are noted here in excerpts from a letter of August 14, 1956, by G.E. Hollinsworth, AITA coordinator, who discusses problems of operating Cansos into Hopedale on the Labrador coast: "Several of the carriers who knew this coast and location were definitely against its use ... A so-called ramp cannot be reached in the small cove with a Canso, as taxiing room is too cramped, and there is no room to turn a Canso around at the top and no shore tie-down area for such an aircraft. The presence of fog presents an unknown quantity as to getting in and out, and long periods of inactivity, with no place to remove

(Left) Passenger Dak CF-JMX used on the Timmins-Kapuskasing-Rouyn scheduled service in the late 1950s. (Right) Veteran Austin captain Doug Mackie snapped by CF-JMX at Kap. He had flown in the RCAF in the war, then for KLM. Later he joined in the big Hollinger Ungava airlift flying DC-3s, and eventually came to work for Austin. Gil Hudson remembers him as "one of the smoothest pilots I ever flew with." (Both, Jim Pengelly)

aircraft from the sea water for protection. The unprotected position of the area required for landing and takeoff make such an operation extremely hazardous at times. A recent landing at the end of July was effected only by landing in the open sea and taxiing in due to the fact that floating ice blocked the area close to the harbour...."

Hollinsworth's report on conditions at Great Whale about the same time further illustrates the airlift difficulties: "The weather visited upon Great Whale this summer has been the poorest of any for some years. The fact that the ice was so late breaking up, and its continued floating around in the bay, accounted for a larger amount of fog which was a holdup for each day's commencement of flying. A very high percentage of unfit days of mixed fog and rain over the summer made for very poor conditions. Weather charts indicate this in periods of four to five days in succession cancelling flying operations."

In spite of such difficulties, the Mid Canada airlift was carried out to the contractors' satisfaction. Thousands of flights were made carrying supplies and personnel into numerous sites between Labrador and the western mountain region. The safety record was good, due largely to the standards set in the operations manual, something that included much of the Austin Airways philosophy of running an airline.

Some of the Boys

Jack Humphries spent many years as a DC-3 and Canso captain with Austin Airways. He began flying in the RCAF, spending a while on C-119s with 435 Squadron before joining 408 Squadron at Rockcliffe for over three years on Cansos. He left the RCAF to join Austin in August 1957 with his first trip being on Canso CF-IHB with Jim Bell in charge.

In his first season with Austin, Jack was kept busy as there was a prospecting rush underway between Hudson

Period	Aircraft	Destination	Hrs. Flown	No. Trips	Tonnage	Days U/S	Days Weathered Out
June 15—30	CF-FAR	Moosonee	17:25	10	12	0	0
	CF-IHB	"	80:15	35	42¾	0	1
July 1—31	CF-FAR	Great Whale	11:40	7	12	0	3
July 1—31	CF-FAR	Moosonee	141:20	78	82¾	0	1
	CF-IHB	"	41:30	18	17¼	0	0
Aug. 1—31	CF-FAR	"	182:35	81	88½	2	1
	CF-IHB	"	45:25	22	25¼	0	0

Mid Canada Line, Canso airlift for 1956, Austin Airways involvement. Other Cansos involved on the airlift at this time were: Dorval Air Transport, CF-IHJ; Eastern Provincial Airways, CF-HFL, CF-HGE; Quebecair, CF-IHA, CF-IHD; Transair, CF-IEE, CF-SAT, CF-HTN; Wheeler Airlines, CF-EMW, CF-ILK, CF-IHC; World Wide Airways, CF-IZU, CF-IZZ; for a total of 15 commercial Cansos used over the airlift period that year.

Bay and Ungava Bay. There were hundreds of prospectors in the region and it was steady work keeping them all supplied. He recalls one trip from Mosquito Bay (to the north of Povungnituk) and Timmins. He and Jim Pengelly had to fight their way south through the roughest of weather. Ice broke the HF antenna, and as they bore through the clouds for the 7:20-hour trip the antenna banged noisily on the fuselage.

On another trip Jack went in to Lac Bienville to move out an Indian family. They had two canoes but only one would fit in the Canso. The head man asked Jack how short he needed the canoe to get it to fit. Jack figured that 12 feet would do. Right on the spot, the Indian sawed four feet off his canoe and they prepared to cast off, with the usual load of kids, dogs, sleds and so on. But as co-pilot Stirling Tugwell was hauling up the anchor, he fell overboard. The water was dreadfully cold but Jack managed to get him back aboard. Helper Brian Robertson got ''Tug'' out of his wet clothes and into some pajamas, then extracted a wad of bills from his pants pocket, the cash which the Indians had paid for the charter. The dripping wet money was hung on ropes and wires crisscrossing the cockpit and left to dry as the Canso lumbered off.

Jack was involved with Austin's water-bomber Canso in its early days, beginning on May 19, 1960, with some test flying off Mississquoi Bay in Lake Champlain, with test pilot John Brown of Aircraft Industries also aboard. The airplane was CF-JTL, fitted with two big removable external water tanks, each capable of a 350-gallon load. This system, devised by Jim Bell and Joe Lucas, enabled

Canso CF-IIW (below) leased by Austin Airways loads at Moosonee. (Left) The crew of CF-IWW in October 1963: Bill McInnis, Murray McMann and Captain Jack Humphries (Both, Bill Eccles)

Joe Lucas of Aircraft Industries was a close associate of the Austins and Jim Bell in the aircraft engineering/maintenance/repair end of the operation. (Jim Bell Collection)

Jim Bell conceived the idea for a Canso water bomber. The system, developed for Austin Airways by Aircraft Industries, is seen being demonstrated at Toronto Island Airport in June 1960. (via Jack Austin)

Two views of the water-bombing Canso. Test and development flying was carried out mainly by John Brown and Roger Goudreau of Aircraft Industries and Jim Bell and Jack Humphries of Austin. (via John Brown, Jack Austin)

conversion without a costly internal modification. Next Jack flew up to Janine Lake in Quebec for more demo flying; then, June 8, he and Jim Bell flew 'JTL into Toronto Island to show off their brainwave. A month later they were working on fires in northwestern Ontario. Jack notes that the Canso wasn't always given a proper chance to show its stuff, as the forestry people would wait until a fire was burning furiously before calling in Bell, Humphries and 'JTL. Throughout August 'JTL also operated on fires in northern Manitoba and away over in the Gander area. Leaving Gander on August 17 they made a long trip into headwinds, landing at Dorval

9:40 hours later.

Jack Humphries was to spend a lot of time with Jim Bell during his Canso years at Austin. Like many others, Jack developed great respect for Jim as one of Canada's leading airmen. He remembers Jim (as most do) as a quiet, often elusive personality. Like any veteran bush flier, Jack had met plenty of the other kind — the blustering heroes of the clouds. Jack put it this way: "Jim had his own show, but being the kind of pilot he was, he didn't even realize that it was going on."

One night Jack Humphries and Jim Bell had Rusty Blakey along on a trip and handed their DC-3 over for Rusty to try for a while. Now anything bigger than Rusty's 'BSC was a bit unfamiliar to the company's top VFR pilot. Rusty had a go at the DC-3 but couldn't see out too well, sitting as he was away down in Jack's seat. After a while the Norseman driver looked at Jack to summarize the state of affairs: "If I could see where I was going, I could keep this thing right side up!"

In February 1964 Austin Airways acquired DC-3 CF-AAL as a replacement for CF-ILQ, which had crashed. Its first revenue trip was made on February 14, a Great Whale-Povungnituk medevac with Humphries and Gwynn. At Pov their DC-3 became frozen up in the cold and the engines wouldn't start. The Austin crew assembled a crowd of Eskimos; they rigged a rope around one prop and upon the signal "Pull like hell!" everyone gave it all they had. The prop spun and the engine kicked over and started. Once again, Austin got its patient to the hospital.

Another trip Jack recalls was a passenger charter with Bill Gwynn and Frank Russell aboard. As Jack approached to land he reached for the landing lights switch but instead hit an alarm bell switch. A loud ringing filled the cabin to the passengers' consternation but in the darkness nobody could find the switch again to turn it off. After a while, Frank came up and politely said to the captain, "Nice flight, Jack. But is the bell really necessary?"

Jim Pengelly flew Austin's Cansos and DC-3s during the hectic Mid Canada days. He started flying just after the war, taking his training at Buttonville, then a grass strip northeast of Toronto run by Fred Gillies. Soon after, the job of building the Seven Islands-Knob Lake railway began and Jim took the train to Seven Islands where John Lutty gave him a job with Hollinger Ungava as an apprentice engineer. He was soon at work under one of the well-liked veteran HUT engineers, Tony Leriche.

Date	Aircraft	Routes	Time
2	CF-JCV	Moosonee-Albany-Moosonee	1:25
3	CF-IHN	Moosonee-Winisk	2:45
4		Winisk-Moosonee-Great Whale-Ft. Harrison-POV-Sugluk	8:00
5		Sugluk-Dorset-Frobisher-Pangnirtung	4:25
6		Pangnirtung-Frobisher-Clyde River	5:00
7		Clyde River-Pond Inlet-Igloolik	3:50
8		Igloolik-Fox Main-Sugluk	3:50
8		Sugluk-POV	1:10
9		POV-Ft. Harrison-Great Whale-Fort George-Moosonee	4:20
10		Moosonee-Albany-Moosonee	1:15
10		Moosonee-Nemiscau-Moosonee	2:35
11		Moosonee-Hannah Bay-Moosonee	1:30
12		Moosonee-James Bay Goose Camp	:10
13		James Bay Goose Camp-Moosonee-Timmins-James Bay Goose Camp	3:00
14		Moosonee-Ft. George-Great Whale-Ft. Harrison-Great Whale	5:40
15		Great Whale-Moosonee	3:25
15	CF-JCV	Moosonee-Nemiscau-Moosonee	2:30
15		Moosonee-James Bay Goose Camp	:50
16	CF-IHN	Moosonee-Porquis Jctn.-Ft. Albany-Moosonee	3:45
16	CF-JCV	James Bay Goose Camp-Moosonee (2 trips)	:40
18	CF-IHN	Moosonee-Great Whale-Ft. Harrison-POV-Ft. Harrison-Great Whale	7:15
19		Great Whale-Belcher Is.-Great Whale-Lac Bienville-Great Whale	4:10
19		Great Whale-Moosonee	1:50
20		Moosonee-Lansdowne House-Moosonee	4:30
23		Moosonee-James Bay Goose Camp-Ft. Albany-Moosonee	1:20
27		Moosonee-Timmins-Moosonee-James Bay Goose Camp-Moosonee	3:10
28		Moosonee-Great Whale-POV	4:55
29		POV-Sugluk-Dorset-Sugluk-POV	4:45
30		POV-Ft. Harrison-Great Whale-Ft. George-Moosonee	4:50
30	CF-IIW	Moosonee-James Bay Goose Camp-Timmins	1:50

Summary of Canso flying, September 1963, for CF-JCV, CF-IHN and CF-IIW; Captain Humphries, with Gwynn and McInnis.

Before long, Jim moved up to flight engineer on Hollinger's Canso, CF-DIK, and held that post for 832 hours until promoted to co-pilot in 1952. But 'DIK was sunk, and Jim moved on to Wheeler Airlines to fly another Canso. The summer of 1955 Jim had been flying a Cessna 170 from Kenogami when he got a letter from

Two takeoff views of CF-AAD: leaving the water at Rupert's House; and leaving Mount Hope on September 7, 1968. (Paddy Gardiner, Larry Milberry)

Austin Canso pilot Jim Pengelly (below) while flying for HUT in the early 1950s. Jim was Canso-flying as recently as 1983. (via Jim Pengelly)

Jim Bell inviting him to work for Austin. The two had met flying for HUT. Pengelly made his first trip with Austin on August 28/29, going out with Jim Hobbs in CF-FAR, flying Moosonee-Winisk-Great Whale-Moosonee. Jim was to remember Hobbs as "the greatest guy in the world to fly with." He claims that, when he got home from a trip, his wife could always tell with whom he had been flying by the mood he was in. If he came in the house cheerful, she knew that he'd been out with Hobbs.

Jim Pengelly stayed with Austin Airways until 1959. His busiest time was the Mid Canada airlift, as the logbook shows for a typical month, April 1957. For this month he was flying with pilots McEachern or Hobbs:

April 9	7 trips	April 21	10 trips
April 16	4 trips	April 22	4 trips
April 18	4 trips	April 23	7 trips
April 19	2 trips	April 28	2 trips
April 20	10 trips	April 30	5 trips

Fifty-five trips on 10 flying days. That June he was on Canso CF-IHB and over 23 flying days logged 76 trips. Through part of the next year Jim flew CF-JMX on Austin's scheduled run serving Kapuskasing, Timmins and Rouyn.

Over his flying career Jim became one of Canada's Canso experts, with over 30 years on the plane. After some 11,000 Canso hours, he has a head crammed with flying boat memories. There are, of course, all the recollections about the crash of CF-FAR. And memories of

the three other earliest Canso's in his flying career — CF-DIK, CF-EMW and CF-AAD. Each was also lost in a crash!

Jim has all the fine details down about every Canso version, including various mods — the PBY-5A, PBY-6A and Model 28-5ACF. He notes, for example, that CF-AAD came to Canada from San Diego in 1957, arriving at Toronto Island. That season it continued working under its US registration, N68746. It had arrived in poor shape but was gradually spruced up. It was nice to fly, and as a former PBY-6A (a relative lightweight) modded back to 5A standards to meet Canadian DOT requirements, was 1200 lb. lighter than CF-IHB, a standard 5A. Thinking of 'AAD reminds Jim of engineer Bob Kerr. Bob was hard at work on 'AAD at Austin's Kapuskasing base one day when he was hit by a painful gall bladder attack. As Jim comments, "Being Bob, he finished the job before going off to hospital!"

Typical of the young pilots who worked their way up the ladder with Austin Airways during the fifties and sixties were Jim Hall and Terry Monk. Jim summarizes his Austin years this way: "My stay with Austin Airways wasn't what you would call colourful by any means. Just a lot of hard work combined with some valuable experience and lots of enjoyable memories. Hal McCracken had hired me in May 1957 as a helper for Herbie Kohls, who was base engineer at Sudbury. Of course, Rusty Blakey was chief pilot there. My job was working around the dock. At the time I was just out of high school. Seventeen years old! I had obtained my private pilot's licence in February of that year at Sudbury Aviation. Several other young pilots were to join the Austin ranks that year — Dunc Robinson, Nick Robertson, Bill Gwynne and Jim Keane to name a few; and we were to have the pleasure of meeting many of the company veterans as they were dispatched to their summer bases through Sudbury, men like Bill Cram, Harry Metzloff and Rudy Hoffman. All this provided me with a romantic outlook on aviation which I was never to lose.

"Needless to say, the financial rewards were no match for the romance! At one point, I was the only man looking after two Norsemen, a Husky and a 180. That August, one of the Norsemen logged 140 hours, and I calculated my pay at 35 cents an hour! Do you think my grandchildren will believe that?

"I served my apprenticeship under the best in the business — Frank Russell, the Kohls brothers, Mark Nieminen and others — and travelled far and wide as a helper and engineer, visiting all the bases at one time or another. For a couple of winters, Great Whale was 'down south,' so after getting my 'M' licence in 1961 I decided to leave Austin for greener fields.

"In February 1968 I returned to Austin where Hal McCracken checked me out on the Beaver. Then it was off again to the barren lands. I flew the 180, Beaver, Norseman, Otter and even the 'Bamboo Bomber' (the Anson). In 1970, deciding that airplanes with washrooms were a better bet, I moved up to copilot on the Canso and DC-3, making captain the following year.

"During this time, Captain Steve Hryniuk and I went to England, took a course on the 748 and, with the help of a couple of senior Hawker Siddeley pilots, managed to find Hamilton (Mount Hope) after many gruelling hours of staggering across the Atlantic. This was Austin's first venture into really modern equipment. I was proud to be involved, even though it was just a brief interlude. In 1973 I left Austin Airways to join Air Canada and 'civilization.' Even though my bush flying years are long past, that's where it all started for me. I owe a lot to Austin Airways."

In 1959 Terry Monk was a young lad taking flying lessons at Central Airways, Toronto Island Airport. Since he had come over from the UK a few years earlier, he had been prospecting in places like Utah and the Arctic but was now venturing into something new. That July he earned his private pilot's licence and asked at the Austin office for a job. Sure enough, if he was willing to spend the summer as a dock hand at Moosonee, he was in.

As many a young pilot had done before, he wangled some flying as helper. His first ride was in Norseman CF-OBN on July 22, then he got on as Dunc Robinson's helper on the Otter, CF-EYY, and later with Don Stewart on the Norseman, CF-JIN. Meanwhile Jim Bell had been taking him out in the Canso and letting him do the odd bit of flying.

In November Terry headed back to Central Airways to get his twin rating. The DOT check pilot who gave him his endorsement was amazed at how well this young fellow handled Central's little Piper Apache. Terry didn't

School children arrive home at Mistassini, Quebec. Pilots Hobbs and Pengelly brought them in aboard this Austin Canso. (Jim Pengelly)

(Left) Austin staff house cooks at Moosonee around 1960: Frances McNamara, on the left, and Mildred Brough. (Right) Jack Humphries, on the left, and John Croker rolling 45s of 80/87 avgas from 'ILQ at Baffin Island site during the spring of 1960. (Moe Sears, via Jack Humphries)

breathe a word that someone he knew had been letting him play with a Canso!

Terry was soon regular crew on the Canso from Moosonee, working the skeds up and down the east and west coasts, servicing drill and survey operations, and flying on the goose hunt. Periodically he would crew with Jim Bell, but more often he flew with Jack Humphries. Terry recalls that his early experiences with Jim Bell were a bit harrowing. Jim was strict and demanding, and there were days with him on the Canso when Terry would come home wondering if he really wanted to be a pilot after all. Once he came to know Jim better, he too discovered that he was the best possible teacher and, as he put it years later, "a fellow with a heart of gold."

In June 1961 Terry found himself crewing with Jim Bell during further evaluations with CF-JTL. At first they did a series of routine passenger/freight runs from Moosonee to demonstrate the "quick change" feature of the Austin water-bomber: the tanks were easily detachable in case the plane was needed for other duties. These flights were made June 2 through 17. Then the Canso went to the Red Lake/Sioux Lookout region on fire fighting. Terry recalls that the Canso had one operational drawback using the external water tanks. To take on water, the pilot had to let it drop off the step while the probes scooped up the load. Then he would pour on the coal and take off. This was hard on the engines when executed dozens of times a day. Cylinder head

temperatures would constantly be in the red and Terry as F/O would be busy tending the manual cowl gills, trying to keep the engines from overheating.

From August 8 to 11 Terry was involved in flying the first group of tourists into Baffin Island. The group was headed by Jim Houston (by now the famous author of such books as *The White Dawn*), who was promoting Eskimo carving, print making and other art forms.

Many of Austin's charters in the 1960s were in support of government projects such as the Dominion Observatory Baffin Island survey. Two others which involved the company were geological studies of the Chubb Crater in Ungava and of a crater in Richmond Gulf. Most of the Baffin work was putting in gas caches in the spring. Ships would put gas ashore along the east coast, then Austin would use a DC-3 to move it inland to sites where it would be used that summer by helicopters flying the scientific parties around the island. In April and May 1961 Terry Monk and Jack Humphries were operating CF-ILQ on this work. John der Weduwen was along to keep the airplane in trim and to help with the muscle work. Day after day (weather permitting) they would heft 18 barrels at a time into the Dak and make their rounds. Along one stretch of coast, north of the Foxe Peninsula, the geography was almost featureless, and unless the light was just right the unmarked sites were sometimes indiscernible and the plane would have to return to base with its load.

When a load of drums was delivered to a cache, it was up to the three Austin crew to offload since nobody was ever there. They carried along a small toboggan which they used to man-haul each drum up to the cache above the high water line. This was work!

One day 'ILQ landed at a cache to take on fuel itself, its supply having dwindled to about 30 minutes. The crew started digging where the drums were supposed to be but found none. They probed around for hours with no luck. Then an Eskimo appeared with his dog sled, and he was able to locate the fuel buried under 10 feet of snow. Once found, the drums had to be extracted and this meant more hours digging out a long snow ramp so that the 400-lb drums could be rolled out of their hiding place.

During the fuel-hauling operations Jack Humphries got a call that an Okanagan helicopter had been forced down on desolate Resolution Island. The S-62 had run short of fuel. On May 28 the Austin Dak flew into Resolution, with its notorious landing strip (an uninviting rocky overshoot at one end and an 800-foot drop into the sea at the other), and delivered jet fuel for the stranded Sikorsky.

From January 25 to February 1, 1963, Terry Monk was copilot with Bob "Pappy" Hamilton on a DC-3 leased from Nordair, flying drill crews and gear from Great Whale into Clearwater Lake at Richmond Gulf. This was a government survey studying the crater at Clearwater to determine whether it was of volcanic or meteoric origin. Then, from February 8 to 28 Bill Coons and Terry did the annual fuel haul into Fort Albany, flying 98 trips. This was a 24-hour-a-day operation flown by two crews, each working 12 hours and averaging 6 return trips each per day. Fuel was hauled 750 gallons at a time in a big rubber bladder, using Nordair's CF-NAH.

On one trip into Fort Albany Terry noticed something dripping from the DC-3's wingtip. Since it was so cold, it couldn't have been water; a whiff of the drippings con-firmed it was stove oil. Soon the crew determined what had happened. Checking under the bladder after it was empty they found a shattered coffee cup, left by someone while taking on fuel at Moosonee. As the bladder filled, the cup shattered under its weight, punching a hole in the rubber. Totally drenched in fuel, the DC-3 was ferried back to Moosonee then on to St. Jean, where Joe Lucas' crew cleaned it up. CF-NAH was soon back in service and spent most of March hauling fuel and freight into Nemiscau for Inco.

Towards the end of 1965 Terry left Austin Airways and joined Air Canada. Soon he was flying DC-8s and today is on 747s. Austin's loss was, once again, Air Canada's gain, for when the big airlines snatched away another of Austin's pilots, they were getting one with his PhD in the practicalities of commercial flying, and certainly one who knew the meaning of hard work. Whenever he lost one of his key men, Jack Austin must have sighed in disappointment. So many young pilots who had learned the ropes with his airline were eventually to take their know-how to the "people's airline."

Bob Pettus became another of Austin's regular Canso drivers. He had flown during the war, training out west on Cornells and Cranes before going overseas where he instructed on Oxfords and Anson Is. After the war Bob came home to St. Thomas in southwestern Ontario and opened up a garage with a friend as partner. One day he received a brochure from War Assets advertising aircraft for sale. There were Cranes and Cornells available in Saskatchewan for a few hundred dollars apiece. Bob was intrigued and drove west to make a deal. He bought a Crane and two Cornells and ferried them home. He formed Elgin Airways at St. Thomas and for a time operated a training and charter business. But, as with many a post-war flying venture, very little was going on, and when he was offered a job as copilot on a Canso for

A 1956 view of the winter strip put in alongside the ONR at Moosonee under Jim Bell's supervision to serve the Mid Canada line airlift. (Jim Bell Collection)

129

(Above) A fine in-flight portrait of DC-3 CF-AAM being flown by Bill Ross. This aircraft was later completely rebuilt, using the wings of CF-AAL. (Left) CF-AAM near Clyde on Baffin Island. (Both, John der Weduwen)

Kenting, he grabbed the opportunity. It was 1950.

So began Bob's 29-year association with the plane he grew to love above all the others, the Canso. Through the fifties he flew for Kenting in such places as New Guinea, the Falkland Islands and the Arctic, and interspersed that with time on the B-17. In 1959 he began studying at the University of Toronto, assisted by Kenting paying him a retainer to secure him as a summer pilot. His studies led him into teaching and in 1963 he took up a post at R.H. King Collegiate in Scarborough. Summer after summer he flew for Kenting until 1968 when a call from Jim Bell

(Below) Canso CF-IHB inland from the east coast on a fuel delivery, Humphries, Lejeune, der Weduwen and Hazeldine crewing. (Eric Hazeldine)

Sledding fuel drums up to a cache on Baffin Island. DC-3 CF-ILQ is in the background. (John der Weduwen)

Evening at Moosonee as an Austin Canso passes over the river. Another Canso bobs at the buoy. (Neil O'Brien)

Bob Pettus holding fort in his Canso at Kovik Bay. His Bermuda windbreaker seems quaintly out of place. (via Bob Pettus)

brought him into the Austin fold. For the next decade it was Moosonee, Winisk, Pov and the rest of those exotic places that would fill Bob's summers, while he continued teaching the rest of the year.

Bob's first Canso trip with Austin took place July 1, 1968, from Timmins. Next day he was hard at work, flying as F/O on the east coast sked with Stuart Tugwell. The summer was to be one of intense flying. Up at the crack of dawn and down to the Canso, off up one coast or the other, then back by dusk, dog tired — 130 hours in July, 82:10 hours in August. Quite a switch from the automotive shop at R.H. King!

Bob's memories of Austin days include Jim Bell. They first met at Kapuskasing, where Jim was running Austin's Mid Canada maintenance base. He characterizes Jim as a flier from out of the past, representing the best of bush flying tradition. He and Jim always got along, but he recalls that Jim used to put up quite a front for the younger pilots. They all thought he was a mean old so-and-so. Says Bob Pettus, "It was all a big act!"

One day Bob was flying a Canso up the coast. Back at Moosonee he had been assigned a new young helper who hardly knew one end of an airplane from the other. Bob's first landing was on the water and upon splashdown there was a yelp from the helper. He was scared silly and didn't exactly inspire the passengers with his scream. It seems that nobody had informed him that a Canso could land on the water.

The Canso operation was basic bush flying. Some days it was like an old-time travelling medicine show. The Canso would plunk down at some little settlement and Bob and his two crewmen would start unloading or loading. Passengers would show up with the usual trappings of canoes, skidoos, dogs, or whatever, and the

copilot would pull tickets from his pocket and sometimes have to dicker around to make change. Someone would owe two or three dollars for this package or that. One day there was a salesman on board with his sample product — a three-wheeled motorcycle. This hefty item had to be offloaded into a waiting freighter canoe at Eastmain. Hard on the back and definitely no job for a pilot with white glove pretensions! Many an evening, upon returning to Moosonee, Bob would be asked to fly yet another leg, maybe over to Rupert House and back. And that still wasn't the end of the day's work. After a bite to eat, he had to do his bookkeeping, recording all the details of the day—legs flown, description of loads, number of passengers, fuel taken on en route, revenue, etc.

Besides Canso flying, Bob did plenty of work on the DC-3. A trip on August 16, 1969, is noted in his logbook. He and F/O Glen MacMillan had a charter to a drill site on remote Akpatok Island in Ungava Bay. After the load was picked up at Earlton, CF-AAL headed for a refuelling stop at Knob Lake, then north to Ungava. The plan for the return trip was to fly straight to Great Whale, a three-hour leg. It was nearly dark on arrival there and, worse still, the place was socked in with fog. Bob couldn't raise the Great Whale radio. The attendant had knocked off for the day. Luckily someone walking past the radio room heard his calls and soon Bob had contact. Great Whale radioed Port Harrison to determine the weather there. It was fine, so Bob turned north. Flaming oil drums marked the runway and Bob got 'AAL down, but not without a good bit of sweat.

Bob Pettus likes to recall a group of young pilots he helped train on the Canso. These were lads fresh off

Shenanigans. A UFO alights on Austin's waterbombing Canso "somewhere" up north. (Jim Bell Collection)

Heave! A passenger (above left) is helped aboard an Austin Canso at Great Whale. Anything to please the travelling public! (Right) Night-time shot of an Austin DC-3 at Sudbury. (Bill Eccles, Peter Marshall)

(Left) Another pair of DC-3/Canso drivers, Ray McLean and Jim Sheldon, relax at Moosonee, June 1964. Ray stayed with the company to become a senior 748 captain while Jim moved to Air Canada. (Right) Austin Airways hangar complex at Ramsey Lake. The main building was 60 x 60 x 18 feet and supported by heavy beams once used in a mine. A second building was 18 x 36 x 12 feet. This base was opened in 1945 and was used until a fire in 1971 totally destroyed the buildings and everything in them, including Cessna 180 CF-JNC and Beaver CF-MAP. (Dave Russell, Frank Russell)

Beavers and 185s. They had proven themselves by hard work, determination and reliability and now it was time to step up to the Canso and DC-3. Bob was proud to work with these pilots — Bill Pullen, Don Beamish, Jim Hall and others. Most eventually left the north, becoming top pilots with the major airlines crisscrossing the country and the world.

August 19, 1977, was a historic day in Bob Pettus' flying career: he flew CF-DFB from Moosonee to Timmins, touched down, and walked away from the Canso. It had been his final trip with Austin Airways. He did a bit more contract flying out west, his last on Canso CF-CRR in August 1979. That month he retired from

active flying and headed back to his teaching career. The nearly forty years since he first joined the RCAF had been a happy time, especially the Austin years.

Spencer Woods worked as a helper, mechanic, then engineer with Austin Airways between 1960 and 1965, with the last three years on the Anson operation. He also made many trips crewing on the Cansos, generally with Jim Bell and Jack Humphries. Spence recalls how they would work their way up the east coast of Hudson Bay and usually refuel at Pov. After the aircraft was tied up, Jim and Jack would cheerfully head into town for lunch, abandoning Spence. The big "boat" was now all his and that meant work! Worst job of all was refuelling, for he would have to wobble-pump 10 drums of gas up into the plane, 450 gallons in all. That was great for developing biceps.

One day at Pov, Jim and Jack had just returned from lunch. Time to take off again, right? Wrong! Spence reported trouble. "We can't go, Jim. Something's unsafe." "Oh," replied the captain, "what seems to be unsafe?" Deadpan, Spence answered, "My stomach. It's empty."

DC-3 C-GNNA up on its nose at Kenty Lake, a mining site inland from POV. The incident occurred in the spring of 1975. In spite of many a bent airplane, Austin Airways boasted what was probably the safest airline operation in Canada.
(John der Weduwen)

And with that he played pilot and trudged off to town for something to eat.

Another day Spence was with the same crew at Fort George. They were about to get away and it was windy and rough. Spence and Jack were out on the nose struggling to get the anchor in. All of a sudden, Capt. Bell decided the time was right to open the throttles. End result: two half-drowned and none-too-happy deck hands!

Ice Patrol

In 1961 Austin Airways won a major federal government contract to provide ice reconnaissance flights in the Hudson Bay-Hudson Strait region. These flights would aid ships navigating the ice-filled waters during the brief shipping season. Such flights had been conducted in the region since the famous Hudson Strait expedition of 1926 when several Fokker Universals and a Moth went north to conduct surveys in connection with commercial navigation between the new grain port at Churchill and Europe.

Jim Bell established Austin's ice patrol guidelines based on what the government required, and a DC-3 was suitably modified for the contract. Ray Lejeune was appointed chief pilot for the first season, and he describes the operation: "The Dak that we used was fitted with a 400-gallon long-range tank that gave us a good 12-hour endurance. A plastic observation dome and a bench for the ice observer were installed just behind the pilots. We had no radar and most of our navigation was done with the ADF when we were close enough to a beacon to allow us to get a fix. At other times we used dead reckoning, flying our track for a fixed time and then turning onto another track hoping that we were close to where we were supposed to be.

"The crew on ice patrol included two pilots, a navigator and the ice observer. The operation was strictly visual and at times we had to fly low down to get underneath the overcast so that the observer could plot the ice flow. When the weather was clear we would fly at about 5000 feet.

"We were based at Frobisher and on patrol we covered Hudson Strait, Davis Strait and Baffin Bay. On a clear day over Davis Strait we could see the mountains of Greenland. At the end of each patrol the ice observer would send out his daily ice conditions map, transmitted to ships at sea using the same equipment for transmitting weather maps.

"Flying the ice patrol was hardly an exciting job. It was valuable work, but all those hours and hours in the middle of nowhere, peering out across ice floes broken only with the occasional iceberg."

In the 1961 ice patrol season Ray Lejeune logged 242 hours between July 1 and September 6. Most trips averaged 8 to 9 hours.

Apart from flying the DC-3 on ice patrol, Ray Lejeune flew it on many other jobs. One flight is remembered by some of Austin's oldtimers. There had been a bad accident involving Alan Rose, a miner at Timmins. A plane was needed urgently to get the man to hospital in Toronto. It looked as though there was no plane available or at least handy. Ray was in Kap at the time and heard of the trouble. Without wasting a moment he fired

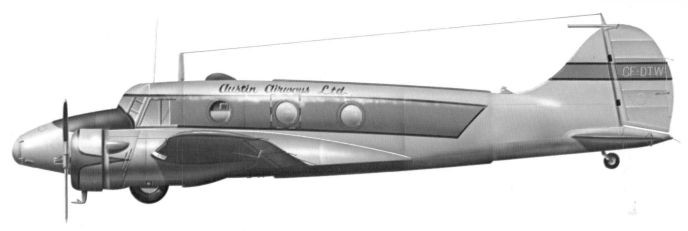

One of Austin's Anson survey aircraft. The Anson served the company into the 1970s.

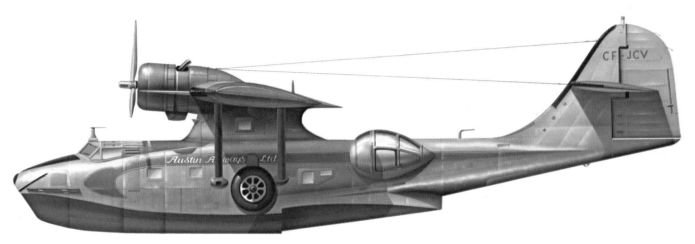

Another Austin "fixture" for many years was the Canso amphibian.

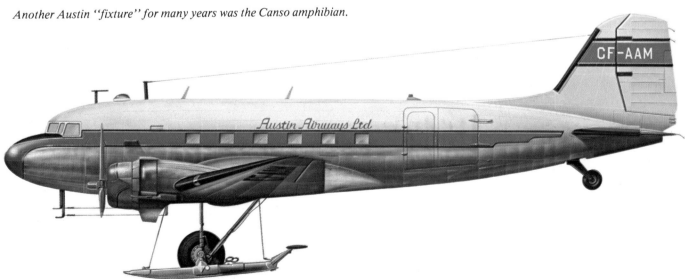

The DC-3 has been part of the Austin scene for over 30 years.

Illustrations by Peter Mossman

Engineer Walter Bray, hard at work on one of DC-3 ILQ's P&W engines at Frobisher during ice patrol duties. The unusual observation dome was devised by Jim Bell. (via Walter Bray)

up the DC-3 on his own, as there were no other crew on hand, and flew straight to Timmins. He hadn't bothered waiting around for orders. While everyone else at Timmins was wondering what could be done, Ray touched down solo with the DC-3, and Rose was soon on his way to Toronto with the crew of Jack Humphries and Al Scully.

More Canso Woes

CF-FAR ran out of luck on December 27, 1956. Pilots Jim Hobbs and Jim Pengelly with engineer Stan Cramer were called at Timmins to take a load of flour from Nakina to Winisk. The crew took a cab around to Kapuskasing where the Canso was stationed. They refuelled with 700 gallons of fuel and took off for Nakina. There the cargo was loaded and the plane taxied out, but two problems arose. It was hard to taxi with the fully loaded Canso, which kept breaking through the hard crust of snow, and one engine wasn't developing full power. Some de-icing fluid was added to the gas, the flour was offloaded, and the Canso flew back to Kapuskasing. Then, after consulting by phone with Jim Bell, Capt. Hobbs and crew took off for Timmins, where a thorough check could be made of the problem.

CF-FAR was about 20 miles from Timmins at 2500 feet when trouble hit. Without warning, one engine, then the other, suddenly quit. In the darkness of a cold December night, all was quiet as the big amphibian sank rapidly. Then, as Jim Pengelly remembers it, there was a terrific din. He recalls thinking, "We can't take much more of this." Things went black for him, till he heard a voice over the radio, "FAR give your position."

Jim found himself pinned in his seat. Hobbs was still in his and conscious, but not looking too alert. Pengelly and Cramer soon helped him out of the plane. Cramer retrieved the survival gear and he and Pengelly set up camp as Hobbs was clearly in shock from the crash. One look at the Canso and each of the crew realized he was fortunate to be alive. The cockpit was a mangled wreck — not the sort of crash scene people often walk away from.

The downed trio settled in for a cold night's stay but was pleasantly surprised to hear a DC-3 fly over low at 10:30, about two hours after the crash. They later found out that it was Hollinger's aircraft, CF-FBS, flown by Don McClintock and Jerry Foster. Next morning CF-FAR was spotted by Kenting's Canso CF-DFB flown by Frank Smith. Jeff Wyborn had been in the area a bit earlier in a Beaver, but it was snowing and he couldn't see the wreck hidden below in the trees.

Meanwhile Austin Airways was already planning a large-scale search, and Search and Rescue HQ in Trenton had been alerted. At Sudbury everyone was instructed to be ready to go out on the search at first light. Most were down at the base before sun-up, clearing snow from wings and generally getting ready to go. At 8:35 the first aircraft, Cessna 180 CF-IBQ, got airborne for Timmins, flown by Jim Keane with Chuck Austin as spotter. Ten minutes later two more aircraft departed: Norseman CF-IGG with Eric Blackwood at the controls, and Bill Montgomery and two other spotters; and Norseman CF-BSC with Rusty Blakey, Frank Russell, Mark Nieminen and Dick Blakey aboard. These were followed at 9:35 by Beaver CF-GBC, flown by Frank Ross with Gordy Kohls and Romeo Belanger. All the aircraft arrived at Timmins shortly, but even while en route heard over the air that the Canso had been found. Late in the afternoon two para-rescue experts jumped to the crash site from an RCAF Dakota and they were soon joined by Jim Bell and Gordy Kohls, who flew in in a 180. As it was almost dark, everyone spent that night in the camp, but come morning the rescue was completed. Jim Hobbs was taken out in a snowmobile, while Pengelly was flown out by Ontario Hydro Bell 47 helicopter. Both injured men spent time in hospital recuperating. The DOT investigation concluded that a faulty electrical fuel valve had led to the crash. The mishap ended the days of the Canso, though some years later it was partially salvaged.

Another Canso incident involved CF-IHB, which was holed by rocks and sunk in the river at Winisk with Doug Mackie at the helm. It looked like a total loss, but bush

(Top) Canso CF-IHB holed and partially sunk at Winisk. The salvage crew of Frank Russell, Bob Kerr, Charlie Williams, Bob Haggert and Mark Nieminen refloated the plane, and Jim Bell ferried it out for repairs. (Below) Ice-bound at Cape Dorset. (Mark Nieminen, Jim Bell Collection)

fliers' ingenuity prevailed. Under Frank Russell, a crew set to work using a scheme devised by Jim Bell and Jack Austin. Quick-drying cement was poured down a stove pipe to plug the holes in the partially submerged plane. Then small fire fighters' pumps were used to refloat it. Just as it floated clear Jim Bell fired it up and steered into midstream. He applied power and took off with water cascading from the hull, headed for Moosonee. There he refuelled and pushed on for St. Jean, where repairs were made by Aircraft Industries.

Engineer Eric Hazeldine tells a lighter story about Canso CF-IHB. In July 1958 he, Jim Bell and John Reid had landed at Cape Dorset on Baffin Island. The bay there was clear, but to play it safe Jim posted an Eskimo on the cape to watch lest ice blow in. As it turned out, ice did appear and clogged the bay before the Canso could escape. As a result, the Austin trio was stranded for a month. When Jack Austin heard of the predicament down at his Toronto office, he was tempted to wire his boys, "Commence your holidays immediately!"

CF-IHB was lost in a crash at Povungnituk on July 2, 1959. The crew that day was Captain Jack Humphries, F/O Colin Grant and engineer Eric Hazeldine, and nine passengers were aboard. Just after takeoff the Canso flew into a fog bank, at which point there was trouble with the starboard engine. This was quickly aggravated when the port engine failed as the captain executed a 180-degree turn. An emergency landing in shallow water was made, breaking the Canso's back. Though the crew was shaken up, the passengers hardly realized they had been in a crash. The DOT accident report notes fuel contamination as the cause of this unhappy Canso story. The airplane was a total loss. Since it was built during the war by Canadian Vickers, it had logged just over 4000 hours.

Canso 'AAD also met an ignominious end. On September 24, 1972, it was in the hands of captain Al Seaward, with copilot Morley McArthur and crewman Dave Craw. Over Great Whale there was trouble with one engine and a serious emergency soon arose. Down came the Canso, with a choice between hitting the rocks or going into the trees. The trees it was, and 'AAD cut a swath through a stand of spruce. The plane was thoroughly torn to pieces, but in yet another miracle

nobody was hurt. The next day Morley was at home nursing a badly bruised hip. There was a knock at the door. It was his smiling life insurance salesman with the good news that his new policy had been approved. "You're almost a day late with that," said Morley, without elaborating.

Story of a Canso: CF-DFB

One of Austin Airways' Cansos was CF-DFB, which served the company between 1971 and 1976. This aircraft had been built in the US by Consolidated in 1942 as serial number 605. It served in the military through the war then was sold as surplus equipment. Between 1949 and 1952 it flew in Iceland with Loftleidir, operating domestically as TF-RVG, christened *Vestfirdingur*. In 1952 it came to Canada as CF-DFB, operated by Aero Magnetic Surveys Ltd. and Photographic Surveys Ltd. of Toronto.

In 1960 ownership was transferred to the Hunting Survey Corp. Ltd., also of Toronto, and in April 1962 it was taken over by Kenting Aviation for survey work around the world, wherever the company was on contract

"The engineer fixes it, the pilot breaks it," reported one Austin engineer. Of course he was only joking! But then, scenes like this one of Canso CF-DFB "hors de combat" at Moosonee could make one wonder. Not to worry, though—engineers Kerr and der Weduwen had things straightened out within a day. (John der Weduwen)

and a Canso was required. On June 2, 1971, Austin Airways took over CF-DFB for use on its passenger and freight routes; to this point the aircraft had accumulated 8459.2 hours. It was next transferred to Wheeler Northland Airlines on March 1, 1976. Total time had by then reached 10,577.3 hours. Records indicate that Austin last flew this Canso on October 18, 1977, likely on lease.

After about another 800 hours 'DFB was acquired by the government of Newfoundland from Field Aviation on

Fuel haul woes. DC-3 ILQ wrecked in the bush near the Rupert River. Captain Bob Hamilton and copilot George Charity were badly hurt in the crash. The hulk of 'ILQ is still there. John der Weduwen notes that many times over the years he has gone in to salvage parts. (George Charity Collection)

October 17, 1978. It was converted by Field to water-bomber configuration and has served Newfoundland since then. To July 25, 1983, it had logged 11,842.4 hours and will likely see many more years of service protecting the province's forests.

So Long to ILQ

A serious mishap struck Austin Airways on January 9, 1964. Captain Bob Hamilton and copilot George Charity were transporting avgas for Inco from Moosonee to Levac Lake in DC-3 CF-ILQ. At about 08:00, about 30 miles from Rupert House, an unnoticed fuel feed problem led to the sudden loss of power in both engines. The aircraft glided in from 2500 feet, and as it neared the ground with the skis lowered, it began slicing through black spruce and there was a terrific racket. George blacked out and awoke feeling miserable. He had two broken ankles but didn't find that out until he tried to get back into the cabin. Bob Hamilton had also survived but he too was banged up.

As the plane crashed, it spun 180 degrees around. It was later learned that Hamilton had tried to do just that to prevent the 45-gallon fuel drums behind from crashing into the cockpit. Unfortunately no distress call had been sent so the two pilots prepared for a long wait in the bush. Hamilton organized sleeping bags from the survival pack, but other than a bag of prunes, no food could be found. The grub box had been thrown somewhere outside in the waist-deep snow.

It wasn't long before aircraft were in the air searching.

In the early afternoon Bruce Cochrane, flying a Cessna 180, spotted the wreck. He landed on the nearby Rupert River but couldn't get through to the crash site because of the snow. He slept in his plane overnight, and while trying to get off the next morning, dinged his prop. A Beaver came in to help him out. Next day Lindy Louttit arrived in a Beaver and Hamilton fired flares to attract his attention. Lindy landed and got the two downed fliers safely out to hospital in Rupert House. They spent the next six months recovering from their injuries.

Soon after this, George Charity left aviation. He moved to the West Coast and built, of all things, a 39-foot salmon fishing boat. He spent the next three years on Vancouver Island, fishing from Tofino and other ports before realizing that he was in as precarious a profession as bush flying. He packed up and moved back to his retirement in South Porcupine. George Charity died on January 25, 1983.

More on Maintenance

As the Austin fleet grew through the years, its maintenance organization had to keep pace. What had started as a small operation in Toronto and at Norm Irwin's farm had progressed to a major float plane base on Ramsey Lake, then an even bigger operation for the DC-3s and Cansos at Kapuskasing. When the hangar at Kap burned in the 1960's, Austin Airways purchased facilities at Hamilton's municipal airport, Mount Hope. This served the company in the early seventies until Jack Austin retired. During all the 40 years since the company started, Frank Russell had been a leading light in maintenance, in fact, chief engineer for many of those years. The following listings are Frank Russell's maintenance schedules for two periods. One looks at bushplane main-

CF-AAB gets some attention at Timmins. The time is the winter of '71-'72, before Austin had a hangar here. (Al Beaupré)

tenance at Sudbury commencing in April 1959. The other is work done on Otters, Ansons and a DC-3 at Mount Hope commencing November 1973. They nicely illustrate a side of aviation too often overlooked in favour of the actual flying that usually absorbs the writer's interest.

Work Program, April 4, 1959

The following is our work program commencing April 4th until ?? The aircraft are listed in order of priority. Also any known work has been listed but not in detail. Any additional work must be authorized by F.W. Russell before proceeding with same. Weather conditions will have to be considered as a factor if any changes in this program are to be made.

Each aircraft as received at the hangar must have a snag sheet signed by the pilot who has been flying the aircraft and also arrangements will be made for Rusty Blakey to test the aircraft and check the snags as listed before the aircraft is taken out of service.

As soon as the aircraft is delivered to the hangar a list of all equipment and parts on board must be made on the equipment list.

All log books must be properly totalled and delivered with the aircraft.

The following aircraft will be changed over at Sudbury: BSC, GMM, JIN, IGG, OBN, MAP, JFE, GBC, FYQ, JNC, SAQ.

In addition to above we will also have the following not of our own: IBM (Butchart), ACK (Forbes), 108 (Cecutti).

(1) GSR   Floats to be completed and shipped to Nakina.
(2) GBC   Engine to be removed and shipped to P and W. Rush.
(3) JFE   The floats for this aircraft should not require any work other than painting. The aircraft will require

Frank Russell and Jack Austin at Mount Hope, May 20, 1971. (via Hal McCracken)

the MacMurray name removed and white top painted on. No other work should be required at this time.

(4) FYQ The floats for this aircraft should not require too much other than painting. The aircraft should require a minimum of work. Gas vent mod to be carried out and C. of A. renewal.

(5) BSC The floats for this aircraft should be ready before it is taken in. The tops of wings and tail surfaces are to be painted. Engine requires a thorough check (See FWR). C. of A. renewal and wing inspection.

(6) GMM Floats should not require much more than cleaning and painting. Aircraft should not require any work other than visual inspection.

(7) JIN Float work at present unknown. Airframe and engine will be as required but should not be of serious nature.

(8) IGG Float work at present unknown. Airframe and engine should be minor.

(9) OBN Float work unknown. Possibility of complete paint job if time and conditions permit.

(10) MAP Floats are ready. Airframe and engine should be normal, check C. of A.

(11) JNC Float work unknown but should be minor. Airframe and engine should be normal check.

(12) GBC Floats should be normal check and clean. Engine installation and minor check for C. of A.

(13) SAQ Floats will require fair amount of work. Engine nil work. Airframe overhaul to continue as time permits.

(14) IBM To arrive after ice leaves to be checked and work decided later.

(15) ACK To arrive after ice leaves. C. of A. and normal check.

(16) 108
Cecutti Floats to be installed.

It is essential that upon arrival and receipt of snag sheets each aircraft be inspected completely and all work assessed and listed.

In view of the large program of work ahead of us and for economical reasons a small staff, it will be very essential that each man ascertain that each day be used to produce the utmost.

Any shortcuts or suggestions without sacrificing safety or quality will be greatly appreciated.

F.W. Russell

Anticipated Work Program as of November 1, 1973

The following aircraft are scheduled to be processed through this hangar from November 1 to approximately January 1, 1974.

Otters—MIT, SOX, BEW, HXY
Ansons—IVK, HQZ
Daks—AAH

(The known work on these aircraft is listed starting at Item 7.)

1. Complete AAB ready for delivery to Timmins. This will include —
   Carpet on floor,
   Dapple paint headlining as per AAM

The following bits and pieces are to be on board —
All equipment as received with aircraft
All cargo nets from JCV
Spare Jr. cylinder for Moosonee
All log books, etc.

Make a complete list of all contents of aircraft as it leaves here. Also have accepting pilot sign a copy of list for our records.

2. Ship both engines as removed from AAB.

3. Ship all accessories.

4. Place hoses, etc., from these engines in a suitable container and store with each engine mount for the time being. These will be overhauled at a later date.

5. Collect and assemble all Otter skis. These are to be complete and ready for installation. They are to be stored in sets c/w all hardware. No shortages please.

6. It is suggested at this time that all benches and work areas be cleaned up and some planning done as to where the various jobs will be done and aircraft parked. This with the thought of avoiding waste motion and increasing efficiency.

7. The following is the known work on the aforementioned aircraft —
   7.1 MIT
       600 hour seasonal check. Replace flap and aileron, install skis, check and repair brakes.
   7.2 SOX
       600 hour seasonal check. Change engine. Install skis. Check and repair brakes.
   7.3 BEW
       600 hour seasonal check. Install heater. Install skis.
   7.4 HXY
       To be painted. HF and VHF radios to be installed. Complete inspection. Ground run. Test fly. Paper work and licence. Complete ski installation.
   7.5 IVK
       Possible engine change if high oil consumption still there. Annual clean up and inspection.
   7.6 HQZ
       Annual inspection and clean up.
   7.7 AAH
       General clean up. Wing pull.

8. JCV
   One engine to be removed, aircraft prepared for winter storage.

9. DFB
   Same as JCV. Both these aircraft to have engines removed as soon as possible for overhaul.

It is to be noted that the foregoing is a very rough listing and that there is possibly more to come. Itemized work lists will be issued at a later date on all above aircraft. The possibility of overtime work is to be anticipated.

F.W. Russell

Austin Airways Today

J.A.M. "Jack" Austin in a 1962 portrait by Toronto photographer Les Baxter. Jack remained with Austin Airways until February 25, 1975, 41 years to the day after he and brother Chuck formed it. The company was sold to Stan Deluce in November, 1974.

Over the years Jack Austin had had several enquiries from parties interested in buying his company, including one in 1970 from former railroader and owner of White River Air Services, Stan Deluce. At the time, Jack was not interested in selling out, but the two kept in touch. As time went by, Jack thought more of retirement. He had been a long time in the business. Many of the original faces on the Austin Airways "team" were no longer on the scene for one reason or another, and those remaining were not getting any younger. Periods of ill health had not helped matters for Jack, Jim Bell, Frank Russell and others still with the company. So it was that in 1974 Jack Austin and Stan Deluce sat down for some serious bargaining. The outcome was a deal completed that November that saw Jack sell all company shares to Stan. Three months later he left Austin Airways for good and began his well-earned retirement. The following year, Jack was awarded the famous McKee Trophy, a fitting tribute indeed for his 40 years of service to Canadian aviation.

Twin Otter C-GOVG of Austin Airways but in Norontair colours is seen boarding passengers at Timmins as an Air Canada DC-9 and an Austin DC-3 await. (Larry Milberry)

Now it was Stan Deluce's turn, and he took over with a plan to change the company image from bush operator to regional airline. Stan had joined Canadian Pacific as a young man, but the Second World War found him flying Hurricanes for the RCAF. After the war he returned to railroading, but in 1951 formed White River Air Services with a lone Stinson 108. This operation was mainly aimed at the summer tourist trade in Lake Superior country. Business grew and Cessna 180s, Beavers and Otters in

(Left) Spring scene, 1975, on the Albany River at Ogoki Post. Bill Ross has just landed CF-IAX with a load of fuel oil. Soon after, he took off for Nakina with school children returning to Toronto. Their baggage waits on the ice. (Larry Milberry)

(Above left) DC-3 Alpha Alpha Mike taking off at Detour Lake, August 31, 1982. (Right) C-GQSV lifts off from the gravel strip at Fort Albany, September 9, 1982. (Below) An Austin 748 offloads freight at Fort George, August 1979. (Larry Milberry)

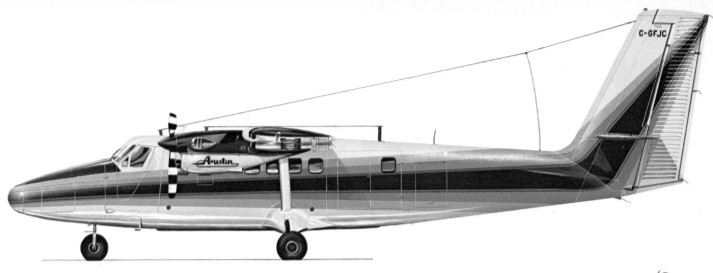

A de Havilland Twin Otter in Austin's garish "pizza" paint job.

Austin's first Cessna Citation as fitted with an ambulance door, and operated for the Ontario Ministry of Health.

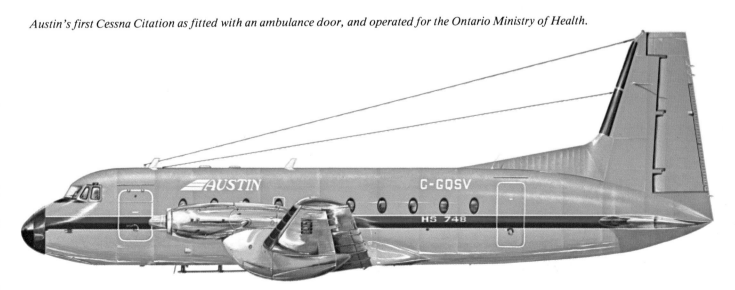

BAe 748 in the colours of Maersk, a Danish airline which had it on lease in the early 1980s.

Illustrations by Ron E. Lowry

White River livery soon were familiar sights. In 1971, Stan's company won the first Norontair feederliner contract from the Ontario government and began operating Twin Otters.

Soon after the Austin deal was completed the Deluce family moved to Timmins, by then Austin's main base. Expansion and modernization began immediately. Not the least of innovations was the simple presence of the Deluces, a large aviation-minded family, all of whom were somehow involved with the family business. Stan's boys began as youngsters. As they grew up they worked summers gassing airplanes, loading and unloading at the dock, guiding, and generally becoming jacks-of-all-trades. Thus did they work their way through school. The first five attended St. Michael's College at Toronto, and took their flying instruction from the Wong brothers at Toronto Island Airport. Each received his private pilot licence at age 17 and gradually developed the knowledge and responsibility needed to be a professional pilot and businessman. All seven boys gained Airline Transport Ratings, and went to work for Austin Airways.

Austin's fleet modernization after 1974 saw the return of the British Aerospace 748 to the skies of Northern Ontario. The first was purchased in 1976, and seven others soon followed. The 748 was now a viable proposition thanks to a big airport upgrading and construction program initiated by the government of Ontario in 1968 which offered subsidies to municipalities for airport construction and maintenance; and a remote airport development program focusing on the isolated areas of Northern Ontario. Under the latter scheme, many new airports were established. As well, the federal government funded other airports in the Austin Airways operating region.

The arrival of the 748 led immediately to a cutback in older types. The company's last Canso was sold in 1977 and the DC-3 fleet was reduced in size. Meanwhile the Twin Otter fleet was expanded and several Cessna 402s were added. In 1979 Austin bought Ontario Central Airlines, a big DC-3 operator in northwestern Ontario, and established a major base at Pickle Lake including a 120 x 160-foot $1 million hangar and a 4700-foot paved runway, serving a host of small native communities to the north.

Austin's 748s had come from a variety of countries. The first, C-GMAA, was the same aircraft evaluated by Jack Austin in 1972. This time it returned through Air Gabon. Another came from Argentina where it had been the presidential VIP aircraft. Two others came from Aero Mexico and four from LAN-Chile. The LAN deal included the airline's inventory of spares, tools, and 23 technicians.

(Top) G-ATAM was the 748 demonstrator originally evaluated by Austin Airways in 1971. This photo shows it at Mount Hope, September 11, 1971, when it was at work doing goose hunt charters. (Below) A former LAN Chile 748 gets a check at Timmins. (Jack McNulty, Larry Milberry)

They and their dependents, 91 people in all, came to Canada and settled at Timmins.

There might be some resistance to referring to the 748 as a bush plane but, in fact, that's what it is in the Austin Airways context. Most of the strips it goes into are gravel, with only basic navaids. Even so, the 748 makes itself at home and has been a boon to the company. Its freight and passenger load is twice that of the DC-3 and it is faster, cruising around 180 knots. Most of its work is freighting, where the airplane plays a greater role than ever in remote northern communities. In former years winter tractor trains lumbered overland carrying everything needed for the coming year, or else people had to wait patiently for the once-a-year supply ship that served coastal centres like Winisk. But such operations are now losing propositions. Even the once-lucrative James Bay barge service has declined in recent years. These days it's the airplane that has taken over, and the 748 is the key in coastal resupply along the Bay.

Food hauling has been one of Austin Airways' chief activities for decades, and today there are weekly food haul flights throughout the Hudson and James Bay region. Customers include the Hudson's Bay Company, which has had posts on the Bay for over 300 years, native co-ops, free traders, government ministries, religious missions, mining camps, communications firms like Bell Canada, and tourist operators. Every meal served up to workers at the big Detour Lake mining project near James Bay initially arrived on the Austin Airways food haul—the site is isolated except for its 3,500-foot gravel strip and its winter road.

A typical food haul on which I rode in 1980 departed from Kapuskasing carrying six tons including fresh blueberries, frozen pizza, chocolate eclairs, 2,250 loaves of bread and hundreds of quarts of milk. From "Kap" the 748 headed for Moosonee for fuel, but weather forced a diversion across James Bay to La Grande. Then it was on to Fort George, where 250 boxes were offloaded, then Attawapiskat (156 boxes) and Fort Albany (87 boxes) for a total day's flying of 966 miles. On another trip we left Timmins at midday for the short hop to Kap. While the 748 was taking on its 11,813 pounds of food, an Austin DC-3 lifted off for Great Whale. The 748 took off, tailing the DC-3 on the 292-mile leg to Great Whale and catching up with it just as it crossed the threshold. Once down we added fuel and offloaded some food. Meanwhile the DC-3 departed for the Belcher Islands and an Austin Twin Otter arrived. Especially along the east coast of the Bay, where several communities have marginal runways, the DC-3

(Far left) An Austin 748 about to swallow a pallet of cement at Pickle Lake. The destination was Webequie. (Right) Ray Lejeune gases up an Austin Cessna 402, August 1982 at Timmins. Ray was one of the company's IFR "old timers" for two decades. (Both, Larry Milberry)

(Below left) A 748 is refuelled at Cape Dorset using the water/particle filter devised by Bob Isaacson. (Centre) High above Hudson Bay and bound for Cape Dorset, 748 captain Bob Isaacson studies his charts. (Right) Freeloader Larry Milberry enjoys a midnight snack prepared by the captain as C-GSXS hums along at 20,000 feet. (Larry Milberry, Bob Isaacson)

and Twin Otter are vital in redistributing supplies brought in to Fort George and Great Whale by 748.

Within an hour the 748 was airborne again, this time for Cape Dorset on Baffin Island. Over Inoucdjouac the captain called for the weather at Frobisher and Coral Harbour for an idea of what to expect at Cape Dorset. The Dorset approach was from the sea, with prominent "cumulo granites" looming ahead. Icebergs bobbed below and turbulence bounced the plane around. Crosswinds added to things, making for a typical northern arrival.

As we taxied in near darkness, a stream of headlights came out from the town—vans and trucks to take the 748's load. Unloading was quick, although one of the locals was unhappy when he found that his two long-awaited outboard motors had once again failed to arrive. After a break for something to eat we boarded the 748, this time nonstop to Timmins, where after almost five hours of flying, we touched down. It was 4:50 a.m.

Besides hauling food, Austin's 748s carry just about anything else needed in the North—building materials from nails to lumber to tarpaper to cement, machinery, skidoos. It's also a flying tanker. Gone are the days of the Canso tankering fuel in one of its wing tanks, or of DC-3s full of 45-gallon drums. Austin's 748s do the job with twin 830-gallon bladders, doubling the DC-3's capacity. This makes a big difference to the many remote settlements that depend on the annual airlift for their supply of winter fuel.

Pilots Jacques Giroux and Joe Deluce change a tire on their 748 at Ft. Albany as John Nakoqee looks on. The date is August 21, 1979. (Larry Milberry)

Austin later acquired six more 748s from LAV of Venezuela. Some were soon profitably resold to Regionair in Quebec and another to Eastern Provincial Airways. More than anyone else, Austin has been responsible for establishing the 748 in Canada.

Austin has also been developing global experience with its 748s. It leased three 748s to Maersk in Denmark. Crew training and maintenance by Austin were included for this two-year scheme. It also provided a 748 with crew for ser-

An Austin medevac. Personnel prepare a company Cessna 310 for a medical case while an Ontario Hydro Jet Ranger arrives on the Timmins ramp. (Larry Milberry)

Passengers board an Austin DC-3 at Timmins for the west coast sked. The DC-3 has served over 30 years with Austin Airways. (Larry Milberry)

vice on Réunion, an island off Madagascar, and crews for a 748 operation in Tunis. Austin pilot Larry Raymond also spent time in Nepal, training Royal Nepal Airlines' pilots on the 748.

Some of this overseas work took place soon after Austin acquired its first 748s. Stan Deluce explained, ''We used this leasing period to best advantage as we built up our own market for the 748 at home. The demand was there at the time—it was a profitable venture and provided us with some good experience and good contacts.''

Sharing the brunt of the Austin Airways work load is a fleet of Twin Otter 300s. These serve on scheduled passenger service and also haul freight, especially where the bigger twins can't get in due to airstrip limitations. Twin

Otters were operated by Austin for Norontair, serving Timmins, Sudbury, Kapuskasing and Cochrane, but Dash 8s operated by Air Dale now fly this service.

For half a century Austin Airways has been transporting emergency medical cases, first with the little Waco and now with a fully equipped Cessna Citation. This is a dedicated air ambulance flown for the Ontario Ministry of Health. It operates on a 15-minute standby basis, 24 hours a day, and has proven its worth since its dedication as ''Bandage 4'' in July 1981.

Based at Timmins, the Citation flies with two pilots, two medical escorts, and either a doctor or nurse accompanying the patient. Most cases are flown to Toronto, but other centres with major hospitals are also used, includ-

(Left) View from the cockpit of CF-AAM on final approach at Detour Lake August 1982. Below is the camp site with seaplane dock, the gravel strip and, in the distance, the gold mine.(Above) An ex-Austin Stinson, much modified and still at work in B.C. (Skeena Air Guides)

147

(Left) John der Weduwen, Bob Kerr and Jeff Wyborn, three Austin old-timers, still at work in the Austin hangar in 1984. (Right) Austin's famous Sudbury base is now owned by former Austin pilot Don Plaunt. Besides flying bush planes, his company, Ramsey Airways, has a large fleet of helicopters at work throughout Canada. In this 1983 photo Don is on the right. Matthew and Simon Milberry and Rusty Blakey make up the quartet. (Both, Larry Milberry)

ing Kingston, London and Ottawa. Cruising at 340 knots the Citation can reach Toronto in an hour. In some cases it uses Toronto/Buttonville airport, where "Bandage 1," a Bell 212, can rush the patient to one of Toronto's heliport-equipped hospitals.

Backing up "Bandage 4" are Austin's original Citation, C-GRQA, and its fleet of Cessna 402s. 'RQA was the first Citation fitted with an oversized door to facilitate stretcher handling. It entered service in 1979.

The DC-3 still has its place in the Austin operation and has its advantages of reliability and sturdiness. It can get into shorter strips with ease. Its ski capability lets it get into spots over the winter where the 748s can't go. Each winter, for example, a DC-3 goes out from Great Whale, flying inland with Eskimo parties and returning with such loads as three tons of Arctic char or up to 36 caribou. Otherwise, it continues in its role as jack-of-all-trades, hauling food and fuel to clear backlogs, sometimes flying the James Bay passenger routes or flying parties of goose hunters to the James Bay hunting camps in the fall.

The eighties have been years of constant growth for Austin Airways. In 1981 it took over Superior Airways, an historic Thunder Bay operator. Soon afterwards, it in-

augurated daily service from Thunder Bay to Minneapolis, giving Northern Ontarians access to global routes radiating from a major US hub. Fifteen-seat Beech 99Cs are used on this route. The fast 99 has far greater passenger appeal than the Twin Otter which it has been slowly replacing in the Austin inventory.

Also in 1981 Austin bought part of London-based Air Ontario which now serves such centres as Sarnia, Cleveland, Toronto, Sudbury, Montreal and Hartford using Convair 580s. The deal also gave Austin part ownership of C&C Yachts, one of the companies controlled by Air Ontario's J.R. Plaxton. Yachts were simply added to the growing list of Austin's interests, another of which is ultra modern greenhouses near Timmins which produce some 8,000,000 evergreen seedlings a year for the Ontario Ministry of Natural Resources.

In 1983 Austin purchased 50% of Ilford-Riverton Airways. An old-time Winnipeg company, it presently serves northern Manitoba with DC-3s, C-46s and a 748. A more recent Austin interest is in Air Creebec of Val d'Or, an airline set up by the Cree Indians of northern Quebec; another has been the sale to Air Inuit of Austin's historic route from Great Whale northward.

(Left) Old cronies from away back. Rusty Blakey and Hal McCracken were Austin colleagues for over three decades and are seen in this 1982 snap standing by a Beaver at Ramsey Lake. (Right) Rusty brings his Ramsey Airways Beaver to another smooth landing at Sudbury, nearly 50 years after he started working at Skipper Chalmers' dock. (Both, Larry Milberry)

In January 1985 Austin Airways began daily 748 service between Toronto and Timmins, competing head-on with Air Canada's DC-9s. This venture was an overnight success, and has been growing steadily. Since added has been daily 748 service from the booming Hemlo goldfields, linking Marathon, Manitouwadge and Geraldton with Toronto.

From its pair of little Wacos, through the years of the Fairchilds, Norsemans, Ansons, Beavers and Cansos, Austin is about to launch into another era. June 17, 1985 it announced plans to purchase its first jetliner — the Boeing 737, for use between Toronto and Frobisher Bay via Timmins. Traditionally, Frobisher has been served by Nordair from Montreal. With 737s, Austin will have undisputed stature as a regional airline.

To August 1985 Austin Airways' fleet included: 10 BAe 748s (2 leased out), 6 Twin Otters (3 leased out), 3 DC-3s (1 leased out), 4 Beech 99Cs, 12 Cessna 402s, 2 Cessna Citations, 2 Otters, and 1 each of Beaver, Cessna 185 and Cessna 310R. It is now only a matter of time before the VFR floatplane operation disappears — as soon as the

Ontario government's northern airport development plans are complete. Thus will end the era that made Austin Airways famous — old fashioned, single engine bush flying. It has been a half-century journey all the way from biplanes to big jets. And surely all who have read this book will agree that today's big modern airline had its foundations well and truly laid by Chuck and Jack Austin, and all the early Austin pioneers, determined and rugged men who knew their business and simply wouldn't quit.

Jack Austin at his summer place near Bala, August 1980. Jack died December 1, 1984. (Larry Milberry)

Appendices

Excerpts from Austin Airways' operations manual from the 1960s covering flight operations and survival in the North.

FLIGHT OPERATIONS GENERAL

1. All flights are to be conducted in accordance with Air Regulations, Air Navigation Orders and Air Traffic Rules.

2. **Aircraft Instruments and Equipment**

   In addition to the instruments and equipment prescribed in Airworthiness Standards approved by the Minister, the instruments and equipment prescribed in the following paragraphs shall be installed in aircraft according to the aircraft used and the circumstances under which the flight is conducted.

   i. *All Aircraft on all Flights Shall be Equipped With*
      (a) an accessible and adequate first-aid kit; the first-aid kit shall include: a handbook on first-aid, bandages, antiseptic gauze, adhesive plaster, absorbent cotton, safety pins, tourniquet, and haemostatic bandage, scissors, haemostatic forceps, water-miscible antiseptic, analgesic stimulant and remedy for burns;
      (b) at least one portable fire extinguisher if the pilot's compartment is remote from the passenger compartment;
      (c) means of ensuring that the following information and instructions are conveyed to the passengers:
         (i) when seat belts are to be fastened;
         (ii) when and how oxygen is to be used, if the carriage of oxygen is required;
         (iii) restrictions on smoking;
         (iv) location and use of life belts, if carriage of life belts is required;
         (v) location and method of opening emergency exits;
      (d) spare electrical fuses of each rating used, equal in number to 25 per cent of the number installed, or three of each rating, whichever is the greater;
      (e) the following manuals, charts and information:
         (i) the Aircraft Flight Manual for the aircraft, or, if such a manual does not exist, other documents containing performance data required for the operation of the aircraft;
         (ii) information relating to communication facilities, navigation aids, aerodrome, in-flight procedures, and such other information as the operator may deem necessary for the proper conduct of the flight operations over the route to be flown;
         (iii) current charts to cover the route of the proposed flight and any route along which it is reasonable to expect that the flight may be diverted;
         (iv) the ground-air signal codes for search and rescue purposes.

   ii. *All Aeroplanes on Flights Over Water:*

      Seaplanes: All seaplanes for all flights shall be equipped with:
      (a) one life belt, or equivalent individual flotation device, for each person on board, stowed in a position easily accessible from his seat and an additional number equal to at least one-fifth of the number of persons on board, stowed in a readily accessible position near the exits;
      (b) equipment for making the sound signals prescribed in the International Regulations for the Preventions of Collision at Sea, where applicable;
      (c) one sea anchor (drogue).
      Note: "Seaplanes" includes amphibians operated as seaplanes.

      Landplanes: All landplanes when used over routes on which the aeroplane may be over water and beyond gliding distance from shore, except during take-off and initial climb, shall be equipped with: one life belt, or equivalent individual flotation device, for each person on board, stowed in a position easily accessible from his seat; however, the Minister may grant specific exemptions from this requirement in the case of multi-engined aeroplanes when operated over water but not more than 20 minutes, at cruising speed away from shore;
      Note: "Shore" includes bound ice capable of bearing the weight of the aeroplane.
      Note: "Landplanes" includes amphibians operated as land planes.

   iii. *All Aeroplanes on Long Range Flights:*
      In addition to the equipment prescribed in 2.ii. whichever is applicable, the following equipment shall be installed in all aeroplanes when used over routes on which the aeroplanes may be over water and more than ninety minutes at cruising speed away from the shore:

      (a) Life-saving rafts in sufficient numbers to carry all persons on board stowed so as to facilitate their ready use in emergency, provided with such life-saving equipment including means of sustaining life as is appropriate to the flight to be undertaken and equipment for making the pyrotechnical distress signals;
      (b) a portable self-buoyant and water-resistant radio transmitter capable of being operated away from the aeroplane by unskilled personnel after the aeroplane has alighted on the water.

   iv. *All Aeroplanes on Flights Over Undeveloped Areas.*
      All aeroplanes when operated across areas where search and rescue would be especially difficult shall be equipped with such signalling devices, a portable radio transmitter capable of being operated by unskilled personnel, and

life-saving equipment including means of sustaining life, as are appropriate to the flight undertaken.

v. *All Aeroplanes on High Altitudes Flights.*
When aircraft are to be operated at altitudes of ten thousand feet or over, the aeroplane shall be equipped with oxygen storage and dispensing apparatus for all on board. *All Aeroplanes in Icing Conditions.* All aeroplanes shall be equipped with anti-icing facilities when operated in circumstances in which icing conditions are reported to exist or are expected to be encountered.

vi. *All Aeroplanes Operated in Accordance with Instrument Flight Rules.*
All aircraft when operated in accordance with instrument flight rules, or when the aircraft cannot be maintained in a desired attitude without reference to one or more flight instruments, shall be equipped with:
(a) A gyroscopic rate-of-turn indicator combined with an instrument which will indicate acceleration along the transverse axis of the aircraft;
(b) a gyroscopic bank and pitch indicator;
(c) a gyroscopic direction indicator;
(d) means of indicating whether the power supply to the gyroscopic instruments is working satisfactorily;
(e) two sensitive pressure altimeters;
Note: A sensitive altimeter of any type fitted in accordance with Airworthiness Standards approved by the Minister may be included in the two here prescribed.
(f) a means of indicating in the flight crew compartment the outside air temperature;
(g) a time piece with a sweep-second hand;
(h) one airspeed indicator system with means of preventing malfunctioning due to either condensation or icing;
(i) a rate-of-climb and descent indicator.
Those instruments that are used by any one pilot shall be so arranged so as to permit the pilot to see them readily from his station, with the minimum practical deviation from the position and line of vision which he normally assumes when looking forward along the flight path.

vii. *All Aeroplanes When Operated at Night:*
All aircraft when operated at night shall be equipped with:
(a) all equipment specified in vi.;
(b) equipment for displaying the lights prescribed in the Air Regulations;
(c) two landing lamps;
(d) illumination for all instruments and equipment that are essential for safe operation of the aircraft and are used by the flight crew;
(e) lights in all passenger compartments;
(f) an electric torch for each crew member station.
Note: Aircraft not certified in ICAO category which are equipped with single landing lamp having two separately energized filaments will be considered to have complied with vii. (c) *Reference:* ANO Series 11 No. 6.

3. **Aircraft Radio Equipment**
i. An aircraft when operated in accordance with visual flight rules shall be provided with two-way radio communication equipment capable of maintaining communication between airport towers, Air Traffic Control, Radio Range Stations and Company radio stations, on appropriate crystal controlled frequencies.

ii. An aircraft when operated in IFR flight within controlled air space shall, in addition to serviceable radio apparatus adequate to navigate safely within the area in which the flight is to be made, which apparatus shall include the equipment in at least one of the following categories:
(a) two automatic direction finding radio compasses;
(b) one automatic direction finding radio compass and one VOR/ILS receiver;
(c) one low/medium frequency range receiver and one automatic direction finding radio compass;
(d) one low frequency range receiver and one VOR/ILS receiver; or
(e) two low/medium range receivers.

iii. An aircraft when operated in IFR flight elsewhere than within controlled air space shall be equipped with serviceable radio equipment adequate to navigate safely within the area in which the flight is to be made and which equipment shall include an automatic direction finding radio compass.

4. **Flight Preparation**
A flight shall not be commenced until the pilot-in-command is satisfied that:
(a) the aircraft is airworthy;
(b) all instruments and equipment, previously prescribed in this Chapter, are installed and are sufficient for the flight;
(c) the aircraft has been correctly signed out by the maintenance staff;
(d) the weight of the aircraft is such that the flight can be conducted safely, taking into account the flight conditions expected;
(e) the load carried is so distributed and secured that the aircraft is safe for flight;
(f) a check has been completed indicating that the operating limitations on the aircraft can be complied with for the flight to be undertaken;
(g) that the flight plan has been completed;
(h) for Class 11, Non-Scheduled Services, a copy of the weight and balance will be left with a responsible person, at Moosonee base for north bound flights, and at Povungnituk for south bound flights.
(copies of forms attached as addendum this chapter)

5. **Flight Planning**
A flight plan or flight notification shall be completed in duplicate for every flight of company aircraft, whether operated under visual flight rules or instrument flight rules. The original copy will stay with the aircraft, attached to the en route flight log and the duplicate filed with flight dispatch at the point of departure or left with a responsible person.

(a) Except in the case of en route flight plan changes, made with the approval of the area Air Traffic Control, all flight plans must be filed at least thirty minutes prior to departure.

(b) The flight plan shall be approved and signed by the pilot-in-command and shall be filed with the operator, his agent, or the aerodrome authority, or, if none of these procedures are possible it shall be left on record in a suitable place at the point of departure.

(c) Pilots flight planning into remote areas, where communications cannot be maintained, must file a flight itinerary giving planned positions at different times and dates and when they anticipate arriving at points where there are communication facilities where progress reports may be filed.

(d) On flights originating or terminating on a company base, where RCCS or DOT communication facilities do not exist, the flight plan will be filed with the Base Manager or his agent, who will be responsible for initiating action in case of overdue flights.

6. **Flight Plans Shall Contain the Following:**

i. *VFR Flight Plans*
   (a) type of flight plan;
   (b) the flight or aircraft identification and the radio call sign if different from the flight or aircraft identification;
   (c) the type of aircraft or, in the case of formation, the types and number of aircraft involved;
   (d) the proposed true airspeed at cruising altitude;
   (e) the point of departure of position of the aircraft if the flight plan is filed while the aircraft is in flight;
   (f) the abbreviation VFR where no specific altitude is to be maintained;
   (g) the route to be followed;
   (h) the point of first intended landing;
   (i) the proposed time of departure in Greenwich Mean Time;
   (j) the estimated lapsed time until over the point of first intended landing in hours and minutes;
   (k) the amount of fuel on board expressed in hours and minutes;
   (l) the radio frequencies to be used or the word "Ronly" meaning receiver only or the word "Nordo" meaning no radio;
   (m) the type of emergency radio transmitter if carried;
   (n) the total number of persons on board;
   (o) the name of the pilot-in-command or, in the case of a formation the name of the formation commander;
   (p) the name and address of the operator of the aircraft; and
   (q) such additional information as may be requested by the appropriate air traffic control unit or considered relevant by the pilot-in-command.

ii. *Flight Notifications*
   Every flight notification shall contain:
   (a) the type of flight notification;
   (b) the flight or aircraft identification and the radio call sign if different from the flight or aircraft identification;
   (c) the type of aircraft or, in the case of a formation, the types and number of aircraft involved;
   (d) the colours of the aircraft;
   (e) whether the aircraft is a landplane, a seaplane or an amphibian and if it is a landplane, whether it is equipped with wheels, skis or both of them;
   (f) the point of departure of position of the aircraft if the flight notification is filed while the aircraft is in flight;
   (g) the proposed date of the proposed time of departure in Greenwich Mean Time;
   (h) the type of emergency radio transmitter if carried;
   (i) the radio frequencies to be used or the word "Ronly" meaning receiver only or the word "Nordo" meaning no radio;
   (j) the name and address of the pilot-in-command;
   (k) the flight itinerary and duration of stopovers;
   (l) the place, date, time and method of reporting arrival;
   (m) the name and address of the person or company to be notified if search and rescue action is initiated;
   (n) unless such information is otherwise available to the Minister on demand, the names and addresses of passengers carried; and
   (o) such additional information as may be required by the appropriate air traffic control unit or considered relevant by the pilot-in-command.

iii. *IFR Flight Plan*
   Every IFR flight plan shall contain:
   (a) the type of flight plan;
   (b) the flight or aircraft identification and the radio call sign if different from the flight or aircraft identification;
   (c) the type of aircraft or, in the case of a formation, the types and number of aircraft involved;
   (d) the proposed true airspeed at cruising altitude;
   (e) the point of departure or the position of the aircraft if the flight plan is filed while the aircraft is in flight;
   (f) the cruising altitude or altitudes and route to be followed;
   (g) the point of first intended landing;
   (h) the proposed time of departure in Greenwich Mean Time;
   (i) the estimated lapsed time until over the point of first intended landing in hours and minutes;
   (j) the alternate airport or airports;
   (k) the amount of fuel on board expressed in hours and minutes;
   (l) the radio frequencies to be used;
   (m) the type of emergency radio if carried;
   (o) the total number of persons on board;
   (p) the name of the pilot-in-command or, in the case of a formation, the name of the formation commander;
   (q) the licence number of the pilot-in-command;
   (r) the name and address of the operator of the aircraft; and
   (s) such additional information as may be requested by

the appropriate air traffic control unit or considered relevant by the pilot-in-command.

7. Weather Conditions

i. A flight to be conducted in accordance with visual flight rules shall not be commenced unless current meteorological reports or a combination of current reports and forecasts indicate that the meteorological conditions along the route or that part of the route to be flown under visual flight rules are, and will continue to be, such as to make it possible for the flight to be conducted in accordance with visual flight rules.

ii. A flight to be conducted in accordance with instrument flight rules shall not be commenced unless the available meteorological information indicates that meteorological conditions at, at least one airport specified in the flight plan will, at the expected time of arrival, be at or above the airport meteorological minima listed in the Operations Manual for that airport when used as an alternate.

8. Fuel and Oil Supply

i. A flight shall not be commenced unless, considering wind and other meteorological conditions expected during the flight at the altitudes specified in the operational flight plan, at least sufficient fuel and oil are carried:
   (a) under visual flight rules to fly to the airport of intended landing and thereafter to fly for forty-five minutes at normal cruising speed, except in isolated areas where the minimum reserve will be one hour.
   (b) under instrument flight rules to fly to the airport of intended landing and thence to an alternate airport or to fly to an alternate airport by any predetermined point and thereafter, in either case, for two hours at normal cruising speed; however, when adequate intermediate aerodromes and meteorological information are available the fuel and oil need only to be sufficient to fly to the aerodrome of intended landing and thence to an alternate and thereafter for forty-five minutes at normal cruising speed;
   (c) under instrument flight rules and where the aerodrome of intended landing is isolated and no suitable alternate is available, to fly to the airport of intended landing and thereafter to fly for two hours at normal cruising speed.
   Note: Section (c) above applies to specific meteorological conditions not normally found or applied within Canada, however, certain locations may qualify but application of this standard must be approved on an individual basis.

ii. Fuel and oil in excess of any of the minima specified in i. above, shall be carried when there are any indications that additional fuel and oil will be required because of expected circumstances such as traffic delays.

iii. Fuel calculations shall be computed with due consideration to the following factors:
   (a) altitude of proposed flight;
   (b) wind velocities and direction at cruise levels;
   (c) temperatures;
   (d) true airspeeds and resulting ground speeds;
   (e) distance between stations;
   (f) calculated elapsed time off to over;
   (g) let down times;
   (h) reserves and alternates;
   (i) additional fuel required due to circumventing storms and icing conditions;
   (j) reserves for isolated area operations.

iv. Fuel consumption to be used for Flight Planning Purposes:

Aircraft	*Fuel Consumption*
PBY 5A	75 imperial g.p.h.
DC-3	75 imperial g.p.h.
Anson V	35 imperial g.p.h.
Norseman	28 imperial g.p.h.
Beaver	20 imperial g.p.h.
Otter	28 imperial g.p.h.
Cessna 180	11 imperial g.p.h.

v. Notwithstanding any weight limitations an extra 20 gallons may be loaded on the PBY 5A or DC-3 aircraft to offset the amount burned off in the start, warm-up and taxiing into position. Five gallons may be loaded on the single engine aircraft.

vi. Fuel tanks must not intentionally be run dry in flight. Should this condition occur care must be taken at the next re-fuelling to ascertain that there is no air lock in the line.

vii. *Canso PBY 5A Aircraft*
The following will be added to the normal run-up and power check prior to take-off.

   1. *Proposed Operation Both Fuel Tanks*
      (a) Port fuel valve closed, interconnect open, check fuel flow both engines.
         Starboard fuel valve closed, interconnect open, check fuel flow to both engines.
      (b) Interconnect closed, both fuel valves open, crossfeed off, carry out normal run-up to ensure fuel flow starboard tank to starboard engine and port, port tank to port engine.
      (c) All crews operations to be carried out with interconnect off and both tank valves on and draining easily.
      (d) Check crossfeed.
      (e) Fuel tanks to be dipped prior to every take-off.

   2. *Single Tank Operation*
      (a) Inoperative tank plugged and fuel valve off.
      (b) Operative tank valve open, interconnect on.
      (c) Check crossfeed.

7. SURVIVAL

General Procedures to be Followed when an Aircraft is Forced Down or Lost

Through experience it has been proven that it is better for the pilot or passengers of a lost aircraft to stay with the aircraft rather than attempt to walk out. If the aircraft is forced down for reasons other than being lost, it will be on or very close to track and even if the pilot knew his position he would no doubt be found by searching aircraft before he could have walked out. If the pilot stays with the aircraft he has the advantage of being able to have his signals ready in the event of searching aircraft being heard or sighted. If he is travelling he has very little time to get a signal ready by the time the search aircraft has passed. A search will be continued for at least 21 days after the date the aircraft went missing. The pilot will be expected to stay with the aircraft for this period of time.

Action When Lost - Float & Ski Equipped

When float or ski equipped aircraft become lost it is important to choose a suitable landing area while plenty of fuel is still remaining aboard the aircraft. A safe landing may then be made and fuel is available to run the engine so that the radio may be used.

Remaining with the Aircraft

Since a search for a missing aircraft will continue for at least 21 days, it is imperative that crews remain with their aircraft for this period of time. The aircraft should be abandoned only when the crew are certain of their position and when shelter and help are within reasonable distance.

Travel in Winter

The major obstacles to travel will be soft deep snow, dangerous river ice, severe cold weather and a scarcity of native foods. If the snow is deep do not try to travel without snowshoes. It may be possible to improvise a pair from boughs or from metal panels of the aircraft. Do not travel in a snowstorm or in extremely cold windy weather. Stay with the aircraft and conserve energy.

Travel - in the Mountains

When travelling on glaciers care must be taken against snow-bridged crevasses. Men should be arranged in groups of not less than three and they should be roped together at intervals of thirty to forty feet. An ice axe or a stout stick may be used to locate crevasses as an aid to travel. Usually it is better to travel on ridges, when possible, where the snow may be firmer and a better view of the route can be obtained.

Shelter

1. When choosing a site to make camp, make sure it is sheltered from the wind and is not likely to be drifted over and buried by snow. In mountains, camp should not be set up below steep snow-covered slopes as snow may slide suddenly.
2. In timbered country build a lean-to, "A" tent, paratent or paratepee, using boughs or fabric covering. In summer, fabric shelters are desirable because they will keep out insects.
3. In timberless country make a shelter of aircraft parts or dig a snow cave. Snow caves and snow trenches are warm and comfortable because snow is an excellent insulator. Use cowling, doors or other parts of the aircraft to make shelters. If poles are available put up a fabric shelter. The aircraft cabin will be too cold for shelter in winter.

Heat

1. *Fuel* In timbered country dry wood from dead standing trees or the lower limbs of evergreen make good fuel. Green wood also will burn if split fine. In timberless areas fuel may be obtained from scrub bushes growing along valleys and in other sheltered places. Dry lichens, moss, dried and shredded peat, heat tablets, gas and oil all make good fuel.
2. *Stoves* Improvise stoves for burning gasoline, oil and fats. Use great care when burning 100-octane gas. Never add gasoline to a burning fire. If food is scarce never burn potential food-stuffs, such as fats and hides.

Food and Water

1. *Emergency Rations* The officer in charge will ration food immediately. Go on half rations by the end of the first week unless native foods are plentiful. If travel is in prospect save light concentrated foods for camping.
2. *Native Foods* Practically all native foods in the North are safe to eat. However, it is difficult to live off the country especially in winter. A great deal of energy can be burned up searching for small game. Depend on emergency rations if they are available.
3. *Animals* Small animals such as rabbits, squirrels, wood-chucks and muskrats are easier to catch than large game. For such small game snares or deadfalls may be set along runways in brush or snow and arranged so animals cannot avoid them.
4. *Birds* Grouse and spruce hens are found in timber areas. They usually stay on the ground and are not difficult to stalk and shoot. They can also be snared or sometimes killed with a club. In summer waterfowl can be obtained along lakes and rivers. Bird eggs are also good emergency food.
5. *Fish* Fish are the most reliable food. They are plentiful in the streams and lakes, and can be hooked, trapped, netted or speared. Almost anything will serve as bait including lures made of feathers, pieces of tin or bits of cloth. You can make spears, build fish traps, or set nets along streams. If more fish are caught than sufficient to eat at one time, smoke and dry the surplus.
6. *Plants* Plants such as lichens, berries, roots and leaves can be eaten but the following are not edible:
   (a) Mushrooms.
   (b) Water Hemlock (the leaves resemble coarse carrot leaves) which grow in swampy places.
   (c) Baneberries (long clusters of cherry-red or ivory-white berries held conspicuously above delicate, non-woody plant) which grow in moist woods.
   (d) The thick roots of two members of the lily family: the Blue Flag or Iris (stiff, grass-like leaves about one inch broad) which grow in swampy places; the death-camass (onion shaped bulk without onion odor and narrow, grass-like roots clustered at the base) which grow in the rich black soil of mountain crevices.

Signals

Signalling devices should be set up as soon as possible to attract rescuers. Every available device is to be used.

154

Smoke Signals White smoke makes good daytime signal against bare ground and evergreen trees. White smoke can be made by adding green boughs and moss to the fire. Black smoke should be used when the ground is covered with snow. This can be made by adding engine oil, oil-soaked rags, pieces of rubber matting or electrical insulation to the fire. Build smoke fire in an open place; in timber areas the smoke must rise above the tree tops to be seen. Keep a small fire going all the time and have plenty of dry wood and smoke-producing materials ready for use as soon as an aircraft is heard.

Signalling Mirror During the daytime the signalling mirror is very effective. Even after being located, keep on signalling as long as the aircraft is in sight. When an aircraft is heard at night, point your flashlight at the mirror and flash an SOS. Wait a few seconds and then repeat, but do not wait until the aircraft has passed. Use the light on the Gibson Girl the same way.

Health Hints

Frostbite Avoid over-exertion and perspiration. Frostbite generally can be prevented by keeping face, ears, nose, wrists and especially hands and feet *covered* and *dry*. Avoid wearing tight-fitting clothing, particularly tight-fitting shoes. If leather shoes or fleece-lined flying boots are being worn, remove the shoes and replace with heavy socks or line flying boots with grass, feathers, fur, or similar materials. Keep snow out of boot tops.

Exercise frequently all parts susceptible to freezing. Watch out for stiffness, loss of feeling or telltale whitish-gray patches of skin. If any of these symptoms appear, thaw the affected part at once. *Do Not Rub.* Thaw frozen parts of face or ears with your warm hand. Apply sufanilamide powder to deeply frozen areas. Do not open blisters. Keep frozen parts elevated at rest and no warmer than body temperature.

Snowblindness Snowblindness is caused by reflected glare from snow, and is painful and dangerous. To prevent it, wear sunglasses if available, or improvise a pair by cutting two narrow slits in a thin piece of wood or soot-blackened canvas and wearing it over the eyes. Blacken area around the eyes with soot or charcoal.

The best treatment for snowblindness is darkness and rest. If pain is severe you can get relief by placing moist compresses over the eyelids.

Carbon Monoxide Poisoning Carbon Monoxide Poisoning can result from the use of an improvised gasoline stove in an unventilated shelter. Be sure to provide some ventilation in any enclosed shelter in which a fire is kept going. If you feel a slight headache combined with drowsiness get into fresh air at once. Do not exercise. Just breathe regularly and keep warm.

General Survival Advice

The following procedures have been compiled to aid in general survival when an aircraft has made a forced landing during the winter. These are to be applied immediately after landing and when the aircraft has been abandoned.

Stay away from aircraft until engines have cooled and danger of fire has passed.

Check injuries. Give first aid and keep injured persons warm.

Prepare signalling devices and have ready for immediate use.

Avoid frostbite. Keep feet dry and keep out of the wind.

Build a fire a safe distance from the aircraft. Calmly consider the situation and plan a course of action.

If the aircraft is still flyable, dilute, insulate wheels from ice with boughs or other materials, anchor aircraft securely and leave brakes off.

Get regular and emergency radios working if possible. Try to keep one engine in working order to generate power for radio. Try to keep battery from freezing.

Prepare shelter, collect wood, gasoline, oil, lichens or heather for fuel.

Check emergency equipment and consider what you have to live with.

Examine surroundings. Think back over the flight, look for landmarks and try to locate position on chart.

Do not over-exert in extreme cold. Sweating is dangerous because it leads to freezing.

Start a log book for future reference.

The following should be kept in mind when forced down:
  (i) The radio does not work if the batteries are dead.
  (ii) Transmitting is hard on aircraft batteries.
  (iii) If the engine is operative, start the engine by manual means and run the generator while transmitting.
  (iv) If radio conditions are generally poor, save your batteries until conditions are good.

Fleet List—1934-1974

Aircraft	Type	Serial	Acquired	Disposed	Notes
CF-AAB	DC-3	12289	1964	1976	ex USAAF 42-92483 (C-47A-5-DK), ex RAF FZ683, ex RCAF 961, sold to Florida dealer.
CF-AAC	DC-3	25369	1965	1970	ex USAAF 43-48108 (C-47A-30-DK), ex RCAF 974, crashed at Val d'Or July 1970.
CF-AAD	Canso	1658	1967	1972	ex N68746, crashed at Great Whale Sept. 24, 1972.
CF-AAH	DC-3	12528	1972		ex USAAF 42-108868 (C-47A-10-DK), ex NC16839 Northern Airlines, All American Airlines, ex N91226 Allegheny Airlines, ex N146A Allegheny Airlines, Southeast Airmotive, Caribbean Helicopters.

Aircraft	Type	Serial	Acquired	Disposed	Notes
CF-AAL	DC-3	26828	1964	1968	ex USAAF 43-49567 (C-47B-15-DK). Crashed near Timmins killing both pilots.
CF-AAL	DC-3	10202	1970	1977	ex USAAF 42-24340 (C-47A-60-DL), ex RCAF 663, damaged in ground fire at POV in Mar. 1977. Salvaged and ferried to Timmins. Cannibalized and parts used in rebuild of CF-AAM. Derelict on farm near Timmins.
CF-AAM	DC-3	9862	1968	Current	ex USAAF 42-24000 (C-47A-40-DL), ex RAF FD941, ex G-AGHO BOAC, Airways Training Ltd., Scottish Aviation, Northwest Airlines, ex N9993F A.J. Leeward.
CF-AMO	Bellanca CH-300	177	1944	1945	Imported by Bellanca Aircraft of Canada May 1930, ex McIntyre Porcupine Mines, Hennessey Airlines, Baillie-Maxwell, Wings Ltd. Registered to Austin Airways Aug. 30, 1944. Crashed at Nakina Jan. 11, 1945.
CF-AND	Bellanca CH-300	178	1939	1944	Imported by Bellanca Aircraft of Canada July 1930, ex Coastal Airways, General Airways. Registered to Austin Airways June 24, 1939. Destroyed by preheating fire at Nakina Feb. 8, 1944.
CF-AOC	Fleet 7	5	1935	1939	ex Fleet Aircraft of Canada and flown in Trans-Canada Air Pageant of 1931. Later Eclipse Airways. Registered to Austin Airways June 4, 1935. Later Saskatoon Flying Club, Toronto Flying Club. Crashed at Edgley, Ont. Aug. 6, 1941. To Central Technical School, Toronto, as instructional airframe.
CF-APL	DH-60T Tiger Moth	1726	1934	1935	ex G-ABNI. Imported Sept. 1931 by DHC. Registered to Austin Airways July 27, 1934. Sold to Walter Deisher. Later Toronto Flying Club, then donated to Central Technical School.
CF-ATX	DH-83 Fox Moth	4049	1934	1935	ex Bobby Cockeram (Prospector Airways). Registered to Austin Airways Oct. 11, 1934. Later H. Watt, B. Watt, Elmer Ruddick, A. Fecteau, J.N. Stevenson, P. Larivière, W.F. McQuade. Fate unknown.
CF-AVL	Waco UKC	3863	1934	1946	Registered to Austin Airways April 14, 1934. Delivered at Troy, Ohio. Sunk at Little Current Oct. 24, 1946 and damaged beyond repair. Austin Airways' first aircraft.
CF-AVN	Waco UKC	3869	1934	1942	Registered to Austin Airways May 26, 1934. Delivered at Fort Erie (Fleet Aircraft). Broke through ice near Biscotasing Dec. 8, 1942. Salvaged by F. Fowler but not restored.
CF-AWI	Waco YKC	3976	1935	1937	Imported by Jack Sanderson of Fleet Aircraft Nov. 1934. Sold to Eclipse Airways. Registered to Austin Airways June 4, 1935. To Fleet Aircraft Aug. 1937 as trade on CF-BDW. Later A.E. Jarvis, Algoma Air Transport, Ed Ahr, Leitch Gold Mines, Salmita Northwest Mines. Destroyed by fire during preheating at Yellowknife Oct. 15, 1946.
CF-AWP	Fairchild 51/71	28	1938	1949	Originally owned by Johnny Fauquier. Registered to Austin Airways May 28, 1938. Crashed at Nakina June 17, 1949.
CF-BDN	Waco VKS-7	4672	1937	1942	Registered to Austin Airways Aug. 6, 1937. Crashed near Chapleau Jan. 8, 1942.
CF-BJW	Fleet 50K	203	1945	1946	ex Fleet Aircraft, CPA. Registered to Austin Airways May 12, 1945. Burned upon startup at O'Sullivan Lake near Nakina Oct. 6, 1946.
CF-BLM	Aeronca 50	C-2529	1942	1943	Imported by J. Dunkelman March 1939, later W. Siple and Leavens Bros. Registered to Austin Airways Aug. 3, 1942. Crashed at Indian Lake March 26, 1943 and bought for scrap by F. Fowler. Restored but crashed May 14, 1945. Sold to Leavens Bros. and restored; thence to M.S. Phillips and back to Leavens Bros. Later Georgian Bay Airways and A.H. McDonald. Submerged and wrecked at Wasaga Beach June 17, 1954.
CF-BLN	Aeronca 50	C-2569	1939	1941	Registered to Austin Airways Feb. 28, 1939. Wrecked at Ramsey Lake Feb. 9, 1941 when aircraft ran away as pilot swung propeller.
CF-BLO	Aeronca 65	C-4539	1939	1940	Registered to Austin Airways July 3, 1939. Crashed at Ramsey Lake Oct. 11, 1940, killing two aboard.
CF-BSC	Norseman V	N29-17	1946	1958	Registered to Austin Airways Aug. 23, 1946. Purchased from Canadian Car as replacement for Fleet 50. Sold to Cargair in Quebec in 1973 after 13,959:20 hours service with Austin (over 10,000 hours flown by Rusty Blakey). Completed 14,564:45 hours before acquired by Canadian Museum of Flight and Transportation in 1983.

Aircraft	Type	Serial	Acquired	Disposed	Notes
CF-BSJ	Norseman V	N29-25	1948	1958	ex USCAN Engineering. Registered to Austin Airways July 2, 1948. Crashed at Nakina Sept. 15, 1958. Structural failure.
CF-BVI	Fairchild 71	674	1944	1949	ex RCAF G-CYWH, ex RCAF 674. Later operated by Wings Ltd. and CPA. Purchased by Austin from Babb Co. and registered to Austin Feb. 19, 1944. Sank in English Lake, Ont. July 17, 1949. Salvaged by G.H. Hughes in 1962.
CF-BVY	Fairchild 51	23	1942	1947	ex RCAF G-CYYT, ex RCAF 627. Built as model FC-2. Purchased from RCAF and delivered at Trenton. Registered to Austin March 3, 1942. Scrapped at Sudbury 1947.
CF-DCK	Norseman V	188	1946	1954	ex USAAF 43-5197. Purchased from War Assets Jan. 1946, with log showing 615:55 hours on airframe. Time to April 15, 1954, 4748:50 hours. Burned in hangar fire at St. Jean, Quebec, Dec. 8, 1954.
CF-DFB	Canso	605	1971	1976	Built 1942 by Consolidated. ex TF-RVG of Loftleidir 1949-52. To Aero Magnetic Surveys 1952 as CF-DFB. To Kenting 1962. Taken over by Austin June 2, 1971. To Wheeler Northland March 1976. Later leased by Austin and last Austin trip made Oct. 18, 1977. Sold to Newfoundland as water bomber Oct. 1978.
CF-DJI	Beaver	27	1963	1970	Acquired from White River Air Services. Burned at Moosonee.
CF-DNZ	Cessna 180	30054	1953	1954	Bought from Jack Sanderson. Wrecked at Sudbury—ran away without pilot and hit shoreline. Wreck sold to Superior Airways.
CF-DTW	Anson V	MDF-282	1952	1969	ex RCAF 12470. Purchased by DOT from War Assets Aug. 26, 1946. Purchased by Austin from Babb Co. Sept. 30, 1952, with total time logged 975 hours. Total time to May 7, 1968, 7117:30 hours. Damaged beyond repair Severn Lake March 3, 1969.
CF-EIB	Norseman VI	137	1947	1957	Acquired from Mr. Kashower of Oshawa. Later traded to Noorduyn for CF-JIN.
CF-EIQ	Husky	7	1952	1954	ex Nickel Belt Airways. Burned in hangar fire at St. Jean Dec. 8, 1954. Total time 4268 hours.
CF-EJX	Anson V	BRC 1134C	1951	1952	ex RCAF 12224. Crashed Flin Flon.
CF-ESM	Stinon 108		1947	1948	Bought from Canadian Car. Later sold to McMurray Air Services.
CF-ESP	Stinson 108-2	2671	1947	1953	Bought from Canadian Car May 23, 1947. Sold Dec. 1953 to G.J. Quinlan. Crashed at La Force, Quebec, Aug. 25, 1957.
CF-FAR	Canso	CV415	1952	1956	ex RCAF 11083. Forced landing near Churchill March 28, 1952. Overshot runway at Timmins March 11, 1956. Landed short at Timmins Jan. 14, 1956. Crashed near Timmins Dec. 27, 1956.
CF-FHE	Beaver	9	1954	1958	Bought from Aircraft Industries. ex North Shore Timber. Replaced CF-EIQ. Crashed in northern Quebec after running out of fuel.
CF-FHP	Beaver	57	1971		ex Irving Oil Transport, ex Laurentian Air Services. Purchased as replacement for CF-MAP. Sold to Horne Air Ltd. Current.
CF-FHX	Beaver	60	1949		Purchased new from DHC. Sold to Lakeland Airways. Crashed on Maple Mountain June 6, 1981, with loss of all aboard.
CF-FJU	Stinson 108-2	2670	1950	1952	Bought by Austin from Don Milne. Later traded by Austin to Jack Sanderson. Later owned by G. Thompson, Mr. Maisey, Jack Elsworth. Currently owned by Collingwood Bros. (Skeena Air Guides), Smithers, B.C. Converted to "Super Stinson." Total time to Dec. 31, 1983: 4995 hours.
CF-FNT	Aeronca 15AC	327	1949	1953	Bought from Art Grout of Chapleau. Traded in on deal for CF-FYQ.
CF-FYQ	Cessna 180	30154	1953	1964	Sold to Oscar Cecutti.
CF-GBC	Beaver	199	1952		Bought from DHC for Inco work from Churchill. Current, White River Air.
CF-GMM	Norseman VI	246	1949	1959	Made up by Austin from set of wings acquired at Dorval, and fuselage from St. Jean.
CF-GQQ	Beaver	119	1951		Bought from DHC. Current, Falcon Leasing, Smithers, B.C.
CF-GRU	Anson V	BRC-1476C	1949	1957	ex RCAF 11990. Registered to Austin Dec. 9, 1949. Total time to Jan. 21, 1952, 1144 hours. Total time to Nov. 28, 1953, 1854:05 hours. Ran off runway into Schist Lake at Flin Flon June 25, 1956. Total time to Jan. 30, 1957, 3116:10 hours. Damaged beyond repair at Desolation Lake, N.W.T., June 14, 1957.
CF-GRV	Anson V		1949	1951	Not used. Scrapped at Sudbury.
CF-GSR	Norseman	N29-47	1960	1970	Bought from Ray McLeod of Dorval. Formerly Wheeler Airlines. Current, Bearskin Lake Air Service, Sioux Lookout.

Aircraft	Type	Serial	Acquired	Disposed	Notes
CF-HDX	Cessna 180	30362	1953	1954	Crashed in Snow Lake region of Manitoba when ski failed on takeoff.
CF-HQZ	Anson V	MDF-289	1969		ex RCAF 12477. ex Transair fish hauler. Purchased as replacement for CF-DTW. Donated to Canadian Warplane Heritage. Presently in Vancouver for restoration.
CF-HZR	Norseman VI	843	1955	1958	Purchased in San Antonio by Ontario Central Airlines in 1955. Bought by Austin June 1955. Crashed 53° 12'N, 86° 32½'W July 31, 1958. Hit trees while landing on winding river and tore off left wing. Sold to Superior Airways. Later to Parsons Airways. Crashed 70 miles WNW Frobisher Bay April 9, 1964.
CF-HXY	Otter	67	1971	1977	Longtime DHC demonstrator. To Eastern Provincial Airways,, then bought by Austin. Current, Lac Seul Airways, Ear Falls.
CF-IBQ	Cessna 180	31765	1955	1963	Purchased from Laurentide Aviation.
CF-IEE	Canso	1566	1967	1970	Purchased from Transair. Damaged in storm at Sugluk while at anchor. Refloated with 45-gallon drums. Stripped and disposed of by sinking.
CF-IGG	Norseman V	CCF 51	1955	1969	Built up from misc. components at Sudbury. Registered to Austin July 29, 1955. Destroyed by fire at Moosonee in 1969.
CF-IHB	Canso	CV294	1955	1959	ex RCAF 11016. Purchased from Babb Co. Total time to May 11, 1959, 3993:15 hours. Crashed POV July 2, 1959, after engine failure.
CF-ILQ	DC-3	12377	1955	1964	ex USAAF 42-92563 (C-47A-5-DK), ex RAF KG368. Purchased from Lund Aviation, Montreal, and registered to Austin Jan. 12, 1956. Total time Jan. 16, 1957, 7691:20. Total time Dec. 31, 1963, 13,249:50 hours. Crashed Rupert River area Jan. 9, 1964, due to fuel starvation.
CF-IVK	Anson V		1960		ex RCAF 12082, ex RCN 801. Bought from Pulsifer Bros. of Halifax. Donated to Canadian Warplane Heritage.
CF-JAW	Anson V	4274	1956		ex RCAF 11904. Bought from Leavens Bros. Donated to Canadian Warplane Heritage. Now at Western Canada Aviation Museum, Winnipeg.
CF-JIN	Norseman V	55	1957	1969	Cracked up at Nakina and shipped to Noorduyn. Rebuilt and sold to Labrador Mining. Crashed again and returned to Noorduyn in Feb. 1973. Acquired by Norco Associates and rebuilt. First flight since occurred Aug. 18, 1981.
CF-JKT	Beaver	1023	1956	1979	Bought from DHC. Current, Lakeland Airways.
CF-JMX	DC-3	25615	1956	1958	ex USAAF 43-48354 (C-47B-1-DK), ex RAF KJ831. Acquired by Austin for passenger skeds. Later sold to DOT as CF-DTT.
CF-JNC	Cessna 180	32843	1959	1971	Purchased from Jack Sanderson. Burned in Sudbury hangar fire in 1971.
CF-JQN	Cessna 180	32848	1963	1968	
CF-KAO	Norseman VI	636	1968		Bought from Air Brochu.
CF-LFM	Cessna 180	50484	1963		Bought from Jack Sanderson. Later sold to Don Mortimer of Muskoka.
CF-MAP	Beaver	10	1959	1971	Bought from Manitoba Gov't. Burned in Sudbury hangar fire in 1971.
CF-MIT	Otter	372	1970	1976	Originally Eastern Provincial Airways, thence to Field Aviation and Austin Airways. Crashed at Fraserdale Sept. 4, 1976, after striking hydro wires.
CF-PTV	Cessna 180	51314	1965		Bought from Jack Sanderson. Damage by storm at Sudbury. Also, sank through ice on another occasion; and later damaged in collision with boat on Ramsey Lake. Current.
CF-OBN	Norseman V	N29-19	1954	1967	ex Ontario Dept. of Mines and Forests. Later Ontario Central, then Austin Airways. Stalled and crashed at Winisk Aug. 10, 1968.
CF-SAQ	Husky	8	1952	1965	Originally Saskatchewan Government Airways as air ambulance. To Nickel Belt Airways, thence to Austin. Sold to Parsons Airways Feb. 1966. To Sioux Narrows Airways June 1969. To West Coast Air Services Nov. 1969 and converted to Leonides engine Jan. 1972. To Island Airlines April 1972. Donated to Canadian Museum of Flight and Transportation, Richmond, B.C., Dec. 1980.

Index

Figures in italics refer to photographs.

Aeronca 37-41, *69*
Air Ontario 148
Aircraft Industries 77, 117, 119, *124,* 137
Albany River 42, 43
Alguire, Cliff 81
Anderson, Bill 53, 74, 111
Anderson, Mrs. 48
Anglican church 70
Ashcroft, Les 28, *29*
Attawapiskat 62, *63*
Austin Airways:
  founded 11
  first employees 12
  first aircraft 17
  air ambulance *16,* 17, *33,* 146-148
  incorporated 19
  Sudbury base opens 20
  buys Eclipse Airways 20
  Gogama base opens 25
  Biscotasing base opens 25
  mining operations 23, 25-27
  aerial photography 29, 30, 37, 43, 73
  maintenance 30-33, 139, 140
  competition *35*
  wartime operations 36, 37
  fish hauling 41-43, 97, 98
  Aeroncas 37-41
  Nakina base opens 41, 46
  Aeroncas 37-41
  Fairchild aircraft 43-49
  James Bay opens up 46-49
  South Porcupine opens 46
  mail contract 48
  radio 55
  first Norseman 55
  missionaries 70-72
  goose hunt 74-76
  Inco work 79-96
  EM survey 79-96
  first Canso 117
  first DC-3 119
  ice patrol 134, 136
  new owners 141
  food haul 145, 146
Austin, Allan 11, 19, *20,* 22, 45
Austin, Bill 11, 15, 19
Austin, Charles *11,* 12, *16,* 18-21, 28, *29, 32,* 33, 36, 44, 50, 52, 53, 59, 83, 136
Austin, J.A.M. *11,* 12, 13, *16,* 18, 19, 22, 28, *29,* 33, 34, 36, 37, 46-48, 53, 56, 76, 80, 82, 85, 96, *114,* 117, 120, 121, 129, 137, 139, *141, 149*
Avro Anson *79,* 83-96, *121, 135*
Ayr, Ed 22, 46, 112
Babb Co. 43, 46, 121
Baffin Island 129-134, 136, 137, 141
Baillie, Frank 41
Baillie-Maxwell Ltd. 41-43
Barilko, Bill 68
Baxter, Gilbert *42*
Baxter, Les *41*
Beamish, Don 133
Beatty, Herb 20
Beech 18, *92*
Beech C-99 148
Belcher Islands *66, 116*

Bell, Bill 23
Bell, Irene *23*
Bell, Jim 22, *23,* 25-29, *33,* 37, 46-48, *74,* 77, 78, 85, 89, 90, 109, 111, 112, 118-120, 122-125, 127, 130
Bellanca CH-300 40-43, 50, *54*
Belleterre 31
Bendall, Eric 42, 43
Bennett, Sid *34*
Bickell, J.P. 18
Biscotasing 41
Blackwood, Eric 112, 136
Blakey, Dick 109, *116,* 136
Blakey, Rusty *16,* 21-27, *33,* 37, 40, 41, 52, 56, 59, 62, *64, 65,* 72-74, 78, 105-109, 113, *114,* 125, 127, 136, 139, *148, 149*
Blatchfor, T. *95*
Boreal Airways 77
Boylen, Fred 18
Bradley Air Service 104
Brand, Dave 80-82
Bray, Walter *136*
Brough, Mildred 128
Brown, John 123
Brownlee, Baden 38
Buchanan, Scotty *86*
Buhl *14,* 15
Burke, C.F. 121
Butchard, Charlie 78
Cabbage Willows 104
Cairns, Elsie *25*
Cairns, James T. 23-25, 28-30, 36, 38
Campbell, Hugh and Mary 98
Canadian Aeroplanes Ltd. 39
Canadian Airways 11, 50, 60, 62
Canadian Aviation 48-50
Canadian Aviation Historical
  Society 45, 50
Canadian Colonial Airways 12, 15
Canadian Nickel Co. 83, 117
Cape Dorset *137, 145*
Capreol and Austin Air
  Services 11
Capreol, Leigh 11, 13, *16,* 17-19, 23
Carroll, Andy 21
Carter, Fred 96
Caughill, B. *95*
Central Airways 80, 89, 127
Central Technical School 56
Cessna 180 80, *82*
Cessna 310 *146*
Cessna 402 144, *145*
Cessna Citation 143, 147, 148
Chaput, Sybil and Fred 112, 113
Chaput, Kipp 113
Chalmers, Al "Skipper" 20, 23, 25
Chandler brothers 39
Charity, George 54, 56, 58-61, 72, 73, 78, 80, 138, 139
Charleson, Jack 22
Christianson, Mrs. 108
Chubb Crater *58, 78, 110,* 128
Churchill 118, 119
Cleverley, Sid *16*
Cockeram, Bobby 17
Cochrane, Bruce 139
Coddere, Larry *96*
Compton, Les 36, 41
Conn, Hugh 46
Consolidated Canso *61,* 111, 117-138
Convair 580 148
Cook, Gary *95*

Coons, Bill 129
Copper Cliff *100*
Cordingly Lake 42, 64
Cormack Lumber 64
Coté, Emile 42, 97, 98
Cowan, Matt 46, 48
Cram, Bill 127
Cramer, Stan 136
Craw, Dave 137
Croker, John *128*
Crosley, Carl 22
Cryderman, Felix *56, 57,* 64, 65
Curtiss HS-2L *24*
Curtiss-Reid Rambler 23
Davis, Bill 78
Davoud, Paul 22
Dawson, Ken 44
de Havilland:
  D.H. 60T 11, *15, 17, 19,* 20
  D.H. 61 *24*
  D.H. 83 *17, 42, 57*
  D.H. 84 25
  D.H. 87 25
  D.H. 89 *12*
  DHC-2 *69, 74,* 77, 80, *87,* 99-105, *107, 110, 149*
  DHC-3 100-105
  DHC-6 *95, 141,* 144, 147
Deluce, Joe *146*
Deluce, Stan 97, 141, 142, 144, 147
der Weduwen, John 105, *112, 128, 130, 138, 148*
Desolation Lake 86
Detour Lake *142,* 145, *147*
Dillon, Jack 22, 27
Dinnin, Ab 99, 100, 112
Dominion Gulf Exploration 60
Dominion Skyways 11, 27
Douglas DC-3 117-138, *141, 147,* 148
Douglas DC-9 *141*
Drew, George 18
Dryden, Fred 84, *85*
Dunbar, Don 81
Dunkelman, J.B. *37*
Dutchburn, R. *95*
Earlton *86*
Eclipse Airways 15, 19, 20
Edmison, Kelly *14*
Edsel, Bruce *95*
Elgin Airways 129
Elliot, J.V. 13
Ennadai Lake *84, 86, 87,* 90
Eskimos 108
Esnagami 98
Evershed, W. *95*
Fairchild *27,* 43-49, *51, 54, 58, 60*
Fairchild 24 *68,* 70
Fairchild 51/71 *26,* 27, 29, *30,* 37
Fairchild Cornell 36
Fairchild Husky 76-78, 79, 80, 81, *83, 84*
Faires, Eddie 107
Farrendon, Mr. 38
Fauquier, Johnny 29, *35,* 43
Fennell, Jim 103
Ferguson Lake *67,* 80, 83, *86,* 117-119, 121
Fiddler, Alex *95*
firefighting 20-22
Firebirds, The 30
fish hauling 41-43, 97, 98
Fisher, Frank 12-14, 16, 18, 21-23
Fleet Aircraft 17
Fleet 7 20, *21,* 27

Fleet Freighter 50-53, 55
Flin Flon 84, *85, 91,* 92
Fokker *14*
Fort Albany *142, 146*
Fort George *115, 116,* 142
Foster, Jerry 136
Fowler, Frank 34, *35,* 38, 39, 41
Fraleck Lake 28
Garratt, Phil 13
Gauer Lake *96*
Gauthier, Bob 101, 103
General Airways 11, 14, 15, *35,* 41
Georgian Bay Airways 105
Gibb, Kelly 77, 80-82
Gibson, Frank 88, 89
Gillard, Vern 22
Gillies, Fred 56, 125
Giroux, Jacques *146*
Globe and Mail 12, 18, 22
Gogama *45*
goose hunt 74-76
Gosby, Don *64*
Goudreau, Roger *124*
Grandy, Roy 46
Grant, Colin 137
Great Whale *65, 66, 108,* 122, 132, 133, 137
Griffin, Fred 22
Groome, Don 28, *29*
Grzelak, Alex *95*
Guest, R.C. 24
Gunner, Alex 112
Gunner, Jimmy 72
Gwynn, Bill 91, 97, 98, *124, 125,* 127
Haggert, Bob *137*
Halcrow Swayze Mine 20, 25
Hall, Jim *86,* 127, 133
Hamilton, A.J.C. 92
Hamilton, Bob 129, 138, 139
Hamilton F. 25
Hannah Bay 74, 104, 107
Harper, Dr. B.H. 72, 73, 107
Harper, Leonard 72
Hawker Siddeley 748 127, *142,* 144-147
Hayes, Paul 90
Hazeldine, Eric *130,* 137
Heath Parasol *39*
Henderson, Bill *95*
Henry, Walter 19
Hepburn, Mitch 41
Hickson, Earl 22
Hill, Frank *87*
Hill, Stu 27
Hobbs, Jim 64, 70, 77, 80, 82, 90, 126, 136
Hoffman, Rudy *96,* 127
Hollinger Mines 26
Hollinger Ungava Transport 80, 109, 125
Hollinsworth, G.E. 121, 122
Horden Lake *94*
Hornick, Jim 48-50
Horwood Lake *26*
Houston, Jim 128
Howe, C.D. 36
Hudson, Dr. Albert H. 68, 70
Hudson, Gil 84, *86,* 90, 118, 119
Hudson Bay Railway 118
Hudson's Bay Company 42, 46-49, 55, *64,* 71, 72, 97, 107, 109, *116*
Hughes, Gordon H. 45, *53*
Hughes, Len 74
Humphries, Jack 122-125, 128-130, 133, 136, 137
Hunt, John 73

Hurd, Don 64
Hyrniuk, Steve 105, 112, 127
Ilford-Riverton Airlines 149
Inco *31,* 74, 78-96, 100, 107, 117-119, 129, 138
Irwin, Norm 17, 19
Isaacson, Bob *145*
Jarvis, Jock 22
Jeffreys, Roy 109
Jellicoe *26*
Jerome, Bert *27*
Jerome Mine *21, 25, 27,* 40
Johannesson, Konnie 91, 118
Johnson, R.N. 37
Joy, Col. Douglas 12, 13, 18, 39
Kallio, Einar *80*
Kapuskasing 136, 145
Kaverna, Vic *93, 96*
Keane, Jim 108, 112, 127, 136
Kearns, W.H. 29, *30,* 37, 48, 73, 74, 111
Keating Aviation 130, 136, 137
Kenyon, Ed 84, *85,* 118, 119
Kern, Norm 90, 91, *94,* 96, 112
Kerr, Bob 85, 127, 137, 138, *148*
Kirkland Air Services 38
Knox, Fred 81-83, 91
Kohls, Charlie 41, *109*
Kohls, Fritz 27, 48, 49, *64*
Kohls, Gordy 136
Kohls, Herbie 127
Krochel, Frank 97
LAN-Chile 144
Lac la Ronge *96*
Laflamme, Joe 28, *29*
Lahti, John *96*
Lakeland Airways *69*
Lamb, Tom 119
Lambair 79
Lansdowne House 71, 72
Lapointe, P. 121
Larry, Cliff 91
Laurin, Peter 37
Leavens Bros. 38, 39, 46
Leblanc, Jim *96*
Lee, James R. 93
Lejeune, Ray *88,* 89, 90, *95, 96, 130,* 134, *145*
Leriche, Tony 125
Levac Lake 91, 92, 138
Loening *14*
Louttit, Lindy 139
Louttit, Rev. Redfern 70-72
Lucas, J.H. 111, 121, 123, *124,* 129
Lundberg, S.T. *57*
Lutty, John 125
Lymburner, J.H. 121
MacDougall, Frank 77
MacMillan, Glen 132
MacKenzie Air Service 11
Mackie, Doug 90, *121,* 136
Maersk 143, 146
Maple Mountain *69*
Massey, Denton 18
Mathews, Jack 21
Mattinen, Taumo 35
Maxwell, Roy 41, 42
McArthur, Morley 137
McCarthy, Bill 32
McCarthy, Marg *25*
McClatchey, B. 46
McClintock, Don 136
McCracken, Hal 53, 56-59, 64, 73, 100, 112, 127, *149*

McCray, Red 22, *23,* 36
McCullagh, George 18
McDougall, Archie 56, 64
McElrea, W.G. 121
McGregor Lake *91*
McInnis, Bill *123, 125*
McIntyre, Don 78, 79, 119
McIntyre, M.L. 45, 50-53, 55
McIntyre Mines 31, 50
McKee Trophy 141
McLean, Harry 18
McLean, Ray 105
McLeod, Ray 104, *133*
McMann, Murray *123*
McNamara, Frances 128
McTaggart, Lloyd 79, 81
McVicar, Don 121
Merwin, Ben 77
Metzloff, Harry 112, 127
Michalak, Gary *92, 95*
Michelchuk, Joe *96*
Michener, Dr. C.E. 79
Mid Canada Line 90, 120-122, 126
Milberry, Matthew and Simon *148*
Millard, Jim 112
Ministic Lake 107
Mitchell, Gord 33, 34, 42, 46-50, 56, 72, 97
Molson, K.M. 43
Monk, Terry *59,* 96, 127-129
Montgomery, Bill *65,* 97, 136
Moore, Bob *74,* 111
Morrison, A.C. 121
Morrison, Ed *96*
Moose Factory *47, 55, 59,* 108, 109, *114, 116*
Moose River, N.S. 22
Moosonee 62, 105, 113-115, *120, 121, 123,* 131, 132, 138
Mount Hope *119*
Munger, John 113
Munro, J. *95*
Murphy, J. *95*
Musselman, Jim 84, *85*
Nakina *36,* 43, 97-100, 102, 136, *142*
Nakoquee, John *146*
National Air Transport *14,* 15, 20
Neal, George 77
Nelson, Tommy 82
New Golden Rose Mine 25
Nicholson, G.B. 11
Nickel Belt Airways 39, 64, 74, 75, 77, 78
Nieminen, Mark *86, 93,* 127, 136, *137*
Noorduyn Norseman 55, 56, *58, 60,* 61, *62, 64, 65, 66, 97,* 99, 100, *105, 106, 109,* 110-113, *115, 116*
Noranda *35*
Nordair 129
Norontair *141,* 144
North American Harvard *56*
Northern Aerial Mineral Exploration 11, 14, 17
Northern Miner 18
Northland 70
Oaks, Doc 14
O'Brien, Neil *106*
Ogoki Post 42, *142*
Okanagan Helicopters 129
Old Factory *64*
Ontario Central Airlines 144
Ontario Hydro 136
Ontario Northland Railway 74, *114*

Ontario Provincial Air Service 14, 15, 22, 24, 29, 30, 60, 62
Orange, Bill 27
Orford, Dr. Tom 46, 47, 48, 72
O'Sullivan Lake 52
Ottawa Flying Club 22, 23
Overbury, Dick 22
Papp, George 53, 54, 73
Parisotto, Ray *95*
Parke, R.D. 117
Parsons, Holly 29, 30, 37, 48, 58, 112
Payne, L. *78*
Pengelly, Jim 123, 125-127, 136
Perron, Theodore 38
Pettus, Bob 129, 130, 132, 133
Phillips, George 22
Pickle Lake 144, *145*
Pierce bros. 18
Piggot, Bill 21
Pineland Timber 39, 81
Pioneering in Canadian Air Transport 43
Pipe, J. 56, 59-62, 78
Plaunt, Don *113, 148*
Polack, Dr. Stanley *33*
Porcupine mine *26*
Port Harrison 47, *61,* 106
Povungnituk *63,* 137
Prass, Hans *95*
Preston, Dick 12-14, *16,* 18, 19, 23, 24, 27
Propair 104
Prospector Airways 17
Prouls, Fred 38
Pullen, Bill *113,* 133
Ramsey Lake 22, 25, *31, 32,* 37, *104, 113, 133, 148, 149*
Raymond, Larry 147
Redmayne, R.N. 121
Reed, Doug *23,* 38
Reid, John 137
Richardson, James A. 11
Richmond Gulf 53, 54, *62,* 71
Robertson, Brian 123
Robertson, Nick 127
Robinson, Dunc 112, 127
Rogers, Lee *96*
Rose, Alan 134
Rose, Chuck 90, 92, *96*
Ross, Bill *130,* 142
Ross, Frank 136
Ruddick, Elmer 34, *40,* 41, 42, 52, 53, 70, 71, 97
Rupert House *61,* 68, 139
Russell, Dave 106
Russell, Frank 12, *13,* 18-22, 28, 30-33, 43, 50, 52, 53, 55, *57,* 59, 76, 81, *88,* 98, 99, 108, 125, 127, 136, 137, 139, 140, 141
Rychlicki, R. 121
Sainsbury, Sam *14*
Sanderson, Jack 17, 20, *21,* 34, 50
Sauvé, Phil 19, *20,* 22, 23, 25, 27-29, 34, 36, 41
Schiller, Duke 18
Scully, Al 136
Sears, M.L. 84-89, 92, *94, 95,* 104, 105, 112
Seaward, Al 137
Senior, Tom 23
Severn Enterprises 62, *92,* 93
Severn Lake 92-95
Shapland, Ralph *86*

Shebandowan Lake 101, 102
Sheldon, Jim *133*
Sherritt Gordon 118
Shirdown, Ron *110*
Sikorsky S-38 *12*
Siple, Wally 38, 46
Skyview Canada 29
Smith, Frank 136
Smith, Harold 22
Soper, Jim 47
South Porcupine *60,* 68, 69, 100
Spartan Air Services 83
Spears, Glen 48
Spencer, Charlie *96*
Starratt Airways 24
Steed, Brian 100-103
Steeves, Gordy 23
Stevens, Jack *20*
Stewart, Don 127
Stinson 108 57, *65, 147*
Stitts Flut-R-Bug *59*
Sudbury *31, 56,* 133
Sudbury Aviation 127
Sudbury Boat and Canoe 20, 25, *31,* 57
Sudbury Star 73
Sugluk *60*
Sumner, Bill 36, 57
Superior Airways 97, 148
Survair *95*
Taylor, Dave 90, 91
Taylor, Ernie 25
The Pas 81, 118
Thompson, Man. *95*
Thompson, Webb 53
Thomson, Don W. 29
Thorn, Mike 20
Timmins *139, 141, 146, 147*
Toronto Air Harbour *12*
Toronto Flying Club 19, 23-25
Toronto Harbour Commission 12
Toronto Island Airport 50, 56, *76,* 80, 89, 97, 104, 124, 127, 144
Toronto Maple Leafs 68
Toronto Star 22, 48
Transair 100
Tripp, Len 56
tuberculosis 109
Tucker, H. *95*
Tugwell, Stirling 123, 132
Umphrey, Harry 84
Vanhee, Archie 22
Vuori, Hank 78
Wabowden 79, 81, *84,* 89, 90
Waco *13,* 15-17, 19, *20,* 24, 25, 27-29, 31-35
water bombing 123, 124, 128
Webberfield, Frank 38
Weiben, O.J. 62, 97
Wenham, John *95*
Wesser, Paul *95*
West, Bruce 30
White River Air Services *141,* 142
Wicks Lumber 59
Williams, Charlie 137
Williams, Tommy 52
Winisk *116, 137*
Wojnas, S. *95*
Wong, Bob 89
Woodrow, Fred *65*
Woods, Spencer 96, 133, 134
Wyborn, Jeff 56, 62, *64, 65,* 69, 108, 109, 136, *148*
Yesno, John 71, 72